THE GREAT CENTURIES OF PAINTING

COLLECTION PLANNED AND DIRECTED BY

ALBERT SKIRA

Translated by Stuart Gilbert

Library of Congress Catalog Card Number: 55-10592.

★

Distributed in the United States by
THE WORLD PUBLISHING COMPANY
2231 West 110th Street, Cleveland 2, Ohio

PRINTED IN SWITZERLAND

THE GREAT CENTURIES OF PAINTING

THE FIFTEENTH CENTURY
FROM VAN EYCK TO BOTTICELLI

TEXT BY JACQUES LASSAIGNE AND GIULIO CARLO ARGAN

SKIRA

The colorplate on the title-page:

Conrad Witz (ca. 1400-1447). St Bartholomew, detail. Right Wing of the "Heilsspiegel" Altarpiece, ca. 1435.
Kunstmuseum, Basel.

One of the chief aims of this book, as will be clear from the way our subject-matter is presented, is to show that, despite a long-established tradition to the contrary, the Renaissance was not a specifically Italian cultural and artistic movement, which little by little gained ground and made good in other European countries. All the facts point the other way; as early as the beginning of the 15th century the Renaissance was in effect a Europe-wide phenomenon, even if it assumed different forms in Flanders, Italy and Germany; and perhaps, indeed, for this very reason.

The opening years of the century witnessed two events fraught with momentous consequences for all European art, when Van Eyck painted the Ghent Altarpiece and Masaccio his no less epoch-making frescos in the Brancacci Chapel. Such were the advances of the creative spirit manifested in these two great works by men of widely differing origins and backgrounds, a Northerner and an Italian, that with them begins a whole new chapter in the history of art. Van Eyck's technical discoveries enabled him to body forth in rich, translucent colors the manifold beauties of Nature, the inner life of things and figures bathed in light. Masaccio, for his part, built up a world of monumental forms permeated, for the first time in art, with a sense of the moral responsibilities of the human situation. Their successors applied themselves to interpreting emotions and nuances of character with a delicate perceptiveness hitherto unknown; and this, too, was the time when thanks to the science of perspective, man could be located at the very heart of reality and become, in an almost literal sense, "the measure of all things."

None the less the 15th century was not characterized, as the previous century had been, by the diffusion throughout Europe of a single pictorial language, a *lingua franca* valid everywhere; on the contrary, national styles were now in process of replacing the International Style of Late Gothic. Needless to say, there were constant exchanges of ideas between countries; yet each tended to develop its own way of seeing, its own scale of values and the conception of an historic past peculiar to itself. This intercourse between the European peoples took the form of an active give-and-take, but in no case did it sponsor the propagation of a uniform tradition.

The Italians based the value of form on the Idea, in the Platonic application of the term, and made an *a priori* conception of Space the starting-off point of the picture, and indeed its *raison d'être*; the framework into which all the pictorial elements were to be inserted. Flemish artists, on the other hand, based form on what they actually saw and, though seeming to focus their attention exclusively on things existing in Time, and to ignore the spatial frame of reference, likewise developed a theory of Space; but, in their case, an *a posteriori*, empirical conception of it. Yet while Italian art is not, and indeed could not be, pure geometry, Flemish art is equally far from being a factual imitation of things seen. In brief, the Italians sought to define form in terms of a given concept, the Flemings to define it in terms of visual experience. For both alike the supreme aim was the discovery of form—"form" in the widest meaning of the term: a conscious representation of the universe, a means of giving objective reality to constructions of the mind, and a recognition of the temporal and spatial conditions of man's earthly life—conditions which, though imposed from without, permitted him to make good his value as an individual, responsible and autonomous.

G. C. A. AND J. L.

Our aim in planning this series of books was to show the underlying links between the great European schools of painting and to give a complete panorama of the ideas and ideals behind the incomparable achievements of succeeding generations of artists. After having studied the rise of modern art, we were led back to the ancient civilizations of the Mediterranean basin in our search for the origins of the great movements that have determined the course of painting. We also deemed it indispensable to include a study of the prehistoric paintings in the Lascaux Cave of southern France, for these tell the story of the birth of art. With this volume and those in preparation —one devoted to the High Renaissance, the other to the art treasures of the Early Middle Ages—this cycle of books, which forms nothing less than a comparative history of painting, will come to a close. We take pleasure in extending our most grateful thanks to the curators of museums, private collectors and directors of various civil and religious institutions whose friendly co-operation has so greatly facilitated the making of this book and its companion volumes.

A. S.

THE FIFTEENTH CENTURY

FROM VAN EYCK TO BOTTICELLI

I

THE CREATORS OF FLEMISH PAINTING

JAN VAN EYCK - THE MASTER OF FLÉMALLE - MELCHIOR BROEDERLAM
ROGIER VAN DER WEYDEN - PETRUS CHRISTUS

THE PRECURSORS OF A NEW ART IN THE GERMANIC COUNTRIES

CONRAD WITZ - STEPHAN LOCHNER

THE PAINTERS OF THE FRENCH DOMAIN

THE MASTER OF THE ROHAN HOURS - THE MASTER OF THE AIX ANNUNCIATION
ENGUERRAND CHARONTON - JEAN FOUQUET

Text by Jacques Lassaigne

2

PAINTING IN CENTRAL ITALY

MASACCIO - FRA ANGELICO - SASSETTA - GIOVANNI DI PAOLO - UCCELLO
DOMENICO VENEZIANO - ANDREA DEL CASTAGNO - FILIPPO LIPPI
PIERO DELLA FRANCESCA - ANTONIO POLLAIUOLO - BOTTICELLI

Text by Giulio Carlo Argan

3

EVOLUTION OF THE FLEMISH SCHOOL

DIRK BOUTS - HUGO VAN DER GOES - HANS MEMLING - GERARD DAVID

NEW ART FORMS IN GERMANY AND AUSTRIA

THE MASTER OF THE LIFE OF MARY - CASPAR ISENMANN - MARTIN SCHONGAUER
MICHAEL PACHER - RUELAND FRUEAUF

PAINTING IN SPAIN AND PORTUGAL

JAIME HUGUET - BARTOLOMÉ BERMEJO - FERNANDO GALLEGO - NUÑO GONÇALVES

THE PAINTERS OF PROVENCE AND LE BOURBONNAIS

THE MASTER OF THE VILLENEUVE PIETÀ - NICOLAS FROMENT
THE MASTER OF MOULINS

Text by Jacques Lassaigne

4

PAINTING IN NORTHERN ITALY

ANDREA MANTEGNA - FRANCESCO DEL COSSA - COSIMO TURA - ANTONELLO DA MESSINA
GIOVANNI BELLINI - VITTORE CARPACCIO

Text by Giulio Carlo Argan

Page 11: Jan van Eyck (1385/1390-1441). The Madonna of Chancellor Rolin (detail), 1435-1436. Louvre, Paris.

I

THE CREATORS OF FLEMISH PAINTING

When he first sees the clustering spires and belfries of Bruges rising half way up the sky above a vast expanse of grassy plain, the traveler approaching that age-old city may well fancy he is gazing at the landscape of some Flemish Primitive and by dint of some "experiment with time" has broken contact with the modern world. The Flemish scene has, in fact, a timeproof quality and the clean precision of work made to last for ever. But there is more to it than that. Upon the pale immensity of skies spanning the low horizons and shimmering with the first light of dawn, the slightest undulations tell out strongly and are magnified by the imagination into a vista of far-off glittering peaks; and likewise the towns bathed in the glow of sunset seem like cities of a dream. One thing is certain: no other school of painting has built up on a basis of concrete reality structures so finely wrought and rich in intimations as those of the Flemish School. It has given us the most faithful depictions known to art of landscapes marked by the changing seasons, with long roads winding between green meadows and flat fields bordered with gnarled, symmetrically polled willows. No less lifelike are the scenes of city life: streets lined with booths and workshops, peopled with tiny figures, carts and men on horseback; of little gardens gay with flowers. But Flemish painting also provided an ideal vehicle for a sensitive and searching interpretation of the mysteries of the Christian faith and reflected with remarkable fidelity the religious thought of the age. Realistic detail was used as the starting-off point of an art that was idealistic through and through, charged with myths and symbols. Thus within a framework of the pious legends dear to the Flemish populace and of scenes in which the saints of the *Golden Legend* cut homely figures and looked as if they had just stepped forth from some humble booth or cottage, there developed a truly creative art, deeply felt and brilliantly original, an art of erudite piety and esoteric symbolism.

Happily immune from the incessant wars raging between France and England, the Lowlanders could indulge their natural bent towards commerce and industry. The Battle of Agincourt in 1415 spelt the ruin of French power for several decades and the downfall of the French aristocracy. The assassination of John the Fearless, Duke of Burgundy, at Montereau (in 1419) led his son Philip the Good to break with the House of Valois and to transfer his capital from Dijon to Bruges. This great free port, then served by an arm of the North Sea now silted up, was not only a central mart of European commerce, receiving a steady flow of goods from the Mediterranean and the Baltic, from Germany and England, but also the home of a flourishing school of painters and illuminators. From the middle of the 14th century on, the various provinces of the Low Countries—in particular those of the Meuse Valley, Limburg, Brabant and Gelderland—had been prolific of artists; but most of these had migrated to the courts of the French princes, where alone they could count on finding understanding patrons. Thus it was Flemish artists who contributed in great measure to the success of the Parisian artists' workshops and the famous collections of the Duke of Berry and the first Duke of Burgundy (who had married the daughter and heiress of the Count of Flanders). When the great Carthusian monastery of Champmol, near Dijon, was founded by the latter, it provided a welcome field of activity for the genius of Claus Sluter, the Dutch sculptor, and for those two fine painters, Jean Malouel and Henri Bellechose, recruited in Gelderland and Brabant. To Dijon were conveyed the masterworks of Flemish artists, for example the reredos carved by Jacques de Baerze and painted by Melchior Broederlam at Ypres. In such works by Broederlam as have escaped the ravages of time we can see the first attempts made by a northern painter to integrate figures into architecturally ordered, three-dimensional space; to depict edifices viewed simultaneously (in the Italian manner) from inside and from without and to present a landscape steeply rising in echeloned planes.

There is no question that the works of art which were brought together at Champmol formed a collection of all that was most characteristically "modern" in early 15th-century art, and that the presence at Dijon of one of the first and most ambitious pictures by the Master of Flémalle and the close association of Jan van Eyck with the Court of Burgundy had a decisive influence on the leading Flemish painters. Sluter's influence, too, had far-reaching consequences. The will to powerful expression manifested in his *Mourners* lay at the origin of the painters' discovery of volume, while his practice of placing statues in niches surmounted with miniature replicas of large-scale architecture foreshadowed the designs in grisaille on the back of altarpieces (on the lines of Giotto's simulated sculpture in the lowest row of the Arena Chapel frescos).

Philip the Good was undoubtedly the greatest art patron of his age; in the records of the Ducal Treasure figure the names of no less than 176 painters. But perhaps this able ruler's chief claim to renown is that he not only appointed Jan van Eyck his court painter but lavished favors on him and treated him as a personal friend. On being designated Capital of the Duchy, Bruges became a center of luxury and the arts, and there forgathered at the ducal court not only Burgundian notables such as Nicolas Rolin,

Chancellor and Superintendent of Finance, a man of iron will but a versatile diplomatist, whom the Duke regarded as his *alter ego*, but Flemish burghers enriched by seaborne trade, and representatives of the Hanseatic and Italian banks, such as Tani, Arnolfini and Portinari. All were active patrons of the arts and thanks to them the vogue of Flemish works of art spread all over Europe.

Though less cosmopolitan, Tournai was an art center hardly less renowned than the capital. It was the headquarters of one of the oldest schools of Northern sculpture, famed for its funerary art—steles, recumbent figures, effigies of mourners—and for its carved reliefs depicting biblical scenes; indeed the School of Tournai is regarded with good reason as one of the main sources of Burgundian art. The city teemed with skillful craftsmen and, after the decline of Arras, ranked among the chief tapestry-producing centers. There Rogier van der Weyden was born and during the first half of the century the school of painting he inaugurated was not only one of the most prolific but gave the lead to other arts.

In every city painters were banded together in guilds bearing the name of their apostolic patron, St Luke. They were employed on decorating books and altarpieces and polychroming statues, and since they alone were entitled to teach drawing, all other forms of art were to some extent under their control. There were three stages in the painter's education. He began as an unpaid apprentice living with his master, who provided him with food and clothing for a period of from three to five years; next he became a journeyman or assistant, and finally a master-painter. When traveling, painters were entertained by their colleagues and visited their studios. In 1520 Dürer was given a triumphal reception in the Guild House at Antwerp. Painters circulated amongst themselves sketch-books illustrating the various interpretations of the great religious themes made by celebrated artists. They were under strict supervision, compelled to use only high-quality materials and their work was often "vetted" by senior members of the guild.

Most 15th-century pictures were painted on oak, though some were afterwards transferred to canvas, as was the case with Van der Weyden's *Last Judgment* (at Beaune). In the few pictures of this period which were painted directly on canvas a special technique was employed and line plays the leading part. They were perhaps in the nature of preliminary drafts or samples made before a picture was definitely commissioned, or may have been intended for use as decorative hangings.

The panels were primed with a white coat of chalk plaster mixed with glue, which at once provided a smooth ground to paint on and held the colors. Whereas some Italian Primitives began by superimposing on the ground a second coat made of pigment mixed with a binding material, of a color different from that of the undercoat —for example a greenish tinge for the flesh parts—the Flemish painter contented himself with a film of binding material only, which, being non-absorbent, enabled all the details of the picture to be painted on it without any blurring of the outlines. The colors used in the actual—that is to say final—painting consisted of one or several pigments mixed into one or more binding vehicles or media. These binding vehicles, in the case of the Flemings, were composed of a siccative oil into which was mixed some other ingredient such as a natural resin; their pigments were of organic or mineral origin. Laboratory examination has revealed a few places in the Ghent Altarpiece in which a binding material diluted with water was employed (in combination with elements of animal charcoal); these passages give the impression of constituting the preliminary drawing. Sometimes Van Eyck has superimposed tempera on passages first painted in oils so as to give them a richer sheen; as in the lapis-lazuli blue of the Virgin's robe. The reason why the blue in ancient pictures is often fissured is that this upper glaze, being highly fragile, has been damaged by careless restorers. The exact nature of the binding substance employed by Van Eyck has not been determined. Basic to it is siccative oil, but there is also some unknown ingredient, perhaps a natural resin soluble in oil. Painters had long been mixing oil with their pigments but had never so far succeeded in giving the impasto a really satisfactory consistency. Another diluent was called for and this may well have been discovered when, at the beginning of the 15th century, the simple process of distillation had superseded the complicated methods of the alchemists and turpentine was readily available. There is in fact much to be said for the view that what led to the sudden triumph of the oil medium in Europe and enabled Van Eyck to carry this technique to a perfection hitherto unknown, was simply the utilization of turpentine.

JAN VAN EYCK

Jan van Eyck made his first appearance in Holland when he was in the service of John of Bavaria, prince-bishop of Liège, who after the death of his brother William VI had become Count of Holland. Van Eyck was employed on decorating the Palace of The Hague from October 24, 1422, to September 11, 1424. By this time he was already a "master-painter." His patron died on January 5, 1425, leaving his finances in much confusion, and on May 19 of the same year Jan took service as court painter and *varlet de chambre* with Philip the Good, Duke of Burgundy, at a salary of 100 livres per annum. At first the painter lived at Lille and he now married a lady by whom he had ten children. Nothing is known about her except her Christian name—Marguerite—and the year of her birth, 1406. Van Eyck was sent on confidential missions by his princely master on several occasions. One of these journeys took him, it seems, to Aragon (in 1426-1427) with the embassy sent by the Duke of Burgundy to solicit the hand of Isabella of Spain, daughter of James II, Count of Urgel. On his return Van Eyck was given a sumptuous reception on the occasion of the festival of St Luke, October 18, 1427, by the burgomaster of Tournai, a town which he revisited on March 23, 1428. He took part in a second mission of the same kind, this time to Portugal, headed by Jean de Roubaix, whose purpose was to negotiate the Duke's marriage to Isabella, daughter of King John I. Van Eyck embarked on October 19, 1428, landed in Portugal on January 12 and promptly made a portrait of the princess, which was dispatched to Flanders on February 12, 1429. Having returned to Flanders at the end of the year, he was present at the wedding of the Duke and Princess Isabella in January 1430. In the course of his travels he put in a fairly long stay in the peninsula—in Galicia,

Castile and perhaps Andalusia—and took the opportunity of visiting England. In 1430 Van Eyck settled finally at Bruges, where next year he bought a house. The Duke visited his studio on January 19, 1433, addressed him as "our excellent painter and beloved friend," and in June 1434 consented to act as sponsor at the christening of one of his children. Two years later Van Eyck was sent by the Duke on yet another diplomatic mission, perhaps to Prague. Meanwhile he was working for the municipality as well as for his royal patron. In 1432 the Burgomaster visited his studio to inspect a work he was engaged on, and in 1435 he was commissioned to polychrome six statues on the façade of Bruges Town Hall. He died at Bruges on July 9, 1441, and was buried in the graveyard of St Donatian's Church. On March 21, 1442, at the instance of his brother Lambert, his body was exhumed and interred within the church itself. The Duke granted a pension to his widow and a dowry to one of his daughters, who in 1449 took the veil at St Agnes' Convent, Maaseyck. This tends to bear out a local tradition to the effect that the Van Eycks were natives of this hamlet or of the neighboring town of Maastricht (in a document of the period he is referred to as "Jan of Tricht").

Jan's social status was far above that of a mere artisan; his servants were permitted to wear the ducal livery and in state processions he walked next behind the highest in the land. He took a proper pride, it seems, in his official status and—what was exceptional in this period—signed his pictures, often adding explanatory legends and the device which, in imitation of the nobility, he had adopted as his motto: *Als ixh xan* ("As best I can"). In his *De Viris Illustribus* Bartolommeo Fazio informs us that Van Eyck was well versed in chemistry and geometry and even made a terrestrial globe for Philip the Good. But his paintings prove that his knowledge covered a much wider field, including theology, astronomy, anatomy and the science of perspective.

There is an obvious correlation between Van Eyck's technical procedures and his conception of the divine order in the universe. He depicts denizens of the celestial world on a monumental scale and (unlike the Boucicaut Master and, later, Hugo van der Goes and Gerard David) he has no qualms about investing human beings who figure in the scene with an equal grandeur. Behind them, in the far distance, we glimpse a miniature world of Lilliputian proportions, cities with busy streets, green meadows starred with flowers, forests, mountains, glaciers. It is as if we were gazing at familiar scenes of life from an infinite distance, from the heights of the world celestial which holds the foreground of the picture. Only these backgrounds can be described as realistic, accessible at first sight—though sometimes, for a full appreciation of their minutiae, a magnifying glass is needed. The more the sacred theme predominates in the picture, the more these details tend to be reduced in size almost to the point of invisibility. The artist's over-all conception is conveyed by the relations between these various elements of the composition and also by the presence of certain esoteric symbols whose purport, even at that time, only a few initiates could fathom. As he saw it, all that existed in nature was but a fragment of "one stupendous whole," a perfectly integrated universe.

Recognition came quickly to Jan van Eyck; he was acclaimed by his contemporaries as the inventor of a new technique of painting, only one other artist, Rogier van der Weyden, being esteemed his equal. Yet, strangely enough, a tendency has developed during the last hundred years to rank beside him, sometimes indeed above him, another painter presumed to be his elder brother Hubert. Was there really any such person and, despite all the research-work devoted to this problem, can a satisfactory conclusion be arrived at?

Those who saw the Ghent Altarpiece in earlier times, Dürer for instance (in 1520), mention Jan van Eyck only. It was not until 1565 that, for the first time, the name of Hubert was cited as that of the maker of the famous polyptych. Responsible for this was Lucas de Heere, who also spoke of a (purely imaginary) sister of the artist's, Margaret, whom he described as a miniature-painter. It would seem that a tradition was current at this time in Ghent to the effect that the painter had been interred immediately below his masterpiece—which could not apply to Jan, who was buried at Bruges. In 1495 Hieronymus Münzer, a German doctor, was shown the tomb below the altarpiece. When in 1517 Cardinal Louis of Aragon came to see "the fairest work of painting in all Christendom," his secretary was informed by a canon that its painter was a certain "Master Robert" who had come from Germany and died before finishing the work, which his brother took over from him. A stone slab bearing the date 1426 (now in the Ghent Museum of Ancient Inscriptions) is said to have come from Hubert's tomb, where it replaced a previous slab, destroyed in 1578. But the chief argument in favor of the existence of Hubert was the rediscovery in 1824, when the wing-panels which had just been acquired by the Berlin Museum were cleaned, of a Latin inscription on the lower margin of the outer frames. It was a quatrain of which the following fragments can be deciphered:

Hubertus ... Eyck. major quo nemo repertus
incepit. pondusque Johannes arte secundus
...... ecit. Judoci Vijd prece fretus
VersV seXta MaI Vos CoLLoCat aCta tVerI.

The last line is a chronogram, the capital letters denoting the year (1432) in which the work was completed. This fragmentary text (whose existence was mentioned by Christopher van Huerne in his Collection of Epitaphs made in 1615) informs us that Hubert... Eyck, "the greatest painter of all time," began the work; that Jan," second to him as an artist," completed it *(perfecit)* on instructions from Jodocus Vijd; and that it was dedicated on May 6, 1432. In 1882 Hilton questioned the authenticity of these lines, affirming that such chronograms were not in use as early as 1432. Moreover the script has not the clean-cut precision we find in other inscriptions known to be by Van Eyck's hand. Laboratory analysis has revealed that this inscription was painted on silverfoil applied to a part of the outer frame which had originally been gilt (like the inner frame) but whose gilding had worn off. Thus there can be no doubt that the quatrain (whose emphatic tone is reminiscent of the Renaissance rather than the 15th century) should be dated to the 16th century—though of course it may well be the exact replica of a previous inscription that had been rubbed off. There seem

JAN VAN EYCK (1385/1390-1441). GIOVANNI ARNOLFINI AND HIS WIFE, 1434. (33 × 22 ½″)
BY COURTESY OF THE TRUSTEES, NATIONAL GALLERY, LONDON.

XV 3

HUBERT (?) AND JAN VAN EYCK.

THE GHENT ALTARPIECE, 1426-1432. CENTRAL PANEL: THE ADORATION OF THE LAMB.

(53 × 92 ¾″) ST BAVO'S, GHENT.

to be no better grounds for holding the inscription to be genuine than for declaring it a forgery, as has been done by some art historians who regard it as a product of local patriotism on the part of the townsfolk of Ghent, unable to stomach the idea that their greatest art treasure was the work of a painter dwelling in the rival city of Bruges.

Attempts have been made to uncover evidence of Hubert's existence in records of the period. Four documents have been brought to light, in which reference is made to "Meester Luberecht," "Meester Ubrechts," "Hubrechte de scildere" and "Lubrecht van Heyke," respectively. There is no proof that these names, suggestive though they are, relate to the same person, or that this person was Jan's brother. It is strange, to say the least, that Hubert's name nowhere appears in the accounts kept up by the ducal treasury of the House of Burgundy, which had so many dealings with Jan. Finally, those who deny that any such person as Hubert existed stress the fact that there is no room for a tomb in the chapel where the polyptych is placed. But, thanks to the researches of two Belgian scholars, A.P. de Schryver and R.H. Marijnissen, it is now established that the polyptych originally stood in one of the chapels of the Lower Church and was not moved to its present place until 1587. (No trace of a tomb exists in this chapel but, considering the lapse of time, this proves nothing.)

Thus, so far as the facts go, Hubert may well have actually existed. Our difficulties begin when we turn to the works themselves. For the advocates of the existence of an elder brother seem to have let their enthusiasm run away with them in their attempts to build up a coherent œuvre around his—hypothetical—personality. They have begun by attributing to him *a priori* almost the whole of the inside of the Ghent altarpiece; then, by analogy, many other works. Indeed, if we are to believe them, the man of genius who conceived these pictures was Hubert (who is no more than a name to us) and Jan was merely a skillful executant. It has been easy for the opponents of this view to refute it and to reinstate Jan van Eyck in the place that is his due, by using as a basis of comparison works that bear his signature and whose authenticity has never been in doubt. The most that can be said is that the existence of an elder brother Hubert may be surmised, provided we assign the reasonable limits preconized by such authorities as Panofsky to his share in the work and frankly recognize the unique originality of Jan van Eyck's personal achievement.

To him must be attributed the outer part of the Ghent altarpiece, depicting the donors accompanied by the two St Johns (in grisaille) and, above, the Annunciation. These panels are completely homogeneous and should obviously be dated to the time when the rich Ghent merchant commissioned the artist to complete, at his expense, the polyptych, various parts of which had been already begun by Hubert or by Jan.

Hubert's share (if any) in the work must be looked for in the central panel and its wings, the starting-off point of the entire composition. The figures kneeling before the Fountain of the Water of Life seem to follow an early conception of the way of handling figures; their posing, the preponderance of profile views and the heaviness of the drapery bear this out. Similarly the foreground groups and especially the fancifully oriental touches in the prophets' garments (reminiscent of the International Style) may well form part of the initial lay-out of the composition, originally intended to culminate simply with the altar of the Lamb. On the other hand, the angels grouped round the Lamb, the Bishops and Holy Virgins, the luxuriant gardens with a remarkable variety of flowers (some indigenous to the North, some to the South), the highly skillful, detailed modeling of the buildings fretting the horizon—all are characteristic, both as to their details and their execution, of the style of Jan van Eyck in works whose attribution to him has never been questioned. The similarities in the type-forms of faces, the treatment of vegetation, hills and buildings have been analysed in detail by Emil Renders, and his conclusions seem fully justified. The sharply ascending perspective employed in this picture strikes me far less as an archaism than as a demonstration of the artist's ingenuity; it enabled him to depict on different planes, and without any risk of confusion, all the multifarious groups he wished to include in the composition. Nothing could be more typical of Jan van Eyck's genius than the way in which the elements mentioned above, in particular the distant scenes, are treated. The various plants and flowers have all been botanically identified; they comprise, *inter alia*, vines bearing white, translucent grapes, fig-trees, pomegranates, rose-trees in bloom, Solomon's seals, dandelions, clover, lilies-of-the-valley, strawberries and currant-bushes. Laboratory examination of these parts of the picture has confirmed their perfect homogeneity and everything points to their being entirely by Jan's hand. The same holds good for the wing-panels on the left in which the Just Judges and the Knights of the Faith are depicted, and also for those on the right, of Hermits and Pilgrims. (X-ray examination has revealed several pentimenti.) The preliminary work on these panels may have been done by Hubert, and Jan may have modified the lay-out so as to give it more elasticity and to enable him to insert the exotic plants and flowers, so clearly reminiscent of his travels in the South.

Renders had a theory that this polyptych was a combination of several altarpieces originally independent of one another, and attention has often been drawn to the disproportion in scale between the monumental figures in the upper tier and the scenes of *The Adoration of the Lamb*. It is quite possible that, to meet the requirements of Jodocus Vijd, Jan van Eyck incorporated pictures he had painted for other purposes, yet the ultimate version of the work as we see it today does not seem to conflict in any way with his artistic practice; indeed, I would say that the startling contrast between the scale of the celestial figures in the top register and that of the sanctified mortals adoring the Lamb in a sort of earthly paradise was quite deliberate.

There has been almost as much controversy about the figures in the upper row. Though the three monumental forms—of God the Father (some have seen here a Christ in Majesty), the Virgin and St John the Baptist—are placed in similar Romanesque niches inscribed with passages from the Book of Wisdom, there are divergencies in the manner in which these figures are treated. That of God has all the characteristics

PAGE 21: JAN VAN EYCK (1385/1390-1441). GIOVANNI ARNOLFINI AND HIS WIFE (DETAIL), 1434.
BY COURTESY OF THE TRUSTEES, NATIONAL GALLERY, LONDON.

of Jan van Eyck's style, as have the representations of Adam and Eve at each end of the row. The restrained realism of these figures and the typically "modern" sensibility in their presentation are stressed by the ascending perspective. Seen thus from below, they seem to be straining up towards the level of God, who is depicted in inverted perspective. They were probably painted last of all, to complete the polyptych and fill up the space left empty owing to the vaulting of the Lower Chapel in which it stood. On the other hand, the figures of the Virgin and St John are painted in oblique perspective—a procedure which Jan seems to have abandoned at an early date (here perhaps we have vestiges of Hubert's work). But the execution, in particular the modeling of faces, the treatment of the hair, the richly ornate crown, is wholly in Jan's style, and the same is true of the angel musicians.

The whole conception of the Ghent altarpiece, no less than its grandeur and complexity, shows that its maker was profoundly versed in Christian theology. Its leading theme, the Redemption, is basic to the Catholic faith. Two proximate sources of the painter's inspiration have been suggested: firstly, the illustration of a vision of the great mystic St Hildegard, described in a tract on the Communion of the Saints written in 1151; secondly, the liturgy of the Office of All Saints' Day, inspired by the Apocalypse and the Beatitudes pronounced in the Sermon on the Mount. The lines enumerating the Blessed—hermits and monks, patriarchs and prophets, pilgrims, virgins, judges, knights, apostles, martyrs and confessors—apply to the various groups advancing in devout procession towards the Lamb. But what is certainly unique in the history of painting and makes this picture, to quote the words of Fierens-Gevaert, "the religious saga of a race," almost one might say a mystic incantation, is the way the painter has interpreted these texts, the spirit animating this gradual progress towards the Godhead, the expressions on the faces, lit up by the inner light of faith, of all these dedicated men and women. It is this all-pervasive spirit that unifies—and how magnificently!—the various groups and guides them, freely moving yet single-minded, through the varied scenes on the side-panels, through the sunlit forests and green pastures of the central picture. Even if we admit that some portions of this great work may have been designed by some other artist, we cannot doubt it was the genius of a single man that saw it through and that this man was Jan van Eyck.

A certain number of Jan's works, being signed and dated, give us a general idea of the evolution of his art. Amongst these are: *Tymotheos* (1432), *Portrait of a Man in a Red Turban* (1433), *Giovanni Arnolfini and his Wife* (1434), all in the National Gallery, London; the *Ince Hall Madonna* or *Madonna in her Chamber* (1433) in the National Gallery, Melbourne; *The Madonna of Canon van der Paele* (1434) in the Musée Communal, Bruges; *Portrait of Jan de Leeuw* (1436), Kunsthistorisches Museum, Vienna; *St Barbara* (1437) and *Madonna by the Fountain* (1439), both in the Musée Royal, Antwerp; *Portrait of Margaret van Eyck* (1439), Musée Communal, Bruges. It is also possible to date the *Portrait of Bauldoyn de Lannoy*, Kaiser Friedrich Museum, Berlin; de Lannoy, who was Governor of Lille and Chamberlain to the Duke, took part in the mission to Portugal. The portrait was evidently painted after his return, since he is

JAN VAN EYCK (1385/1390-1441). PORTRAIT OF A MAN IN A RED TURBAN, 1433. (10 ¼×7 ½″)
BY COURTESY OF THE TRUSTEES, NATIONAL GALLERY, LONDON.

wearing the Order of the Golden Fleece, which was not created until 1430. Cardinal Albergati, Papal Legate to the Kings of France and England and to the Duke of Burgundy, visited Bruges in 1431 and presumably the famous silverpoint drawing of him now in Dresden was made during this visit. On it are color notes jotted down in the Limburg dialect by the artist. This obviously served as a preliminary sketch for the portrait of Cardinal Albergati now in the Kunsthistorisches Museum, Vienna.

Jan van Eyck brought about vital changes in the art of portrait painting and here, too, succeeded in reconciling opposites. True, his drawing is meticulously accurate, he spares us no details, everything, even the texture of skin and the stubble on ill-shaven cheeks, is set forth with almost photographic verisimilitude. None the less we feel that his main interest lay not in externals but in the personality of his sitter, his inmost self. For though the facial expressions seem studiously non-committal, almost enigmatic, there is always something in the gaze that tells us of the man's or woman's character: of anxiety or self-interest, cunning or candor. Moreover Van Eyck was first of all artists

JAN VAN EYCK (1385/1390-1441). THE MADONNA OF CANON VAN DER PAELE, 1436. (48×61½")
MUSÉE COMMUNAL, BRUGES.

JAN VAN EYCK (1385/1390-1441). THE MADONNA OF CHANCELLOR ROLIN, 1435-1436. (26×24¼″)
LOUVRE, PARIS.

to paint a portrait (the *Man in a Red Turban*) in which the sitter's gaze is directed straight towards the spectator, establishing personal contact with him. It is thus that a painter making a self-portrait sees himself in the mirror; indeed there are grounds for believing it to be a self-portrait—which lends this picture even greater interest.

Unique of its kind, combining as it does a full-length double portrait with an interior scene that is a genre piece in itself, is the famous *Giovanni Arnolfini and his Wife*. A merchant hailing from Lucca, Arnolfini had settled at Bruges in 1420 and been appointed a Councillor to Philip the Good. He and his wife Jeanne Cenani are standing, clad in sumptuous garments, in the foreground of a comfortably furnished room. The man, who is holding himself very straight, conscious of the solemnity of the occasion, wears a fur cloak and a huge, wide-brimmed hat, while his wife, whose hand he lightly clasps, is clad in a voluminous green gown trimmed with ermine. They are

JAN VAN EYCK (1385/1390-1441). THE MADONNA OF CHANCELLOR ROLIN (DETAIL), 1435-1436.
LOUVRE, PARIS.

not looking at each other; the painter's aim, it seems, was to celebrate the climax of the marriage ceremony when the couple link hands. Though light is flooding in from the window, a candle is alight in the chandelier: symbol of Christ, Light of the World, unseen witness of the pledge expressed by the bridegroom's lifted hand. As Panofsky points out, every detail here has its significance, and there are similar details in Van Eyck's religious works. Thus the necklace of crystal beads and the flawless mirror, whose frame is decorated with scenes of the Passion, symbolize purity and innocence; the fruit in the window, the delights of man's lost paradise; the small griffin terrier, fidelity. The mirror on the back wall gives us a glimpse of two persons entering the room, one the painter himself; hence the inscription on the wall, *Jan van Eyck fuit hic* (was present here).

Van Eyck painted several Madonnas, notable being those at Melbourne and Frankfort, which have much in common. In both we see the Virgin seated well in the center of the composition under a canopy; falling in ample folds, her cloak streams out in front of her, adding a touch of solemnity to a very natural attitude. The setting is a fairly large room in which figure her symbolic attributes: a crystal carafe and fruit without blemish. In *The Madonna by the Fountain* (1439), in which the Virgin is standing in front of a curtain held by angels, with a rose garden in the background, the presentation is simple to the point of homeliness. In this charming little picture Van Eyck harks back to the "closed garden" theme and the touches of archaism are doubtless intentional. In the 1437 *St Barbara* we have merely the preliminary design, drawn with the brush on a white ground; but so detailed and precise is the linework that it well may give us a clearer idea of what the artist was aiming at than would have done the painting, had it been "completed." Indeed it would seem that Van Eyck wished this picture to remain in its present state, since he gave it a simulated marble frame and signed it.

In the *Madonna* of the Dresden altarpiece the architectural elements are treated on a lavish scale, as is the case in his large-size compositions showing the Virgin attended by saints and donors, in the pictures commissioned by Chancellor Rolin and Canon Van der Paele, and in his last (unfinished) works, *The Madonna with a Carthusian* and the Ypres altarpiece. More than any others, these pictures throw light on Jan van Eyck's use of symbols and his antiquarian proclivities. It will be noticed how prominently Romanesque forms figure in his work, though Romanesque architecture had died out over two centuries before, and it is clear he must have studied ancient monuments very attentively. Jean Pucelle had already had the idea of using ruins and intact buildings to symbolize the contrast between Judaism and Christianity. The Master of Flémalle and Van Eyck employed the Romanesque and Gothic styles to signify respectively the Old and the New Testament, and in several of their pictures Gothic and Romanesque forms are combined in meaningful patterns. Van Eyck's *Annunciation* in the National Gallery, Washington, is a case in point. The building is obviously imaginary since its base is Gothic and its upper part Romanesque. From high up on the right of the choir the God of the Old Testament is transmitting his

JAN VAN EYCK (1385/1390-1441).
THE MADONNA OF CANON VAN DER PAELE,
1436. DETAIL: THE VIRGIN'S HAND.
MUSÉE COMMUNAL, BRUGES.

message to the Virgin in the form of rays streaming down from a Romanesque round-arched window into the Gothic interior, symbolizing the New Dispensation. Romanesque stands also for the future as against the present, the heavenly Jerusalem as against the world of men. In *The Madonna of Chancellor Rolin*, the Chancellor kneels in front of the Virgin in a luxurious palace decorated with jasper and porphyry. The elaborately carved capitals of the columns depict Old Testament scenes and incidents of Roman history, suggesting the fusion of the old and new orders. Beyond the arcade is a walled garden of supernal beauty, gay with lilies, irises and roses, an evocation of the *hortus conclusus* of Paradise. Across the crenellated wall we glimpse a river valley and a city rendered with extraordinary minuteness, a bridge dotted with tiny figures, several churches, and roads winding their way across the sunlit countryside towards a far-off line of snowy peaks. Attempts have been made to identify this city with Liège, Maastricht, Lyons and Prague, but to no purpose; it is a symbolic vision of an ideal city, built up of fragments taken from the real cities the artist visited in the course of his travels. In the Dresden *Madonna* there is the same combination of Romanesque arches with Gothic pillars, while the capitals, right and left, depict scenes of Roman history and the Old Testament respectively. In several pictures the floor is patterned with the signs of the Zodiac arranged in view of their appropriateness to the thematic elements; thus in the Washington *Annunciation* the angel is kneeling on the sign of the Ram (i.e. March, month of the Annunciation) while the lilies rest on Capricorn (sign of Christmas).

In *The Madonna of Canon van der Paele* we have a summing-up of the symbolist aesthetic basic to Van Eyck's art. As in the Dresden triptych the Madonna is seated above a deep-piled carpet flowing across a richly diversified tiled floor and rendered with well-nigh illusionist realism. The background (which occupies less space than usual in proportion to the figures) is the interior of a sumptuous Romanesque basilica, with some small Gothic details. The lay-out is almost rigidly symmetrical and the minute delicacy of the brushwork brings out the differing textures and plastic "feel" of precious stones, drapery and gold. Though the figure of St George is ostensibly in movement (he is in the act of raising his helmet as he steps forward to present the Canon to the Madonna), it is a curiously arrested movement and his smile seems oddly

JAN VAN EYCK (1385/1390-1441). THE MADONNA OF CANON VAN DER PAELE, 1436. DETAIL: THE CANON'S HANDS. MUSÉE COMMUNAL, BRUGES.

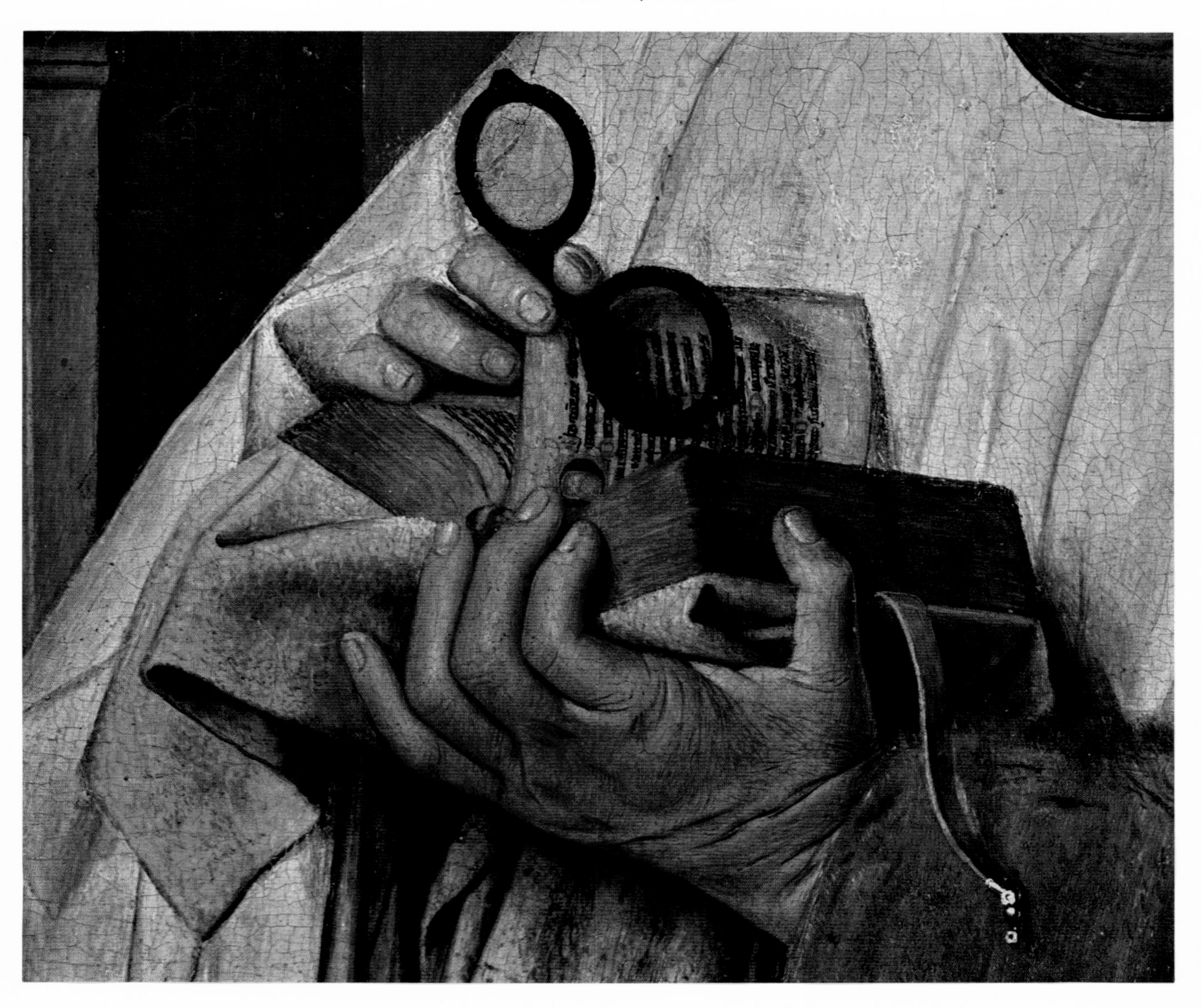

JAN VAN EYCK (1385/1390-1441). THE ANNUNCIATION. DETAIL: HEAD OF THE ANGEL.
MELLON COLLECTION, NATIONAL GALLERY OF ART, WASHINGTON.

petrified. The Madonna and St Donatian in his gorgeous brocaded cope are no less statuesque. On the other hand, the face of the Canon, with its ivory white cheeks which have the suppleness of living flesh, is instinct with vitality.

Suggestions have been made that we may attribute to the hand of Jan and perhaps to Hubert van Eyck certain illuminations whose style has affinities with theirs. Tradition has it that they took part in illustrating the *Très Belles Heures de Notre-Dame* commissioned by the Duke of Berry. These miniatures, now in the Museo Civico at Turin (some were destroyed in the great fire at the Royal Library of Turin in 1904), have been studied by Count Durrieu and Hulin de Loo, who see in them the work of two different artists, one designated as "Hand H" and responsible for four scenes, the other as "Hand G" and responsible for seven scenes. The composition of the miniatures by "Hand H" is dense, strongly expressive—an intensification as it were of Jan van Eyck's style. *The Crucifixion* was inspired by one of his pictures whose original is lost, but a contemporary copy can be seen in Venice in the Ca' d'Oro. The art of the "Hand G" miniatures is at once subtler and more original. In *The Birth of St John* the artist has experimented with two different kinds of perspective; the vanishing lines of ceiling and floor converge, while for the furniture the oblique perspective used by the Master of Flémalle is resorted to. The two seascapes (these were destroyed in the Turin fire but photographs of them are extant), with their flat landscapes and extremely low horizon-line, are—like the small scenes in the lower margins—much in advance of their day. So much so that F. Lyna holds these works to be, very possibly, post-Van Eyckian and to date from the middle or latter half of the 15th century. From which it follows that de Loo's attribution of the "Hand G" group to Hubert and "Hand H" to Jan can hardly be relied on. On the whole it seems more likely that the "Hand G" miniatures were works of Jan van Eyck's maturity, while those by "Hand H" may belong to his last period or were made soon after his death by an imitator or disciple.

Jan van Eyck died relatively young, in his fifties, and his œuvre, spanning a period of some twenty years, is remarkably uniform, showing no tendency to weaken with advancing years. None the less we can see how he gradually individualized the Virgin's face as time went on and made it fuller, though without diminishing its languid grace, emphasized now and then by gentle movements of the delicately formed hands. The massive sweep of garments becomes more fluent; they fall in ampler folds with deeper grooves between them, while colors, however strong, keep their unique translucency. Movement is "fixed" at its most telling moment, arrested at its climax, emotion given full expression in tranquillity. Born of lofty aspirations and impeccable technique, Van Eyck's art is perfect, complete in itself. Though he exercised a veritable fascination on his contemporaries, and not in Flanders only, it was a matter rather of prestige than of any direct influence. True, Luis Dalmau signed (in 1445) at Barcelona the altarpiece of *The Virgin of the Councillors* which contained some panels directly copied from the Ghent altarpiece, but this was an exception. Artists of the latter half of the 15th century were far more prone to borrow themes and take a lead from Rogier van der Weyden or his hypothetical precursor, the Master of Flémalle.

THE MASTER OF FLÉMALLE

ROGIER VAN DER WEYDEN

Such is the number and diversity of the works attributed to Van der Weyden (as compared with the compact, coherent œuvre of Jan van Eyck) that art historians have tended to ascribe the earlier works to an unidentified painter given (by Von Tschudi in 1898) the name of the Master of Flémalle. Nevertheless the Italian chroniclers of the time, Cyriacus of Ancona (in 1449), Bartolommeo Fazio (1454-1455) and Giovanni Santi (1485) couple one name only with that of "the great Jan": that of Rogier of Brussels, his disciple. This obviously implies that Rogier must have been a good deal younger that Jan and that even if he was not Jan's pupil in the full sense of the term, is unlikely to have had any influence on him. No work signed by Rogier is extant and when we seek to glean any precise idea of his life and work, we come up against a problem even more baffling than that of the dubious existence of Hubert van Eyck.

It was in the middle of the 19th century that Alphonse Wauters, keeper of the Public Records at Brussels, conjointly with the scholars Pinchart, Hocquet and Houtart, unearthed some facts concerning the painter's life. We now know that Roger de la Pasture (French form of Rogier van der Weyden) was born in 1399 at Tournai and was the son of Henri de la Pasture, a cutler, and Agnès de Watelos. On November 17, 1426, "Master Rogier" was received with honor by the Burgomaster of that city and presented with "twice four measures of wine"—double the ration given Jan van Eyck a year later on a similar occasion. From the Register of the Guild of St Luke we learn that on March 5, 1427, "Rogelet de la Pasture" and Jaquelotte Daret enrolled as apprentices with the master-painter Robert Campin. (Daret had been working as a "companion" in Campin's workshop since 1418.) Prior to April 21, 1435, Rogier was registered as a resident of Brussels and subsequently was appointed City Painter. He decorated the Town Hall with the famous pictures of Trajan and Herkinbald administering justice, which were destroyed in 1695 when Brussels was bombarded by the troops of Marshal de Villeroy, but we can get an idea of what they were like from the tapestries inspired by them, now in the Historisches Museum at Bern. However he kept in touch with his native city, investing in its public securities in 1435 and again in 1441. His mother and sister continued living at Tournai, and Rogier acted as guardian to the latter's children. In 1449 Van der Weyden went to Italy, where he visited Rome with a view to obtaining the jubilee indulgence of the Holy Year of 1450, and was, it seems, much impressed by Gentile da Fabriano's frescos in St John Lateran. On his way back to Brussels he spent some months at the court of Lionello d'Este at Ferrara. After 1460 he entertained at his home the Italian painter Zanetto Bugatti, whom the Duke of Milan, Francesco Sforza, had sent to study under him in Brussels. Wealthy, highly esteemed, he bestowed large dowries on his children. He died in 1464 and was buried in the Collegiate Church of St Gudule. The memorial mass, however, attended by all the members of the painters' guild, was celebrated at Tournai—which seems to show that he was always regarded as a citizen of that town. Actually there was a clause in the regulations of the Painters' Guild of Tournai under which a master-painter living elsewhere could continue to enjoy the privileges of membership, provided he paid the statutory dues.

It certainly seems strange that the distinguished artist who was welcomed with such pomp and circumstance at Tournai in 1426 should have enrolled as an apprentice in Campin's workshop in 1427 and been nominated "master" only in 1432. This seeming anomaly has led some art historians (amongst them Renders) to maintain that Rogier is not to be identified with "Rogelet" and that Campin's apprentice led an obscure life at Tournai, while Master Rogier made a great name for himself at Brussels. Those, on the other hand, who believe that Rogier and Rogelet (it was the custom at Tournai to call apprentices by "pet names" derived from their given names) were one and the

MASTER OF FLÉMALLE. THE NATIVITY (DETAIL), BEFORE 1430. MUSÉE DE LA VILLE, DIJON.

MASTER OF FLÉMALLE. THE NATIVITY, BEFORE 1430. (32 ½ × 27 ½″)
MUSÉE DE LA VILLE, DIJON.

same man maintain that the title "master" as applied to the artist in 1426 may either have referred to some branch of art other than painting or else to his having qualified as such in another town. But, despite research, no evidence to this effect has been forthcoming; though the fact that Rogier's son, Corneille, took his degree of Master of Arts in Louvain may be suggestive. One thing anyhow is known: that after a period of varying length during which the young painter was taught the fundamentals of his craft, he had to undergo a course of "administrative" training and not until this was over could he rank as a master and open a workshop of his own. Quite possibly even an artist of acknowledged merit had to go through this formality before being admitted to full membership of the Guild. At any rate, the date of Rogier's promotion to the rank of master-painter, 1432, may be accepted and the works prior to this date may be ascribed to another painter, perhaps Robert Campin—which would account for the stylistic affinities of the master and disciple. The ascription of the altarpiece from the Abbey of Saint-Vaast at Arras (whose panels are now divided between the Kaiser Friedrich Museum, Berlin, the Petit Palais, Paris, and the Thyssen Collection, Lugano) to Daret has made it clear that his style is very different and that he too used themes deriving from the Master of Flémalle. In his *Visitation* is a circular building resembling that in the Master of Flémalle's *Miracle of the Rod* (Prado), and in Daret's *Nativity* in the Thyssen Collection are the same, rarely found figures of the two midwives who are also present in the Master of Flémalle's Dijon *Nativity*. This tends to corroborate the generally accepted view that Robert Campin and the Master of Flémalle are identical.

On the other hand, if the Brussels "Master Rogier" was a much admired painter as early as 1426, he may well have been the author of the works attributed to the Flémalle Master, in which case these would be his early efforts. (This is Renders' and Lavalleye's view.) That there is an intriguing kinship between the works attributed to the Master of Flémalle and those known to be Van der Weyden's is undeniable. A host of examples of identical details—sometimes at many years' distance—has been pointed out, and while frankly admitting that great differences of style exist between the Master of Flémalle's earliest works and Rogier's last, Renders has rightly drawn attention to the fact that this is not the case with the Master of Flémalle's last works and Rogier's earliest, which were contemporary as well as much alike. In both he finds the same method of composition, resemblances in the drawing and color-schemes, striking analogies in the treatment of figures, hands, hair and garments. Renders has also pointed out that several Flémalle pictures depict sacred edifices, in the Brabantine style, which can be identified; for example the Church of Notre-Dame-des-Victoires at Brussels (in *The Miracle of the Rod*), just as the nave of Sainte-Gudule figures in Rogier's altarpiece of *The Seven Sacraments*. But Campin, it seems, led an active and eventful life; there are many gaps in our knowledge of his movements, and he may well have visited Brussels. Finally, when Colin de Coter (in a work preserved in the church of Vieure in the Allier department of France) imitated Rogier's *St Luke painting the Virgin's Portrait*, he incorporated in the background the scene of St Joseph making mousetraps which figures in the Mérode *Annunciation*.

The most cogent argument in favor of the separation of the Flémalle œuvre is based on the evident maturity of certain works which are almost certainly previous to the first known pictures by Van Eyck and may be dated to approximately 1420. Can it be possible that so young an artist as Rogier then was should have painted them? The knowledge we possess regarding the painters of this period, the long course of training they had to undergo and the strict controls of the guild system, practically rule out any such precocity. Rarely does a painter achieve full mastery of his talent before he is in his thirties, and this holds good for Van Eyck no less than for Bouts. So it would seem more reasonable to ascribe the works of the Master of Flémalle to some such painter as Robert Campin, who was born prior to 1380 at Valenciennes and settled at Tournai where he acquired citizenship in 1410, directed a large workshop, became dean of the painters' guild in 1423 and was elected a member of the City Council. Subsequently, owing to the part he played in the political troubles of 1423-1428, he fell foul of the authorities, was accused of "living in concubinage" and banished from the city. However, the term of exile was reduced thanks to the good offices of the Duchess of Hainaut. He died on April 28, 1444. Obviously these dates fit in with the period assigned to the productions of the Master of Flémalle and there is no question that his reputation which, if not international like Van Eyck's and Rogier's, was well established in his day, justifies the attribution to him of an œuvre of such high quality.

It was, moreover, an extremely large body of work, comparable to Van Eyck's and probably more extensive than that which can be positively assigned to Van der Weyden. Tolnay has described the Master of Flémalle as the true founder of the Flemish School, since several of his works preceded those of Jan van Eyck, which they undoubtedly

MELCHIOR BROEDERLAM. THE FLIGHT INTO EGYPT, CA. 1399. DETAIL: ST JOSEPH. MUSÉE DE LA VILLE, DIJON.

influenced—though soon the influence was reciprocal. This painter's art comes very near that of the Franco-Flemish School, Jacquemart de Hesdin's and the Boucicaut Master's miniatures. His first step was to transpose the homely interiors and landscapes of the miniature-painters into big altarpieces which, however, still have gold backgrounds and a lingering primitivism. But in the earliest work ascribed to him, the triptych now in Count Seilern's collection (London), the Master of Flémalle displays a rare power of exact observation. Taking over the discoveries of Broederlam, he develops and generalizes them, stressing contrasts between the various figures, some of which have an almost startling ugliness. These tendencies can be seen in the *Marriage of the Virgin* and *The Miracle of the Rod* (Prado), a twofold composition in which, for the first time, well before Van Eyck, he combines Romanesque and Gothic architectural forms. On the back are two simulated statues in grisaille of St James the Great and St Clare

MASTER OF FLÉMALLE. THE IMPENITENT THIEF (DETAIL), AFTER 1430. WING OF A LOST ALTARPIECE. STÄDELSCHES KUNSTINSTITUT, FRANKFORT.

MASTER OF FLÉMALLE. THE WERL ALTARPIECE, 1438. RIGHT WING: ST BARBARA (DETAIL). PRADO, MADRID.

of Assisi, the first painted imitations of statuary since Giotto's frescos. In these figures, which look like sculpture brought to life, the artist made a great forward stride in mastering the third dimension and pointed the way to monumental forms in painting.

A careful study of works of sculpture—perhaps Claus Sluter's and undoubtedly those of the master-sculptors working at Tournai—probably lay behind those extraordinary figures which make their appearance in the Flémalle Master's work around 1425, in particular that of the Virgin in the Mérode *Annunciation* and the London *Madonna*. Here the majestic presence and grave beauty of the Virgin and the maturity of her face are in striking contrast with the naïve, girlish charm of Van Eyck's Virgins. The figures are placed in interiors painted with thoroughgoing realism and containing objects of common use such as were found, presumably, in most Flemish houses. In *The Annunciation* the room is treated box-wise, space being expressed by the foreshortenings of the fireplace, the wooden bench and the timbered ceiling. The composition is extremely dense, its various elements being so closely dovetailed as to leave no open spaces. The scene is presented in the oblique perspective already used by Giotto, Broederlam and the Limbourgs, which disappeared for good round about 1430. Hence the much foreshortened, almost flattened forms on which the light falls harshly, an illumination very different from Van Eyck's diffused light. As Paul Rolland has pointed out, these forms are clearly reminiscent of the carvings in relief which were being made by the Tournai sculptors about this time.

Most characteristic feature of the Master of Flémalle's art is his highly realistic treatment of religious symbols, which are as frequent and precise in his work as in Van Eyck's. In the London *Madonna* the Virgin is shown seated, apparently on a footstool, in front of a wooden bench adorned with small carved lions—a version of Solomon's throne adapted to the atmosphere of a burgher's home—with a plaited firescreen behind her head to protect her from the heat of the fire. This firescreen is a naturalistic substitute for a halo. Similarly, as Meyer Schapiro has pointed out, the famous scene of St Joseph making mousetraps, in the right wing of the Mérode altarpiece, is an allusion to the Augustinian doctrine that with the marriage of the Virgin and the Incarnation God set a mousetrap baited to catch the devil. In both these works occurs, for the first time in art, the motif of a realistic view of a town with gabled roofs showing through an open window. If the Master of Flémalle is rightly identified with Campin, Van Eyck may well have seen this altarpiece when he was at Tournai in 1427 and 1428. Indeed he seems to have drawn inspiration from it for his *Annunciation* on the back of the Ghent altarpiece.

In the Dijon *Nativity* we have for the first time a landscape background given a large place in the picture. In front is a hut with ragged walls—symbolizing the imminent collapse of the Old Testament—all the structural details being rendered with complete verisimilitude. (Later, in Rogier's Bladelin altarpiece, the Nativity is located in a small

ROGIER VAN DER WEYDEN (1399/1400-1464). THE ANNUNCIATION (DETAIL), CA. 1435. LOUVRE, PARIS.

ROGIER VAN DER WEYDEN (1399/1400-1464). THE ANNUNCIATION (DETAIL), CA. 1435.
LOUVRE, PARIS.

Romanesque temple.) A spacious countryside occupies the entire top of the picture, while on the right a road flanked by a few houses, winding its way through a wintry landscape of bare trees, stresses the effect of deep recession. In the middle distance we see a man riding a horse and, further on, a town—whose purely imaginary architecture is much more conventional than the details of the picture—, a lofty castle on a hill and a lake on which a boat (a subsequent addition, it would seem) is sailing. On the left the sun is rising behind a jagged peak and on one of the foothills bathed in level light are a vineyard and a tiny farmhouse. Particularly striking is the contrast between the symbolic figures of the angels and the simple lifelike renderings of the shepherds; between the ideal beauty of the Virgin and the wrinkled face of St Joseph, who is here the mild old man that Van der Weyden was so often to portray. On his left are the massive figures of the midwives in voluminous Flemish costumes, wearing white head-cloths falling in elaborate folds. (Similar figures can be seen in many of Van der Weyden's works.) Following Broederlam, the color-scheme is light and delicate, the dominant hues being green, red and blue, with skillful interminglings of yellow and lilac.

The Master of Flémalle's greatest work, if we are to judge by the influence it had on several generations of painters throughout the century, was an immense *Descent from the Cross*. We can get a general idea of it from a rather poor copy in the Walker Art Gallery, Liverpool; all that has survived of the original is a fragment of the right wing-panel showing the Impenitent Thief and two Roman soldiers (Städelsches Kunstinstitut, Frankfort). The lay-out of its central scene—reverted to notably by Bouts, Memling and Gerard David and at the close of the century by the Bruges Master of 1500 and by Benson in the Segovia altarpiece—may well have inspired the world-famous *Descent from the Cross* in the

MASTER OF FLÉMALLE. THE WERL ALTARPIECE, 1438.
RIGHT WING: ST BARBARA. (39¾×18½") PRADO, MADRID.

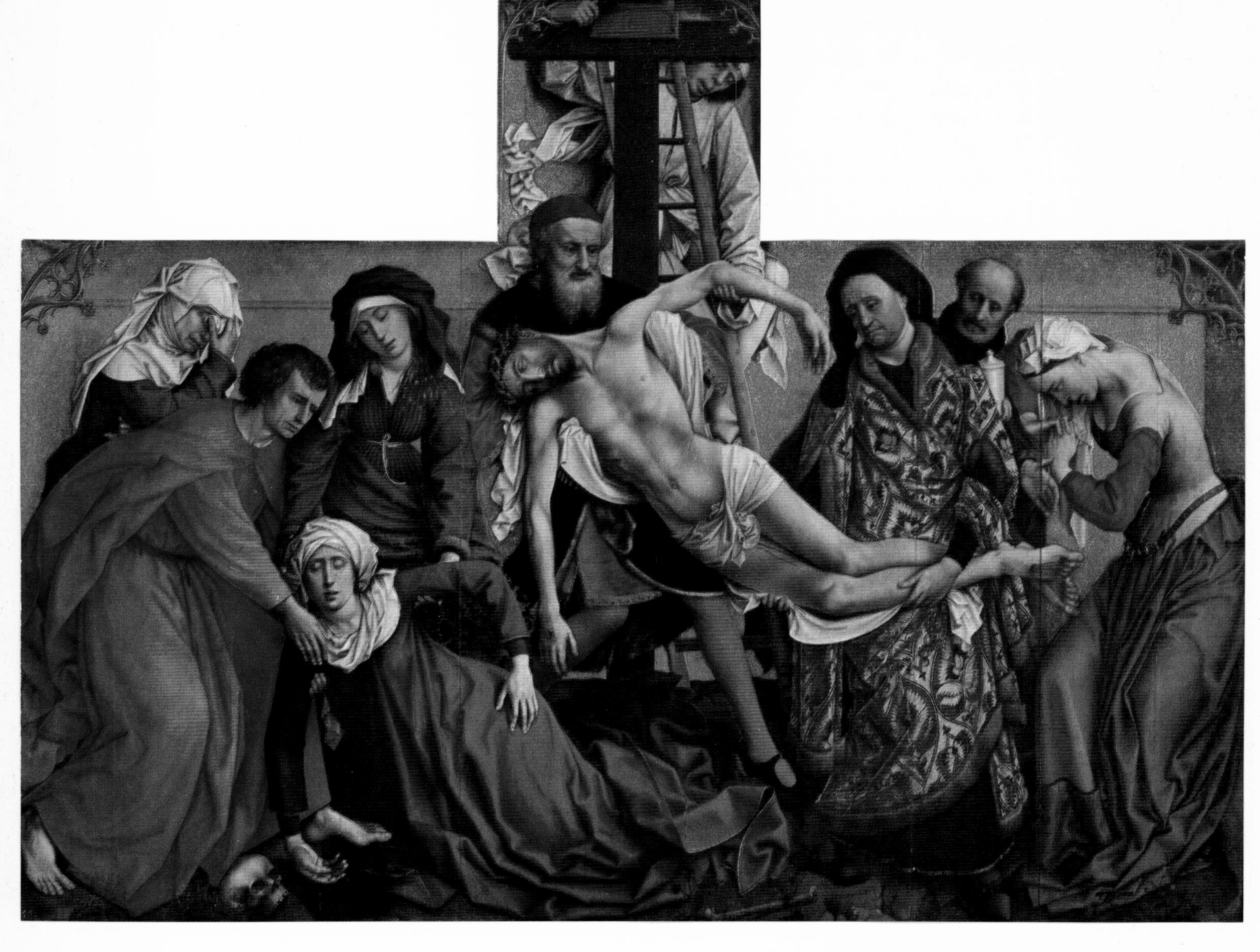

ROGIER VAN DER WEYDEN (1399/1400-1464). THE DESCENT FROM THE CROSS, CA. 1435. (86 ½ × 110″) PRADO, MADRID.

Prado, the first large picture attributed to Rogier van der Weyden. After figuring for many years in Notre-Dame-du-Dehors at Louvain, the last-named picture was bought by Maria of Hungary who presented it to the King of Spain. It contains ten figures grouped as in a bas-relief; volumes are stressed, telling out strongly on a close-up background; the highest point of the composition, the Cross, is but summarily indicated so as to focus attention on the rigid body of the dead Christ, traversing the foreground diagonally, its line being paralleled by the Virgin's drooping form. Noteworthy, too, is the figure of the Magdalen, shown in profile, with which the painter closes the composition on the right. Her anguish is expressed by the movement of her arms, whose curious contortion verges on mannerism. (Van Eyck, too, sometimes used gestures of this sort, for example in the *Crucifixion* in the Metropolitan Museum, New York, but there was still a touch of naïvety in the way he handled them.) Notable, too, is the strongly plastic treatment of the folds of her garment, which form an intricate, sculpture-like arabesque. Panofsky regards this picture as a "painted critique" of the Flémalle-Campin *Descent from the Cross* and in fact it seems that Rogier wished to stress, as against his teacher, the priority that should be given to the expression of emotions rather than to picturesque or anecdotal elements.

Nevertheless there is no denying that the Frankfort fragment of the Flémalle picture is one of the masterpieces of Flemish painting. The look of agony on the thief's face is all the more poignant for its frozen calm, while in the depiction of the dislocated body, the flesh cut into by the thongs, cruelty there is, but firmly kept in hand. No other work of the period contains faces so startlingly lifelike as those of the Roman soldiers, particularly the one with an oriental type of face who has a white scarf tied round his curly hair, and it is easy to understand why a detail such as this was imported bodily into other pictures by Rogier (or his disciples), for example in the right wing of the Bladelin altarpiece. However, the Master of Flémalle's rendering is franker and more vigorous. It should be noted that these figures, though "modernistic," are given a gold background, doubtless because this enabled the painter to individualize them yet more strongly. For in using this background he certainly had no archaistic intent, considering that in other works such as the Dijon *Nativity*, unquestionably earlier, he had included landscapes delightfully true to nature. The fragments of another triptych, also in the Städelsches Institut, Frankfort, depicting the Madonna, St Veronica and the Trinity (in grisaille), likewise contain monumental forms, stripped of all anecdotal elements; they look like figures carved in full round placed in front of a brocaded backcloth. They were believed to have come from an abbey at Flémalle-lès-Liège; hence the name given the artist. It was later discovered that no such abbey ever existed; however Panofsky has pointed out that in this town there was a Priory of the Knights Templars made over to the Order of St John, which may once have owned the triptych.

From approximately 1435 onward, all the works ascribed to the Master of Flémalle show more and more signs of Jan van Eyck's influence. Outlines grow softer, light is more diffused, landscapes become remoter and, though still precisely rendered, are treated with a lighter touch. We see this in the small *Madonna in Glory* (Musée Granet,

Aix-en-Provence), a visionary theme *par excellence*, in which the Virgin appears to St Peter, St Augustine and an Augustinian abbot. Here, however, the artist has indulged in one of the naïve extravagances of his early days when he shows the Virgin seated on a ponderous, carved bench poised on a cloud bank half way up the sky.

Of the triptych made in 1438 for Heinrich von Werl, a professor at Cologne University, only two panels have survived (they are in the Prado): *The Donor and St John the Baptist* and *St Barbara*. Here the Master of Flémalle's stock themes and the symbols of the Virgin, adapted with slight changes to St Barbara—the lily replaced by an iris, the carved lions of the bench omitted—are treated in quite the Eyckian spirit. In the left panel we even find a round, convex mirror reflecting the side window and the backs of St John and the donor, as in the Arnolfini portrait. The *St Barbara* also has points in common with a seemingly contemporary picture by Rogier, the Louvre *Annunciation*, which contains several similar objects, such as a carafe with the light shining through it and an embossed metal pitcher of a peculiar shape. However, the mere fact that these accessories figure in both pictures by no means proves that the Flémalle Master should be identified with Rogier, for in the same picture Rogier reproduces a detail of the double portrait of Arnolfini and his wife, viz. the chandelier —and no one has ever dreamt of identifying Rogier with Jan van Eyck. Nevertheless it is interesting to compare these pictures for the light they throw on the close contacts between the three great 15th-century Flemish masters.

In his *St Luke painting the Virgin's Portrait* Rogier van der Weyden drew once again on Van Eyck's *Madonna of Chancellor Rolin*, but he kept only to the letter of Van Eyck's composition; the spirit is quite different. Thus we find a far greater homogeneity between the foreground scene and the succeeding landscape. There are no "allusions"; the two quaint little creatures leaning on the crenellated wall in the Van Eyck picture have become mere banal *figurants*. On view over a long period in the premises of the Painters' Guild at Brussels, this picture was often copied; yet it strikes us now as a feeble imitation of its great precursor. Though Rogier always showed remarkable adroitness in harmoniously distributing, and diversifying, the figures in his narrative or episodic compositions, these procedures tended to obscure the over-all significance of the picture. With the result that, in order to safeguard it, he had recourse to a rhythm linking up the disparate elements and ensuring their continuity.

When, for example, he wishes to create a close correspondence between the action and the architectural setting or landscape in which it is taking place, he shows much more originality and sense of composition than the Flémalle Master, who lets each of the component parts take care of itself. This is why landscapes in Rogier's works are deliberately idealized, little resembling nature; trees are slender stems with an almost feminine suppleness and delicacy, while in his depictions of the burial of Christ's body (e.g. the Uffizi *Entombment*) rocks and vegetation are given an eerie bleakness. This *Entombment*, which was executed in Italy after a lay-out by Fra Angelico of a kind quite unknown to Flemish painting and completely transformed in Rogier's interpretation, was closely studied and imitated by Giovanni Bellini. In the same spirit Rogier

ROGIER VAN DER WEYDEN (1399/1400-1464). THE LAST JUDGMENT ALTARPIECE, CENTRAL PANEL (DETAIL), 1443-1446. HOTEL-DIEU, BEAUNE.

ROGIER VAN DER WEYDEN (1399/1400-1464). THE VIRGIN AND ST JOHN THE BAPTIST. (71 × 36 ½")
LEFT WING OF A DIPTYCH. JOHNSON COLLECTION, MUSEUM OF ART, PHILADELPHIA.

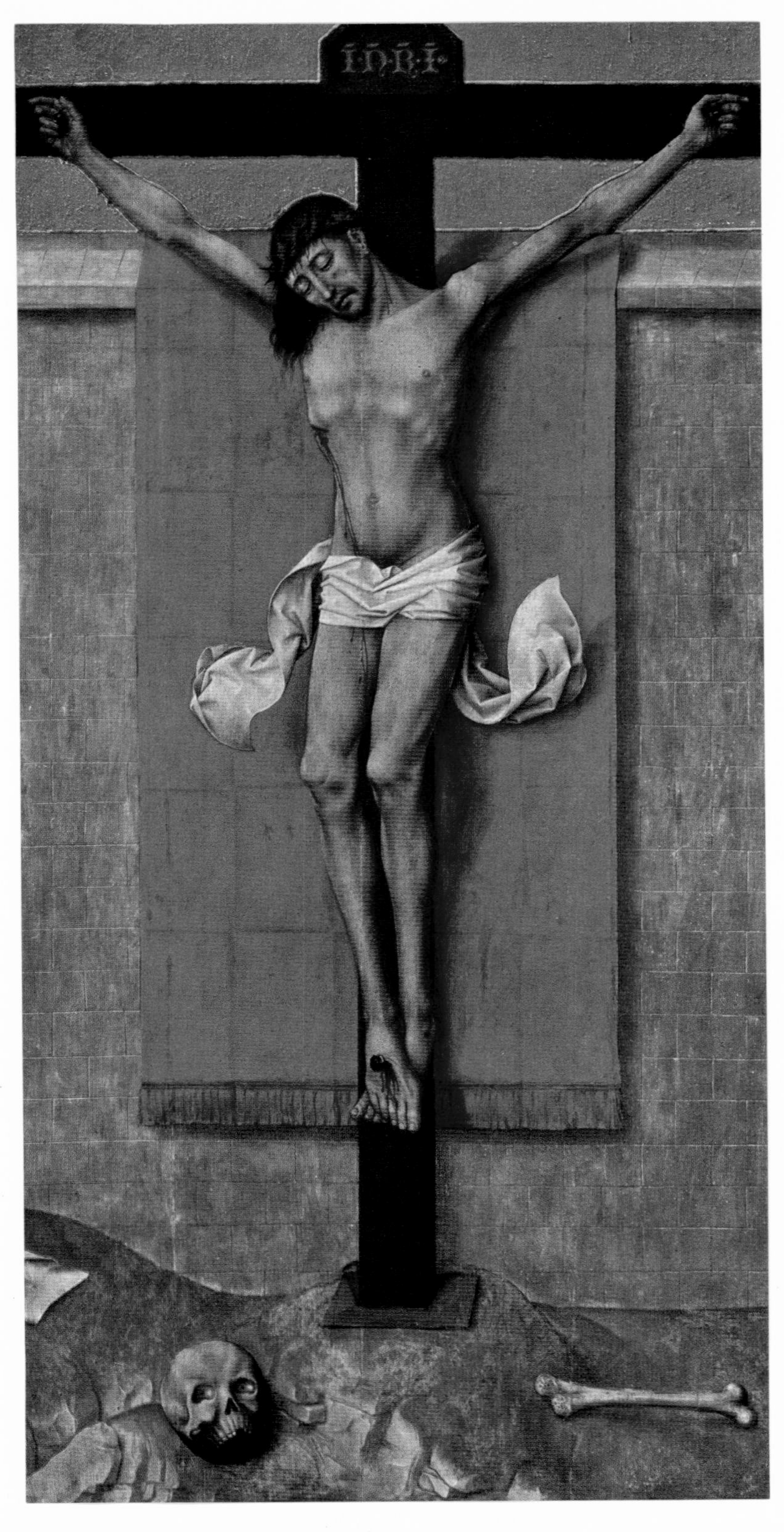

ROGIER VAN DER WEYDEN (1399/1400-1464). CHRIST ON THE CROSS. (71 × 36 ½″)
RIGHT WING OF A DIPTYCH. JOHNSON COLLECTION, MUSEUM OF ART, PHILADELPHIA.

reverted to the use of vast church interiors as settings for his compositions. Thus in the *Seven Sacraments* altarpiece the Calvary and Eucharist are located in the central nave of Sainte-Gudule, while the realistic, smaller scenes—Baptism, Confirmation, Penitence, Ordination, Marriage and Extreme Unction—take place in side aisles. Above these scenes angels are hovering, clad in white, yellow, red, mauve, blue and black, symbolizing the successive stages of a human life.

Rogier was happily inspired when (in the panel in the Escorial) he placed the leading scene of the Crucifixion in front of a stone wall, and (in the Philadelphia diptych) before a wall hung with red drapery. The tall, pale, sculptural forms of the Crucified, the Virgin and St John have now become emotive yet almost abstract representations of spiritual or physical distress; forms stripped bare of any decorative or anecdotal elements locating them in Time. Indeed we are conscious of a sublime indifference to those ever-changing aspects of nature and the picturesque details of ordinary life which still subsisted in the Flémalle Master's vision of the world and in Van Eyck's. Similarly in the huge *Last Judgment* at Beaune, the Dead are arising from an all but barren soil, the scanty signs of vegetation being mere wraiths of flowers and grass. The Blessed and the Lost, whose naked bodies have that detailed yet decorous exactitude characteristic of Flemish painting, are personifications of joy and despair, and have nothing in common with the individualized figures and seething masses of writhing, tortured bodies so forcibly depicted twenty years before in the *Last Judgments* of Jan van Eyck and the Master of Diest.

Thus it seems natural enough that Van der Weyden's basic contribution to the art of his day can best be seen in his portraits. These are elaborate compositions in which the figure is usually shown half-length in a carefully studied attitude, and the position of the clasped or crossed hands holding (for example) an arrow, a ring or a goldsmith's hammer is likewise meaningful. Rogier's portraits show a distinct advance on those of Van Eyck, in which features were not defined by lines circumscribing the zones of color, and the face emerged from shadows forming a patch of shimmering light, in which tiny, superimposed touches were adroitly blended. We get an impression of curious presences emerging from the mists of the past, but there is little to tell us what sort of men these were. Rogier, on the other hand, outlines features, minutely renders the contours of eyebrows, lips and noses, angles and volumes. Moreover these people are given their historical context, as indeed was to be expected, since Van der Weyden was commissioned to paint many portraits of the notables of the day. Even when we know them only by way of copies his portraits of Philip the Good, Charles the Bold, Philippe de Croy or the Grand Bâtard of Burgundy seem wonderfully alive. For the first time a face (that of Francesco d'Este) is made to stand out on a creamy white ground with the sharp precision of a head engraved on a medal. Rogier both discovered the means of individualizing features and explored the secret places of his model's heart, whereas Van Eyck's interpretations of his sitters were, in the main, subjective. Thus in his portraits Van der Weyden never lapses into the stereotyped procedures we find in some of his Madonnas and other religious scenes.

ROGIER VAN DER WEYDEN (1399/1400-1464). PORTRAIT OF FRANCESCO D'ESTE. (11¾×8")
METROPOLITAN MUSEUM OF ART, NEW YORK.

PETRUS CHRISTUS

Jan van Eyck died in 1441, but his workshop at Bruges continued to function some time longer. His unfinished pictures—amongst them the *St Jerome* in the Detroit Institute of Arts (which reproduces with remarkable fidelity a miniature by the Master of Boucicaut) and *The Carthusian Madonna* in the Robert de Rothschild Collection, Paris—were completed by another artist. Some have seen in these works the hand of Petrus Christus and though a theory that this painter never had any personal contacts with Van Eyck and came under his influence at a later date has recently been put forward, everything, in my opinion, points to the fact of Christus' having been Van Eyck's pupil. No doubt he was also familiar with the work of the Master of Flémalle and Rogier van der Weyden's, but so far as the painting of the Bruges School can be said to follow a continuous line of development, it was above all Van Eyck's message that Christus transmitted to his followers.

Born at Baerle, not far from Ghent, Petrus Christus obtained the rights of citizenship at Bruges in 1444. Though he visited Cambrai in 1454 to make some copies in the Cathedral of that city, all other mentions of this artist relate to his activities in Bruges. In 1462 he and his wife enrolled in the Confraternity of the Dry Tree. In 1463 payment was made him by the City Fathers for painting a Tree of Jesse and he took part in organizing the procession of the Holy Blood. In 1467-1468 he received fees for restoring old pictures. He became Dean of the Painters' Guild in 1471 and died in 1472 or 1473. Some have thought to identify him with the "Peter of Bruges" reported to have been in Milan in 1457, but this seems unlikely.

Like Van Eyck, Christus had the habit of signing and dating his pictures; thus we can trace the course of his artistic evolution. In the early works—the *Madonna with a Carthusian* in Berlin and the *Madonna and Saints* in Frankfort—he kept very close to the style of Van Eyck. The portraits of Edward Grimston (on loan to the National Gallery, London), of a Carthusian (Metropolitan Museum of Art, New York) and of a young man (National Gallery, London) are dated 1446, while the striking *Portrait of a Young Girl* in Berlin was made presumably a little later. Perhaps the "young girl" in question was, as Simone Bergmans has suggested, Isabelle de Bourbon (wife of Charles the Bold) who died in 1465. In this work the painted surface has a porcelain smoothness and the colors, especially the blues telling out on a grey ground, remind us of Vermeer. The face devoid of eyebrows, with the hair drawn tightly back and treated as a purely formal element, has a curious inscrutability. Characteristic of the faces in other pictures by Christus is the close-cut hair, and the curiously globular shape of the heads is another of his mannerisms.

By 1449, when he painted *St Eloy in his Workshop* for the Antwerp Goldsmiths' Guild (Robert Lehman Collection, New York), Christus seems to have completely shaken off the influence of Van Eyck. What gives this picture its singular fascination is the wonderfully detailed depiction of a goldsmith's shop and its varied contents. Here, too, there is a convex mirror reflecting the street, but the difference between this and the Arnolfini interior is immense. There is no spiritual significance in the scene; it is simply a genre picture, a faithful replica of everyday life.

The Berlin diptych (1452), which curiously combines on one tall panel a *Nativity* and an *Annunciation*, as well as a *Last Judgment* much inferior to Van Eyck's, while reminiscent of Van der Weyden, shows how narrow was this artist's imaginative range as compared with that of his great predecessors. Unquestionably his finest picture is the 1465 *Lamentation* in Brussels (there is a variant in the Metropolitan Museum, New York). Built up lengthwise, the composition is held together by figures that Christus sets at a considerable distance from the central group, at the two extremities of the picture, notably a kneeling Magdalen who is glancing round in an intriguing attitude, at once expressive and unstudied. Another interesting figure is the burly man with a big round head, a distinctly "proletarian" type. In short there is nothing pretentious in Petrus Christus' art, its chief merits being much nicety of execution and a delicately intimate realism instinct with life.

PETRUS CHRISTUS (?-1472/1473). PORTRAIT OF A YOUNG GIRL, AFTER 1446. (11×8¼")
KAISER FRIEDRICH MUSEUM, BERLIN.

CONRAD WITZ (CA. 1400-1447). THE SYNAGOGUE. OUTER PANEL OF THE "HEILSSPIEGEL" ALTARPIECE, CA. 1435.
(33¾×31¾") KUNSTMUSEUM, BASEL.

THE PRECURSORS OF A NEW ART IN THE GERMANIC COUNTRIES

A MEETING-PLACE of styles, a melting-pot in which the achievements of the naïve sculptors of the French cathedrals and those of the Italian fresco-painters, the discoveries of the Sienese, the delicate art of the English alabaster-carvers and that of the French illuminators intermingled—such was medieval Germany. But the great diversity of the various local schools flourishing in all parts of the country should not blind us to the fact that these artists were among the first to produce works that can be described as "paintings" in the modern sense of the term. As early as the beginning of the 14th century they took to transposing the decorative, delicately wrought productions of the illuminators on to wooden panels, and whereas, in Bohemia, forms tended to become monumental, hieratic, Meister Bertram, in Westphalia, painted ordinary folk just as he saw them, with humor and simplicity while, in Hamburg, Meister Francke stressed the contrast between the elegance of his Virgins and saints and the uncouth faces of the common mortals accompanying them.

In and around the Rhineland, under the auspices of Conrad von Soest and a group of painters whose leader was the Master of the Cologne *Veronica*, there developed an art of mystical effusion, pensive and serene, whose fragile figures seem poised midway between earth and heaven. Here we have certainly the finest flowering of the International Style and the achievements of these artists were brilliantly original. They made a point of treating the picture as a flat surface and it is, in fact, this deliberate exclusion of the third dimension that gives their works an archaic flavor, as against those of Broederlam or the Franco-Flemish miniature-painters. Nevertheless the masters of the Cologne and Westphalia schools need not fear comparison with the latter; thanks to their use of deftly modulated colors, they perfectly suggested the volumes of bodies, while no less attractive is the exquisite finish of their renderings of sumptuous garments, brocades, rich fabrics glittering with pearls and jewels.

The first German work which can be assigned to the "new style" is the St Magdalen altarpiece, still in the little church at Tiefenbronn in the Black Forest, for which it was made in 1431 by Lucas Moser. Clearly the painter was no longer young at the time, for records tell of work he did for the town of Ulm at various times going back as far as 1402. Some have ascribed to him the stained-glass windows in Ulm Cathedral, but the only work positively known to be his is this altarpiece. It has a special form, traditional in this locality, being in fact the door of a closet containing a statue. Four scenes of the life of Mary Magdalen figure on it. *The Meal at Simon's House* (in the lunette) shows the saint wiping Christ's feet with her hair after washing them with her tears. He is seated in front of a trellis covered with flowers like those which Lochner and Schongauer subsequently used as backgrounds, and the still life of a laid table, dishes and a tub containing wine jugs says much for the interest now felt in objects in themselves. The other three scenes take place in front of a single, uniform background in which landscape and architecture link up with one another, but in which the perspective is given a sort of twist enabling us to see, on the right, the interior of the church which in the central panel is shown in side view. On the left are Mary Magdalen, Martha and Lazarus, accompanied by Bishops Maximin and Cedon in a boat, without sail or rudder, making towards Marseilles. Wavelets are racing up towards a background of mountains and a gold sky; a scene suggesting less a sea-coast than the shores of a lake, such as the Lake of Constance from which so many German artists drew inspiration. In the central panel the saints, having failed to find a lodging, are camping in an outhouse annexed to the church in which, on the right, St Magdalen borne by angels is receiving the last sacrament from Bishop Maximin. Above, the buildings are carried over from one panel to the next with the result that the upper parts of all three scenes interlock, a procedure reminiscent of the Master of Flémalle. In his old age, finding himself competed with, perhaps superseded, by younger men like Multscher and Conrad Witz, who had borrowed more than he from the aesthetic of the Flemish masters, Moser was moved to write that curious inscription on the Tiefenbronn altarpiece: "Weep, my art, weep and mourn thy fate, for today, alas, no one desires thee any more!"

Born in 1400 at Reichenhofen, Hans Multscher came in 1427 to Ulm where he obtained rights of citizenship and died in 1467. Given many lucrative commissions for the decoration of cathedrals, he made a great name for himself as a sculptor, his most famous work being the "Man of Sorrows" in the west portal of Ulm Cathedral; but he is also described in records of the day as a "maker of panels." Two paintings emanating from his workshop have survived: the Wurzach altarpiece (now in the Kaiser Friedrich Museum, Berlin), dated 1437, and the Sterzing altarpiece, dated 1457. Suggestions have been made that Multscher confined himself to blocking in the outlines and left the actual painting of the panels to his pupils. Notable in the Wurzach altarpiece is an extreme emphasis on dramatic effects and emotive contrasts. A sculptor in the lineage of Claus Sluter, Multscher was interested above all in the human figure; nature meant little to him and the settings are perfunctory in this respect, though he assigned an important place to still-life elements. Thus in his *Adoration of the Magi* we see shelves stacked with books, pots and boxes of cheese, much as in the triptych of the Master of the Aix Annunciation. This is a feature also of the altarpiece in the Abbey of Klosterneuburg made for King Albrecht by an Austrian master round about 1440. Though this artist's figures have an exceptional sharpness of definition, his landscapes are clumsily handled, but he achieves in his still lifes of books and utensils a naturalism remarkably effective and scrupulously precise. In 1440, at Vienna, realism was carried to its highest pitch in the carvings of the huge Altarpiece of the Passion, and thereafter all Austrian art followed this lead.

But we cannot help feeling that there was still an incompatibility between the ideals of the new art that was emerging and the static, conventional forms that were the legacy of Gothic painting. Only one painter in 15th-century Germany succeeded in reconciling these conflicting trends and that was Conrad Witz.

It is clear that Burgundian influences played a considerable part in his early training, though there is no solid evidence for the theory that his father, Hans Witz, should be identified with the "Hans of Constance" who worked at the Court of Philip the Good between 1424 and 1426. In 1434 "Conrad of Rottweil" (whether this means the village of Rottweil near Brisach or Rottweil-am-Neckar is uncertain), who had been living at Basel for three years, was admitted to the Painters' Guild of that city. Next year he acquired citizenship in Basel and married Ursulina von Wangen, a niece of Nikolaus Rusch who hailed from Tübingen, had worked at Dijon and was regarded as the city's foremost painter. The frescos Conrad Witz painted jointly with Rusch at this time are lost. In 1444, to the order of François de Mies, Bishop of Geneva, he painted the St Peter Altarpiece, now in Geneva Museum. When he died in 1447 at Basel he was under fifty and left five young children.

Thus his active period, so far as is known, spanned twelve years, during which he produced some twenty large-scale pictures. He arrived at Basel just at the time when the famous Council of Basel, which was to make that city the cynosure of Christendom for eighteen years, began its sessions. Cardinals, prelates and eminent theologians came from all parts of Europe to take part, and many not only brought with them portable altars adorned with paintings but were accompanied by their favorite painters. It was here that Witz came in contact with Heinrich von Werl, Bishop of Cologne (for whom the Master of Flémalle painted the diptych now in the Prado), and also struck up a friendship with the Bishop of Geneva.

There is no question that of all the painters of the period Conrad Witz had the clearest understanding of the new style of painting originated by Van Eyck and the Master of Flémalle. Nor, it would seem, did any other artist better transpose into terms of painting the discoveries made by Claus Sluter in the domain of sculpture. But his artistic personality is so strong, so original, that it cannot be accounted for by contacts with the art of France or Flanders.

He has a simplicity, a fine spareness, all his own and he is more sculpturesque than any of his contemporaries. Bodies are presented as volumes, or surfaces, located in empty space, and the human figure interests him *qua* mass, not as a means to the portrayal of an individual. He rejects every detail that is not basic to the structure of the composition, he dispenses with still lifes and reduces symbolical allusions to a minimum. Nor does he indulge in complicated lay-outs, and it is in his simplest works that we see him at his best. Like the Flemish painters and unlike his compatriots who mostly preferred to paint on deal, he used oak panels, but his technique was very different from that of the Flemings. He painted in tempera, not in oils (as was formerly supposed), and by using very finely ground pigments achieved richly luminous effects and—especially in his renderings of breast-plates—a shimmering, silken iridescence.

Of his first known work, the "Heilsspiegel" altarpiece (ca. 1430), thirteen of the sixteen panels are extant (in Basel, Dijon and Berlin). On each panel of the reverse there is a single, monumental, full-length figure shown in a strictly confined space, a bare cubical cell, and each figure has a distinctive color. Thus in the lefthand panel the Church is wearing a red mantle, while the Synagogue on the right is in yellow (this color contrast follows an old hagiographical tradition), the Angel of the Annunciation in the intervening scene wears pink over a white robe, while the Virgin, in a scene which has been lost, was clad presumably in blue. Cast shadows are clearly indicated on the walls. Two figures of the lower register have survived: St Augustine and St Bartholomew holding a red book. The latter figure is noticeably larger, and its monumentalism accords with the surrounding architecture (which, exceptionally, contains no roof). The saint is given an unnatural pose, his feet being thrust forward in a manner impossible to a standing man, yet this anomaly enhances the majesty of his demeanor. The hand whose presence is perceptible under the drapery produces a curiously sculptural effect.

Each scene of the altarpiece, when the shutters are opened, contains two figures, seated or standing, upon a damasked gold ground, and in each case there is a visual dialogue of two meaningful colors. Esther and Ahasuerus are wearing, respectively, bright green and dark pink, the Queen of Sheba and Solomon blue and green. Melchisedec's greenish armor reflects Abraham's crimson robe; there is a subtle concord between Ahasuerus' smiling lips and the dark pink of his garment, while the blue mantle hanging in stiff folds down Sabobai's back stresses his hierarchic dignity. Though the scenes are separate, they are sometimes correlated; thus we see Abishai, Sabobai and Benaiah coming towards David, each carrying a gift, and thus symbolizing the Magi bringing their offerings to the new-born Babe; similarly Esther made queen by Ahasuerus prefigures the Virgin crowned by God. Once again we find episodes of pagan antiquity being given a Christian application; thus Antipater, victim of an unjust charge, shows Caesar his wounds, evocative of Christ's, and the Sibyl reveals to the Emperor Augustus signs premonitory of the birth of Jesus. All wear richly embroidered garments, furs, brocades and jewelry. Their headgear is skillfully diversified, ranging from close-fitting caps to turbans treated in an even more imaginative style than Piero della Francesca's in the Arezzo frescos.

In the Nuremberg *Annunciation* and in the Strasbourg *Sts Catherine and Magdalen* figures are given a deeper architectural setting which, though handled with a like discretion, is stressed by steeply ascending lines. The room in *The Annunciation* is timbered and the physical properties of the wood are brought out with extreme precision. One has the impression that the angel has miraculously traversed the closed door and appeared behind the Virgin, who is somehow conscious of the presence of the celestial visitant. Another curious impression given by this scene is that the perspective pivots on an axis, while the movements of the entering angel are suggested by the position of the transoms overhead, which seem to be descending from the sky.

The St Peter altarpiece (Geneva Museum) contains four scenes. Like Multscher, Witz seems to have an aversion for the traditional altarpiece with its big central panel and side wings and to prefer a sequence of scenes of equal dimensions ranged side by side. On the inner side we see *The Miraculous Draught of Fishes* and *The Liberation of St Peter*. This *Miraculout Draught* is probably the first real landscape in the whole

CONRAD WITZ (CA. 1400-1447). SABOBAI AND BENAIAH BEFORE KING DAVID.
INNER PANEL OF THE "HEILSSPIEGEL" ALTARPIECE, CA. 1435. ($38\frac{1}{4} \times 27\frac{1}{2}$") KUNSTMUSEUM, BASEL.

history of painting (if we leave out of account the Limbourgs' miniatures and those ascribed to Jan van Eyck in the Turin *Hours*). With his visual realism and fidelity to natural appearances Witz anticipates Patinir and the Dutch painters. The lake and city of Geneva and the Petit-Salève bulk so large in the picture and are depicted with such verisimilitude that the landscape may be said to play the leading part. This was a new

CONRAD WITZ (CA. 1400-1447). THE MIRACULOUS DRAUGHT OF FISHES, 1444. (52×60¾″)
MUSÉE D'ART ET D'HISTOIRE, GENEVA.

departure; till now Witz had carefully refrained from inserting scenes of nature even in window openings and the like, so as not to divert attention from the central theme.

In his earlier *St Christopher*, however, the landscape had been highly conventional, the saint being placed between two huge rocks, one of which seems to be pressing against his back and the other touching his forehead, while the water, opaque in the foreground, becomes transparent in recession as if a stretch of clear water were overlaid upon a dark one. But in *The Miraculous Draught* landscape is realistically depicted; we see meadows, fields, roads and tree-lined avenues little different from those of a present-day countryside. However, the artist never overstresses details, and the composition is architecturally ordered throughout. The upstanding form of Christ walking on the water exactly reiterates the line of the postern-gate, and the boat lies parallel to the shore. Thus the picture combines two conceptions, that of monumental lay-out (with a corresponding simplification of forms) and that of visual realism with an abundance of lively anecdotal elements meticulously rendered. There is something here of that ideological dualism which we find in Van Eyck's art, but Witz takes care to integrate these tendencies within a common atmosphere. Thus as between Christ's hieratic figure and the throng of tiny horsemen and washerwomen on the shore of the lake, the boat in which are the disciples acts as a connecting link both on the spiritual and the material plane. Witz does not confine himself to recording externals, the superficial aspects of the visible world, but looking beneath the surface brings out, for example, the intrinsic difference between the inner structure of the rocks and the green-glimmering translucency of the lake with its eddies and air-bubbles rising from the depths. Also he studies with almost scientific precision the optical effects produced by the immersion of solids in a liquid. Similarly bodies are given their full density, with light and shade distributed in terms of different colors, and are modeled with a vigor that brings out their anatomic structure. The position of the hands is always functional, significant of something done or about to be done and sometimes more expressive than a completed gesture.

Notable in *The Meeting at the Golden Gate* at Basel (as in *The Adoration of the Magi* on the back of the St Peter altarpiece) is the extreme precision with which decrepit, crumbling walls are rendered. Here, too, space is not an autonomous element governed by its own laws, but is still built up around the figures, while architectural elements are sometimes given a sort of twist so as to emphasize the movements of the figures and to balance their volumes. In fact Witz bends architecture to his will, adapting it to his figure-patterns. In this respect he was worlds away from Masaccio and Van Eyck, for whom perspective had opened up a new vision of the world. Moreover, he always treated figures as symbols, self-contained, existing in their own right.

And this he did deliberately. No painter of the day was so sculptural as Witz, and none had a stronger feeling for volumes; nevertheless he stood up for the claims of the picture as a flat surface—a stand of capital importance for the future of art, since it reconciled the static quality of pictured forms with the fact of movement and acted as a corrective to the anecdotal tendencies of the then prevailing realism.

STEPHAN LOCHNER

While all Southern Germany and the Upper Rhineland came under the influence of the Master of Flémalle and certain artists even carried his discoveries a stage further, North German art kept much nearer the style and methods of Jan van Eyck. The art of the Cologne School had a second flowering on the lines of its earlier achievement and under the auspices of Stephan Lochner it, too, contributed to the new developments in Flemish painting during the last half of the century. Lochner was born at Meersburg on the Lake of Constance (the exact year is not known, but it was shortly after 1405), but we may assume he migrated to Cologne at an early age, so strongly is his art infused with the distinctive spirit of that flourishing art-center.

"Felix Colonia" was one of the leading capital cities of the day and among the works of its unschooled painters are many charming depictions of its cloisters, spires and the colorful houses along the Rhine banks. But its more accomplished masters kept to idealized renderings of scenes culled from local religious legends, e.g. the martyrdom of the Theban Legion, St Ursula and her eleven thousand Virgins, the exploits of St Gerion (patron saint of the city) and his three hundred knights. It was in this spirit that Lochner painted his celebrated *Dombild* originally commissioned by the municipal authorities for the chapel of the Town Hall which had just been built (in 1428) on the site of a former synagogue. The *Dombild*, now in Cologne Cathedral, is a triptych whose central panel shows *The Adoration of the Magi*, with *St Ursula* and *St Gerion* on the wings. The Virgin is placed in a setting of flamboyant Gothic, with a gold background, and the figures around her, though dressed in the style of rich burghers of the period, have an otherworldly aspect and impersonal faces. Armors, furs and gorgeous raiment, silver and gold brocades, while painted with amazing virtuosity, have a curious air of unreality. In Lochner's dreamworld everyone is young and carefree, each object a delight to the eye, and time at a standstill.

But in his smaller pictures (which have much the same dimensions as the portable altars made by the *Veronica* Master) and his depictions of the Madonna as a demure, almost childish young person, Lochner makes proof of a technical ability that the very greatest artists well might envy. The most famous of these smaller works, *The Madonna and Child in the Rose Garden* (Wallraf-Richartz Museum, Cologne), testifies to the great progress made by German art since the beginning of the century. Here the highly expert handling of volumes, the modeling of the gracefully rounded faces, the strong relief imparted to figures, the smooth flow of the garments, the delicate precision of the renderings of leafage, blossoms, the grassy foreground starred with tiny flowers, and in particular of the medal with an enamel figurine framed in pearls, hanging on the Madonna's bosom—all remind us of Jan van Eyck in those gentler moods when, as in the Antwerp *Virgin*, he as it were comes down to earth and gives his figures a simple, intimate appeal.

However, in a later work, his magnum opus, *The Last Judgment* (probably commissioned for the Church of St Lawrence and now in the Wallraf-Richartz Museum, Cologne), Lochner shows an audacity which, in view of his earlier work, takes us by surprise. Indeed he completely revivifies this somewhat hackneyed theme by a mingling

STEPHAN LOCHNER (CA. 1405-1451). MADONNA AND CHILD IN THE ROSE GARDEN. (20×15¾″)
WALLRAF-RICHARTZ MUSEUM, COLOGNE.

of archaisms and startling innovations. The Blessed are presented as a serried mass of graceful figures, white-skinned, fair-haired, chubby-cheeked—foreshadowing those of Baldung Grien and Cranach—with skillfully placed lights marking the cheeks and nostrils. Gothic elements pullulate not only in the setting but in the forms of the angels with their wispy, undulating bodies and wildly beating wings. Imagination of no mean order has gone to the picturing of the devils and the Damned; some indeed are masterpieces of the grotesque.

Thus at the very time when the Flemings' rationalist conceptions of light and perspective were making good throughout Europe, those ferments of the irrational and fantastic which were to characterize German art at the beginning of the next century already made their presence felt in Lochner's *Last Judgment.*

STEPHAN LOCHNER (CA. 1405-1451). THE LAST JUDGMENT. (48×69¼″)
WALLRAF-RICHARTZ MUSEUM, COLOGNE.

THE PAINTERS OF THE FRENCH DOMAIN

In 1904, in response to the growing interest in the subject, Henri Bouchot organized in Paris, at the Pavillon de Marsan, a large-scale exhibition of "French Primitive Art," which demonstrated for the first time the existence of a school of French Primitives, autonomous and autochthonous. Works from all parts of France were shown and when we examine the catalogue we find that the corpus of French Primitives remains today much as it then was; that in fact (with the exception of the Nouans *Pietà*) there have been no really outstanding discoveries in this field during the last fifty years.

In many cases, despite intensive research, the painters are still unidentified. Long lists of artists have been compiled for many parts of France, with summaries of the chief facts of their lives and the commissions they were given. Unfortunately these data—except in the cases of Charonton and Froment—seldom relate to works that have come down to us. Even the ascriptions of Fouquet's pictures are based in almost every case on stylistic grounds, while the mystery surrounding the origins of such masterworks as the altarpiece of the Aix *Annunciation*, the Villeneuve *Pietà* and the productions of the Master of Moulins has never been cleared up. When, in 1936, Louis Dimier carefully defined the geographical limits of what can properly be styled French art, he went so far as to classify as "foreign," works produced in certain regions such as Burgundy and Provence which at the time were not yet included in the Royal Domain. True, Burgundy (with which Flanders was united in the 15th century) had developed into an independent state frankly at enmity with France; nevertheless all its leading artists, though hailing from the North, had spent some time in Parisian ateliers and their art bore many traces of French influence. As for the City of the Popes, Avignon, and the countship of Provence, a domain of the Holy Roman Empire afterwards incorporated in the Kingdom of Naples, these descriptions were no more than political fictions; in point of fact the southern French schools (after the Popes' departure) were wholly dominated by French conceptions, while at Aix the court of King René of Anjou was exclusively French. This much, however, may be accepted of Dimier's rather arbitrary definition: that French 15th-century art flourished in its most characteristic form in the Loire valley and those central territories which had always been the nucleus of the kingdom. Thus, as against Dijon, Bruges and Tournai, we have Bourges, Angers, Tours and, a little later, Moulins, which ranked throughout this period as the chief centers of French art.

Bourges was already the residence of the Duke of Berry, most lavish of art patrons at the close of the 14th century. It was to him that his brother Philip the Bold turned for advice and assistance when he set to embellishing his capital, Dijon, and he often "borrowed" his brother's artists. Thus the Master of Works at the palace and the Sainte Chapelle of Bourges, Drouet de Dammartin, was called on to make the plans of the Chartreuse of Champmol, while Claus Sluter was sent to the castle of Mehun-sur-Yèvres, one of Jean de Berry's country seats, to work in concert with André Beauneveu.

MASTER OF THE ROHAN HOURS. LES GRANDES HEURES DU DUC DE ROHAN: THE TRIUMPH OF THE VIRGIN. (11 3/8 × 8 1/8″) MINIATURE, BIBLIOTHÈQUE NATIONALE, PARIS.

MASTER OF THE ROHAN HOURS. LES GRANDES HEURES DU DUC DE ROHAN: PENTECOST. (11 3/8 × 8 1/8″)
MINIATURE, BIBLIOTHÈQUE NATIONALE, PARIS.

The Duke of Berry's favorite artists were André Beauneveu (born at Valenciennes), Jacquemart de Hesdin and the Limbourg brothers who came from Gelderland and had been employed in Parisian artists' workshops before coming to Bourges. All these men set up house in the vicinity of the Collegiate Church of Saint-Pierre le Puellier, where also lived Drouet de Dammartin. Subsequently the Limbourg brothers accompanied the Duke to Paris, where he died in 1416. The Dauphin, afterwards Charles VII, inherited the estate of his uncle, whose tomb he completed and whose illuminators he continued to employ. He lived in the Château de Mehun-sur-Yèvres and when he came to the throne made Bourges his capital. His wife was Marie d'Anjou, King René's sister, and he never lost his affection for the Loire valley, spending the last years of his life at Tours. After turning out mediocre work for a while, the artists' workshops at Bourges came into their own again during the second half of the century under the auspices of Jean Colombe, who followed in the footsteps of Fouquet and whose brother, the famous sculptor Michel Colombe, acted as a link between the schools of the Loire valley and the Bourbon court at Moulins.

THE MASTER OF THE ROHAN HOURS

Angers was the capital of Louis d'Anjou, brother of Jean de Berry, Charles V and Philip the Bold. These four remarkable men did much to shape the course of art, and even the territorial distribution of the various schools, for several generations. At Angers Louis commissioned Jean de Bandol to make the famous *Apocalypse* tapestry; his son, that dreamer of romantic dreams, Louis II, who became King of Naples and Sicily, was almost certainly the patron of the brilliant creative genius to whom we owe the *Heures de Rohan.* And his son King René, who incorporated the countships of Lorraine and Provence in his dominions, did more than any other monarch to further the cause of art in the mid-15th century.

The problems set by the book described (inaccurately) as *Les Heures de Rohan* have given rise to much controversy. Containing no less than 65 miniatures, 11 of them full-page, this is one of the largest illuminated manuscripts that have come down to us. Its exceptional size and the highly original way in which the illustrations are presented show that we have here a wholly original artist who can be affiliated neither to the Parisian nor to the Franco-Flemish school. True, some details show that the Rohan Master was acquainted with the productions of the Boucicaut Master and the Limbourgs (in particular *Les Très Riches Heures du Duc de Berry*), and it has been suggested that his iconography derives from an historiated 14th-century Bible. Nevertheless the whole conception of the Rohan Hours is different; the compositional unity is absolute, and architectural or landscape elements combine to form a symbolical arabesque whose sole purpose is to underscore the attitudes and gestures of the figures and expressive distortions of the features. There are no empty spaces, no forms that are not dynamic and significant. The sky is strewn with fluttering wings, plants and trees sway wildly to and fro, flesh is mottled with wounds, garments billow in a great rushing wind. So strikingly expressionistic are this artist's methods that some have thought to find affinities between him and later Dutch or German painters, for example Grünewald.

But this work must be assigned to a far earlier date, 1435 at the latest, and moreover is of western provenance; so the resemblances can only be fortuitous. Originally made for a prince of the House of Anjou, these miniatures came later into the possession of the Rohan family, who had their bearings painted on them. The same artist painted the *Hours of the Dukes of Anjou*, in which appears the first known portrait of King René, and also the *Cambridge Hours*, which once were owned by Francis II of Brittany, who was married to a princess of the House of Anjou. The painter may very well have seen works by the Limbourg brothers in the library of the Dukes of Anjou, so there is no need to assume that he ever worked in Paris. Perhaps he also drew inspiration from the superb tapestries for which already Angers was renowned. His fondness for monumental and strongly dramatic effects, also for forms in movement, certainly suggests that he had studied the essentially "mobile" work of these tapestry makers. Likewise his use of large tracts of flat color (especially vivid reds and blues) may owe something to the stained-glass window. Of particular interest to the art historian is the fact of this artist's contacts with King René in his youth, for tradition has it that the king, too, was a painter, had fully mastered the techniques of the Flemish School, and himself made these known to the Provençals. After his military reverses at Naples René returned, in October 1442, to his fief in Provence and it is an interesting point that his arrival synchronized with the appearance of that other great enigma of 15th-century art, the Aix *Annunciation*.

THE MASTER OF THE AIX ANNUNCIATION

This famous work has been dismembered. The central panel is still at Aix, in the Church of Sainte-Marie-Madeleine; the right lateral panel depicting St Jerome in an alcove with bookshelves above is now in the Musée Royal, Brussels; the lefthand panel has been cut in two, one part, representing the prophet Isaiah, being in the Van Beuningen Collection at Vierhouten, Holland, and the other, the still life above the figure, in the Rijksmuseum, Amsterdam. Originally in the Cathedral of Saint-Sauveur at Aix, this *Annunciation* was made under the provisions of the will of a draper, Pierre Corpici; the will is dated December 9, 1442, and as Corpici died in 1449, we may assume that the painting was made between these dates.

The setting is a Gothic church whose naves are represented in perspective. The reading-desk is an exact reproduction of a similar detail in one of the Limbourg miniatures, while the small carved figures remind us of Sluter and Burgundian art. So perfect is the execution that the Aix *Annunciation* can hold its own beside the noblest achievements of Van Eyck, and it is probably to him that we should turn, rather than to the Flémalle Master, if we seek to trace its pedigree. Opinions differ widely as regards the authorship of this picture. Hulin de Loo believes it to be the work of a Flemish painter who had come in contact with Conrad Witz before going to the South of France. Tolnay saw in it the hand of a disciple of the Master of Flémalle, Lionello Venturi has drawn attention to its similarities with the productions of Antonello da Messina, while Carlo Aru has no qualms about ascribing it to that artist whose very existence is a moot question, Colantonio, the alleged teacher of Antonello.

MASTER OF THE AIX ANNUNCIATION. THE ANNUNCIATION, 1445. (60¾×69") CENTRAL PANEL OF A TRIPTYCH.
CHURCH OF SAINTE-MARIE-MADELEINE, AIX-EN-PROVENCE.

Unmistakable in any case are the artist's affinities with Conrad Witz in his treatment of perspective and his feeling for volumes, especially in the garments with their broad, deeply scooped-out folds. These resemblances are particularly marked in the handling of the secondary figures, for example that of God the Father, those of the angels on the left of the picture and those of Mary Magdalen and Christ on the back of the lateral panels. The soft glow and subtle translucencies of the colors in the figures of the Angel of the Annunciation and the Virgin, who is wearing a sumptuous mantle of gold brocade (in the French style), are typically Eyckian; the forms, however, are fuller, more roundly modeled. Particularly striking is the way in which this artist has humanized his effigies of prophets, abandoning the old tradition of painting them, in grisailles, as statues set in niches. Standing on pedestals and portrayed in color, these prophets have the look, not of stone figures, but of living beings—an effect enhanced by still lifes of common domestic objects placed on shelves, pots and pans and boxes, books piled up in disorder: details obviously stemming from Van Eyck. Thus we have here a painter who learnt much from the Flemings—though, unlike them, he painted not on oak but on deal—and who most probably had practised at Dijon and there seen Sluter's work. At some time he must have come in touch with Conrad Witz, perhaps at the Council of Basel where artists of many nationalities, attached to the households of church dignitaries, had forgathered. This unknown artist's work diverges in so many ways from that of those from whom, up to a point, he took his lead that he may well have been a Frenchman, and there are several facts pointing in this direction—for example the fact that Mass is being celebrated on an altar adorned with fleur-de-lys. In some unpublished notes utilized by Jean Boyer in an article in *Arts* (March 19, 1948), the late Canon Requin suggested that the painter of the Aix *Annunciation* may well have been Jean Chapus, born at Avignon (his father hailed from Chambéry), who worked for King René at Aix. (He also claimed to have ascertained the date when the picture was completed: July 1445.) Records, however, are available giving detailed descriptions of the pictures Chapus was commissioned to paint at Aix and these hardly seem to tally with the style of the *Annunciation*, far less narrative than monumental. Moreover, Chapus must have been a relatively young man in 1442 (he died some time after 1472) and the *Annunciation* seems to be the work of a completely mature artist; one, moreover, who had traveled widely.

Though we have no wish to exaggerate their importance (as, to our thinking, Emile Henriot has done), mention should be made of some peculiarities in this artist's treatment of his subject. The fact that he has inserted in the ray of light leading from God the Father to the Virgin a tiny, fully formed babe, the Infant Jesus, may not have the heretical intention that some have read into it (this naïve symbolism had had a precedent in the Mérode altarpiece), but it is odd, to say the least, that a small carved monkey should surmount the reading-desk in front of which prays the Virgin; that a bat and a small demon should figure on the trefoil arch above the Angel of the Annunciation; and that the window at the back is similarly adorned with the heads of devils. Some have thought to detect alongside the traditional lily various malefic flowers such as aconite, belladonna and basil, and in the angel's wings the plumage of that bird of ill omen, the owl. (One cannot help being reminded of the somewhat sacrilegious flavor of Fouquet's depiction of the Virgin with one breast bared, in the exact likeness of the King's mistress, Agnès Sorel.) Whatever be the explanation of these "eccentricities," one thing is certain: only a painter in high favor with King

René or (if the suggestion does not seem too far-fetched) the royal artist himself would have dared to include such background material in his work. It must not be forgotten in this context that King René's writings teem with intricate symbols and bold flights of fancy—in one of his illuminated manuscripts he had himself portrayed as a crowned skeleton! Anyhow it seems hardly credible that the creator of the Aix *Annunciation* was some humble local craftsman, however gifted.

ENGUERRAND CHARONTON

There is certainly a vast difference between this work and the *Coronation of the Virgin* by the Avignonese artist, Enguerrand Charonton, most famous painter of his day, regarding whose life and artistic career we are relatively well informed. He was born in 1410 or thereabouts in the diocese of Laon. In 1447 he settled at Avignon, renting a house in the Place Saint-Pierre, whence he moved to another in the Rue de la Saunerie. Pierre Cadard commissioned him in 1452 to make an altarpiece (now in the Musée Condé, Chantilly) for the Church of the Virgin of Mercy in collaboration with Pierre Villatte, a somewhat younger artist from the diocese of Limoges. On April 24, 1453, he entered into negotiations with Abbé Jean de Montagnac for a *Coronation of the Virgin*, to figure in the Carthusian Church at Villeneuve-lès-Avignon; it is now the pride of the Villeneuve Hospice to which it was transferred in the 19th century on the initiative of the distinguished French novelist, Prosper Mérimée, who was also an authority on archeology and held the post of Inspector-General of Historical Monuments. The contract (one of Canon Requin's discoveries) shows that the painter was given a detailed program, which he carried out scrupulously. Painted "in oil colors of the best quality," the picture is divided into separate compartments treated on different scales. In the center we see the Virgin crowned by the Holy Trinity, the Father and the Son being represented as of the same age and almost exactly alike. Right and left are rows of angels, saints and the blest in adoration, amongst the latter figuring persons of all ranks and conditions, beginning with the Pope, the King and the Emperor. Below we see the earth, with Jerusalem on the right, Rome on the left, and in the center Christ on the Cross with the donor kneeling before Him. On the extreme left the Mass of St Gregory is being celebrated and we have a glimpse of the Burning Bush. Hell and Purgatory figure in the lowest register. For the composition the painter has obviously been guided by such great traditional models as Orcagna's *Paradise*, and the carved tympana of cathedrals.

Particularly delightful is the almost horizontal landscape, in which the artist has evoked with quite amazing virtuosity the scenery of Provence: the cliffs of L'Estaque, Mont Ventoux, Montagne Sainte-Victoire, a blue expanse of sea. Here, too, we recognize the ramparts, buildings and public squares of Villeneuve-lès-Avignon. Unlike some Flemish landscapes, Charonton's, though rich in details, nowhere seems overcrowded. Bathed in white, almost immaterial light, it is carefully constructed, the large tracts of color (for example the pink, blue and yellow houses) being so placed as to enhance the beauty of the composition, and not for realistic ends. The relatively large figures, such as those of Moses, the shepherd and the Damned, are depicted with forcible, well-nigh brutal directness. Here we have the manifestations of a style that reappears in the group of figures sheltering under the vast cloak of the Virgin of Mercy (Chantilly). Faces are square-cut, with the features stressed, though not unduly so, and their natural expressions strike a telling contrast with the elegantly stylized forms of the celestial beings with their air of strange remoteness.

ENGUERRAND CHARONTON (1410?-1466?). THE CORONATION OF THE VIRGIN, 1453-1454. (71¾×86½")
HOSPICE OF VILLENEUVE-LÈS-AVIGNON.

ENGUERRAND CHARONTON (1410?-1466?). THE CORONATION OF THE VIRGIN (DETAIL), 1453-1454.
HOSPICE OF VILLENEUVE-LÈS-AVIGNON.

ENGUERRAND CHARONTON (1410?-1466?). THE CORONATION OF THE VIRGIN (DETAIL), 1453-1454.
HOSPICE OF VILLENEUVE-LÈS-AVIGNON.

JEAN FOUQUET (CA. 1420-CA. 1480). THE MELUN DIPTYCH. RIGHT WING: THE VIRGIN AND CHILD (DETAIL), CA. 1451. MUSÉE ROYAL DES BEAUX-ARTS, ANTWERP.

None the less we can sense a faintly rustic, provincial tang in Charonton's work, when we compare it with the pictures Jean Fouquet, recently returned from Italy, was producing at the same time in the Loire valley. Fouquet's place would seem to be in the lineage of the humanists and those intellectuals in the noblest sense of the term, Jan van Eyck and Piero della Francesca. And his rise to fame, at the auspicious close of the catastrophic era of the Hundred Years' War, was a welcome token that the national French values still held their own in the field of art.

Jean Fouquet was born at Tours about 1420. The mystery surrounding his birth has been cleared up by the discovery of a letter from Pope Nicholas V in 1449 in answer to a request by the painter for a dispensation from his "defect of birth"—meaning that he (Fouquet) was the son of a priest and an unmarried mother and as such would be debarred from receiving any payment from the ecclesiastical authorities unless and until he could produce a dispensation of this kind. It was perhaps with this in mind that he went to Rome in 1445 or thereabouts. Once in Rome, he stayed there several years and despite his youth made so great a name for himself that when Pope Eugenius IV decided to have a portrait painted of himself in the company of two intimate friends, he had no hesitation about commissioning the twenty-five-year-old artist for the task. No longer extant, this picture was famous in its day for the complete verisimilitude of the likeness. While in Rome Fouquet struck up a friendship with Filarete who was then engaged in completing the bronze doors of St Peter's Basilica; and presumably it was Filarete who taught him the new technique of applying enamel directly to copper (instead of using the cloisonné method, the only one known to French enamelists of the time), and painting on this ground For his self-portrait in the Louvre Fouquet employed this technique. Probably it once formed part of the frame of the Melun diptych commissioned by Etienne Chevalier. In 1447 Fra Angelico was in Rome, painting his Vatican frescos, so Fouquet had opportunities of studying his methods. It is believed that he visited Florence, since details of buildings in that city figure in his work. However, none of the monuments he must have seen in Italy is reproduced entire in his pictures; he merely drew inspiration from architectural details such as friezes, festoons of flowers or fruit, cupids and in particular the columns adorned with leaves said to have been brought back from Jerusalem by Titus, which Bernini imitated in St Peter's.

Fouquet returned to Tours in 1448, married, and rented a house there. He worked for King Charles VII and was in touch with such high dignitaries of the Court as Etienne Chevalier, the King's Treasurer, and the Chancellor, Juvénal des Ursins. In the Louvre there is a portrait by him of Charles VII which bears no traces of Italian influence but is wholly in the traditional French style. It shows the king in three-quarter view between two symmetrical curtains, wearing an expression of morose indifference. This portrait is believed to have been made before Fouquet's journey to Rome. Its inscription "*le très victorieux roi de France*" might seem to allude to the conclusion of the Peace of Arras (1435); actually, however, this description of the king does not appear in official documents until after the victory of Formigny which took place in 1450. It is more probable that the portrait should be dated to 1451 and commemorates the liberation of Guienne. To this time may also be assigned the Melun diptych, now dismembered, the panel representing Etienne Chevalier with his patron saint being in the Kaiser Friedrich Museum, Berlin, and the Virgin and Child in the Royal Museum, Antwerp. Etienne Chevalier was Agnès Sorel's executor (she died in 1450); tradition has it that the Virgin is her portrait and certainly this figure has all the characteristics we find in other portraits of that famous royal favorite: the high forehead with the hair drawn tightly back over the temples, the prominent eyes, opulent bosom and pointed chin. There is no denying the great differences in the treatment of the figures in the two panels: between the telling realism of the portrait of the donor with its warm, lifelike flesh-tints and the ethereal aspect of the Madonna with her ivory-pale skin, and the little pink and blue angels so much like those in Franco-Flemish miniatures and Broederlam's paintings. All the same there is no reason to doubt that these two panels formed a diptych, and we may be sure the contrast was intentional; the painter aimed at lifting his representation of the King's mistress on to a supramundane plane, remote from human passions.

The *Hours of Etienne Chevalier* should certainly be assigned to the same period; it is the only one of Fouquet's works in which we feel that his experiences in Italy were still fresh in his mind. In three pictures figuring in these Hours (*Pentecost*, *The Coronation of the Virgin* and *The Entombment*) he employs Alberti's geometrical perspective, as yet unused by Flemish painters. But the reminiscences of Italy are confined to decorative details; all the edifices depicted were those of Paris or its vicinity: the Sainte-Chapelle, the Louvre, the Temple, the Bastille, the Château de Vincennes, Saint-Denis. This has led Perls to advance a theory that Fouquet had studied in Parisian ateliers or, more precisely, in the one and only painter's workshop that continued to function under the English occupation, that of "the Master of the Duke of Bedford," presumably Hancelin de Haguenau, collaborator and heir of Jacques Coene, whom some have sought to identify with the Boucicaut Master.

Fouquet was also on friendly terms with the great Chancellor of France, Juvénal des Ursins, whose portrait he painted in 1460, showing him at his prayers in an extraordinarily sumptuous setting, glittering with gold. A preparatory study exists, a charcoal drawing on grey paper, heightened by touches of brown and red chalk; now in the Kupferstich-Kabinett, Berlin, it is the first known work in this technique.

It would seem that Fouquet rarely left Tours, favorite residence of the King and his court, where his time was fully occupied with commissions for paintings. Round about 1458, doubtless under instructions from Charles VII, he set to illustrating the *Grandes Chroniques de France* (51 miniatures), and also the Munich "Boccaccio" (80 miniatures) for Laurens Gyrard, a lawyer employed as the King's secretary. During this period he evidently had a considerable staff of assistants and only a limited number of illustrations in these books are entirely by his hand.

JEAN FOUQUET (CA. 1420-CA. 1480). THE MELUN DIPTYCH. LEFT WING: ETIENNE CHEVALIER COMMENDED BY ST STEPHEN, CA. 1451. (36½×33⅜") KAISER FRIEDRICH MUSEUM, BERLIN. ►

JEAN FOUQUET (CA. 1420-CA. 1480). THE BOOK OF HOURS OF ETIENNE CHEVALIER: THE STONING OF ST STEPHEN, 1452-1460. (6½×4¾″) MUSÉE CONDÉ, CHANTILLY.

Louis XI came to the throne in 1461. On August 17 Fouquet, who had been visiting Paris, returned to his hometown to organize the ceremonies for the reception of the new king. Under Louis XI his prestige rose still higher but it was not until 1475 that he was nominated King's Painter, though to all intents and purposes he had held this privileged position over a long period, had designed the plans of all new public buildings, stage-managed festivals, state ceremonies and processions. When in 1469 the King instituted the Order of St Michael, Fouquet was called on to provide the Book of Rules and Regulations of the Order with a frontispiece depicting the King attended by the first Knights of St Michael. He painted a portrait of Louis XI (only replicas are extant) and in 1474 drew up, along with Michel Colombe and Colin d'Amiens, the plans of a funerary monument for this king.

But the key work of this period, indeed the only one which, being ascribed to Fouquet with absolute certainty, has made it possible to identify the rest of his œuvre in detail, is the set of illustrations for a French manuscript of the *Jewish Antiquities* of Josephus commissioned by Jacques d'Armagnac, Duke of Nemours, a descendant of the Duke of Berry. At the end of the book is an entry made by François Robertet, secretary to the Duke of Bourbon who acquired it after Jacques d'Armagnac had been beheaded (in 1477) for high treason. "In this book are twelve tales, the first three [illustrated] by the Duke of Berry's illuminator and the other nine [in reality eleven] by the hand of Jean Fouquet, native of Tours, the excellent illuminator-painter to King Louis XI." It is interesting to find Fouquet being called in to complete an illuminated manuscript begun in the Duke of Berry's ateliers by a member of the Limbourg group, his affinities with which have so often been remarked on.

The illustrations of *Jewish Antiquities* which, throwing light as they do on Fouquet's personal style, have facilitated the identification of his other works, are of an even higher quality than those in the *Hours of Etienne Chevalier*, such is their well-knit, ordered composition into which nothing is allowed to enter that might distract attention from the leading theme. He has a feeling for history and excels in battlepieces, in the depiction of masses of armed men and the measured progress of ceremonial processions. But when he "tells a story" he never clutters it up with details; never, even in his crowd scenes, produces an effect of confusion. (In this respect he is at the opposite pole from the Master of Rohan.) Fouquet always keeps his impulses well in hand; serenity, lucidity, a fine sense of balance and decorum characterize his art, and he aims at saying everything in the fewest possible words.

Perhaps it was the nature of the art form in which he was working, the miniature, that necessitated the selectivity, the carefully arranged color-schemes and the nicety of drawing distinctive of this work. Seeking to impart to his line effects of massive power, he created a new type of figure, simplified, foreshortened, and the same is true of his sturdily built horses. His white has an extraordinary intensity, literally steeped in light. Fouquet goes farther than the great Flemish masters; he does not merely give us glimpses of a distant countryside seen through a window. He takes us into the heart of the country, amongst fields and the familiar scenes of the French landscape, and bids us admire its natural beauties, bathed in limpid, sparkling air. "He too," writes Louis Gillet, "had seen the Alps and Italy, but all he learnt from them was to see his beloved Touraine with an understanding eye." And no painter better brings home to us the smiling grace of the Loire valley,

JEAN FOUQUET (CA. 1420-CA. 1480). THE BOOK OF HOURS OF ETIENNE CHEVALIER: THE BIRTH OF ST JOHN THE BAPTIST, 1452-1460. (6 ½ × 4 ¾") MUSÉE CONDÉ, CHANTILLY.

green hills faintly tinged with blue in the far distance, calm sheets of water, light mists rising through the dusk. His shepherdesses are real French girls, not ladies dressed up for the part, and the naturalness of his peasants anticipates that of Bruegel's.

JEAN FOUQUET (CA. 1420-CA. 1480). JEWISH ANTIQUITIES: THE TAKING OF JERICHO, CA. 1470. (7 ½×6 ½″) MS FRANÇAIS 247, FOLIO 89, BIBLIOTHÈQUE NATIONALE, PARIS.

Unfortunately the few full-size pictures by Fouquet that have survived do not suffice to give an adequate idea of his achievement in this field. Indeed only three such works have been positively ascribed to him: the portrait of Charles VII, the Melun diptych and the portrait of Juvénal des Ursins. These reveal his high abilities as a portrait painter but leave us in the dark as to his larger compositions. That is why so much importance attaches to the discovery—by Paul Vitry, in 1931, in the little church of Nouans—of a large *Pietà* whose style and graphic delineation assimilate it, to say the very least, to the school of Fouquet. The colors have greatly deteriorated, but the superb draftsmanship remains. Is this work entirely by the master's hand? Miss Grete Ring finds its execution rather uninspired and lacking in vigor. In a closely reasoned and to a certain extent convincing study, Abbé de Raulin has sought to identify this *Pietà* with the picture of the Virgin known to have been commissioned by Jean de Bernard, Archbishop of Tours, with whom he also proposes to identify the donor of the *Pietà*. In the portrait of the donor, which is one of the leading motifs in the composition, the drawing much resembles Fouquet's in his *Juvénal des Ursins*; the wrinkles round the eyes and on the forehead are treated in the same way and there are the same close-set lips and long, thick nose. Moreover, the features much resemble those of the archbishop as he figures in a stained-glass window in Tours Cathedral. Finally, the donor's costume, which combines simplicity with studied elegance, is adorned with a handsome lace *godet* like that of Thomas à Becket now in the treasury of Sens Cathedral. Against this it is argued that the Archbishop of Tours, who died in 1466 at the age of eighty, does not look as old as would be expected in the Nouans picture and also that he is accompanied by St James, not by his patron saint, St John. But the latter had already been given a place in the picture—he is supporting the half-fainting Virgin—and thus it was natural enough that, following a fairly common practice, the archbishop should have chosen his patron saint's brother to be his sponsor (nor should it be forgotten that Tours was one of the stations of the pilgrimage to St James of Compostella). Despite the many excellences of this work we cannot help regretting that the artist has made his figures look like statues, whose rounded forms alone convey the idea of Space. This is an extreme instance of the procedure Fouquet followed in his large portraits (whose backgrounds, moreover, are lavishly adorned with gold). There is a vast difference between this and the delightful vistas of the miniatures, in which, while deliberately rejecting the mathematical perspective of the Italians, he achieved such happy effects in his arrangements of successive planes. Nor do we find in his paintings the gay colors, sometimes diversified with gold hatchings, of the miniatures; in the former he usually keeps to neutral, subdued colors, applied in thin glazes. Yet this technique undoubtedly tends to bring out the spiritual, as against the merely mundane, qualities of the model. When Fouquet has a fairly large surface to fill he practises an economy of means enabling him to focus attention on the heart of the matter. We see this notably in the self-portrait; instinct with comprehension, simplicity and kindliness, this face seems to disclose the secrets both of his personality and of his art.

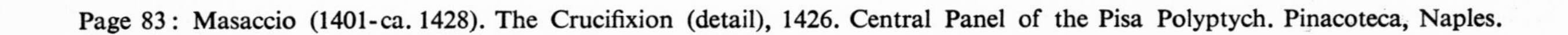

Page 83 : Masaccio (1401-ca. 1428). The Crucifixion (detail), 1426. Central Panel of the Pisa Polyptych. Pinacoteca, Naples.

2

PAINTING IN CENTRAL ITALY

The word Renaissance conveys to us an idea of the rebirth of something which, after having existed in classical antiquity, was subsequently disintegrated by a series of disastrous events—that "something" being the historical legacy of antiquity. For the humanists, the disastrous events in question were the barbarian invasions, foreign domination and the political and moral upheavals of the *media aetas*; all of which violently interrupted and deflected the main stream of European culture.

True, the humanists applied themselves enthusiastically to the study of the classics, but—what was more important and a new departure—they regarded the development of civilization as a natural and logical process, and saw the past not as something dead and done with, of strictly antiquarian interest, but as an inexhaustible source of enlightenment, the vital stuff of history.

When the vast theocratic structure of the Holy Roman Empire and the feudal system fell to pieces and political and economic control passed into the hands of new classes of the community, the lives both of individuals and social groups acquired a new importance and a new scale of values. For now that responsibility was no longer centered in a single person or a small body of men vested with authority from God, each man was personally answerable for his acts. Moreover, a man can appraise his acts only in the light of experience and all experience is founded on the past. Thus if acts are to be conscious, i.e. logical and natural—and this implies a like awareness of their future consequences—it is essential to have a logical, coherent vision of the past as well. And since this vision is selective, since, that is to say, it chooses what is rational or civilized in the past, leaving aside what is irrational or "barbarian," it involves a criterion, that judgment of the data of experience which in fact is basic to history —and history was in fact the paramount concern of the Renaissance.

It was not the memory of the great events of antiquity that perished in the Middle Ages, but the capacity of evaluating them. The story of the past was handed down from generation to generation, but it was accepted unthinkingly, uncritically, and treated merely as a hotchpotch of legendry and fables, having no bearing on the lives and behavior of contemporary man. And indeed when a man's chief aim in life was the salvation of his soul, what help was to be expected from the annals of pagan antiquity? But if on the other hand the value of a man's life derives from the logic of his acts, his full awareness of their causes and effects, what better mentors could he have than the Ancients, repositories of wisdom and "natural philosophers" *par excellence*? However it was also necessary to sort out what was authentic in the legacy of the past and to distinguish between events whose course was shaped by the reasoning faculty and those which were merely incidental. For the permanent values of history are constructions of the critical and logical activity of the thinking mind.

It was not only an objective study of the ancient sources that was called for in this conception of history as the ideal instrument of enlightenment. A knowledge of nature, too, was needed, for the good reason that whatever is logical and rational is also natural. Thus the world brought into being at the Creation (divine archetype of all human action) was intrinsically logical, even though its underlying order was being constantly obscured by "accidentals," just as the logical pattern of history is often blurred by the random course of day-to-day events, themselves illogical. From which it followed that for a clear perception of reality a special frame of mind was needed: that critical, analytical spirit and that consciousness of values which are basic to an understanding of the past. In the time dimension it is history that sets order in the flux of events and determines values; in space it is perspective. Indeed the whole conception of space derives from perspective, that vision of an architecturally ordered world which human reason alone can conjure up within the chaos of appearances.

Nothing could be more erroneous than to believe that a total change in man's outlook on the world came quite suddenly at the beginning of the Quattrocento. Things were far from being as simple as that; as late as the middle of the century there were men like Lorenzo Ghiberti and Cennino Cennini who still refused to admit the importance of the "reawakening" that had taken place some ten years before. Yet they, too, loudly voiced their admiration of the Ancients and were far from regarding themselves as conservatives or die-hard medieval traditionalists. In their opinion the true revolution was that effected by Giotto at the beginning of the 14th century, when he "translated art from Greek into Latin"; it was then that there had been a real break with tradition and the lost wisdom of the past had been retrieved. The tradition they had in mind was that of rigid, iconographic Byzantine formalism, while the wisdom regained consisted of Latin *humanitas* and *pietas*.

So much impressed were Ghiberti and Cennini by the magnitude of the revolution brought about by Giotto that they failed to notice that another great renewal was taking place under their eyes. Indeed even Brunelleschi, Donatello and Masaccio, though they took the lead in bringing about the changes that came over art in the 15th century, would

MASACCIO (1401-CA. 1428). THE ADORATION OF THE MAGI, 1426. (8 ¼ × 24″)
PREDELLA SCENE FROM THE PISA POLYPTYCH. KAISER FRIEDRICH MUSEUM, BERLIN.

certainly have denied that their ideas conflicted in any way with those of Giotto or Nicola and Giovanni Pisano. They, too, were quite ready to admit that a great art revolution had intervened, but to their thinking artists had harked back to the old errors and settled down again into the rut of tradition, despite an air of modernism. When Giotto "translated art from Greek into Latin" he had not merely substituted a new repertory of themes and forms for the Byzantine canon; he had, for the first time, brought "history" into painting and shown that the artist should view his work from an historical angle. Thus as regards "the Gothic" a critical approach seemed called for, with a view to determining its true nature, for though Gothic art might be described as Neo-Latin, a movement so widely generalized could hardly have any precise historic value. What Ghiberti desired was to revive the classical tradition; whereas Brunelleschi, Donatello and Masaccio aimed at establishing "history" on a rational and moral basis. The first objective of these torchbearers of the Renaissance was to resume contact with their specifically Latin background, to distinguish it from the common art heritage of the day, and to re-establish contact with the wisdom of the Ancients, depositaries of all that was most valid in antiquity.

Whereas Gothic art corresponds to the social system of "communities," Quattrocento art reflects the earliest conceptions of "nationalities" (though the nation in question might be merely a township or a district). Thus Florence claimed to be the sole authentic heir of Rome, and this claim seems less extravagant when we remember the chaos prevailing in the Eternal City in the early Quattrocento. It was not until the second half of the century, when the Church of Rome had re-established its ascendancy and made an end of schisms, that Rome regained her exalted place in history. Padua and Venice, too, grew conscious of their historic past and espoused the cause of the new humanism—but only in the last half of the Quattrocento.

This, then, is one of the first things that strike us in Renaissance art: a conflict between exponents of the belated, international forms of the Gothic (styled Germanic), and those on the other hand who championed the new Latinity. By Latinity, needless to say, was meant something quite other than a servile imitation of classical motifs, of which indeed contemporaries had but a relatively vague idea. When they spoke of the new art forms, writers of the day frankly confessed their ignorance as to whether these had been rediscovered or newly invented; indeed they seemed to take little interest in settling the point, since both the process of research and the process of invention involved the exercise of reason.

This awareness of the work of art as being at once historical and new, ancient and modern, gave rise to another, no less distinctive trend of the Renaissance. Since art was no more to be appraised in terms of its compliance with a norm established by tradition, it now was guided by theoretical principles and thus developed theories and an historical pattern of its own. In medieval aesthetic, art was defined as *recta ratio factibilium*, a proper understanding of the feasible, and the artist was merely a craftsman, thoroughly versed in the traditional techniques. In the Quattrocento, however, the artist was a man whose *raison d'être* was discovery and invention, not merely craftsmanship, and who was guided by theoretical and historical principles. Thus the medieval *mechanica* was superseded by the notion of *ars liberalis* and ceasing to be an artisan, the artist ranked among the intellectuals. And there came another change, still more significant. From the viewpoint of medieval aesthetic the concept of "the beautiful" was applicable primarily to God's works and had little to do with art, which was concerned exclusively with the work of men's hands. With the coming of the Renaissance, however, the two views tended to coalesce, "the beautiful" signifying both the perfection of natural forms and a logical proportioning of aesthetic values.

It has often been said that Quattrocento art was essentially naturalistic. This is true only if by naturalism we mean something different from the imitation of reality and read into the word "nature" an ideal form of reality. Governed as it was by laws of space which the artists had deduced from Euclidian geometry, nature was regarded as a counterpart of the human understanding and its rational structure. It was also the field of action assigned to man, regarded as an historical entity. For just as every human action, having causes, objects and definable effects, is conditioned by Time, so it is conditioned by Space, which fixes its limits and provides its setting. Moreover, only when space is rendered in perspective can each element fall into its proper place and be given its proper value, and every act be transformed into an act having its place in history, dramatically significant and possessing universal validity. Thus it was also on the metaphysical plane that the art of the early 15th century differed from the Gothic immediately preceding it. For what Gothic art was for ever seeking was something subtle and elusive, whereas the plastic form distinctive of Renaissance art bears the stamp of certitude, of acts which a man does knowing their causes and effects, knowing, too, that they will hold their place immutably in Space and Time and of whose absolute historical validity he is assured.

The new ideas regarding art had already gained considerable ground at Florence when Masaccio made his sensational appearance on the scene. As early as 1401 Brunelleschi had declared war on Gothic rhythms and forms in his bas-relief, *The Sacrifice of Isaac*, one of the trial pieces for the Baptistery doors, and the structure of the dome of Santa Maria del Fiore signalized the triumph of his theories of perspective. Meanwhile Donatello's sculpture was proving that the study of antiquity could be more than a noble humanistic *otium*, the hobby of an intellectual élite, and could be combined with a forthright realism acceptable to the common man and with the expression of emotion at its most dramatic.

Masaccio was born on December 21, 1401, at San Giovanni Valdarno and died at Rome in 1428. Only one of his works can be positively dated, the polyptych he made for the Carmine church at Pisa in 1426. No sooner was this finished than he started work on the frescos in the Brancacci Chapel of the Carmine church in Florence, which may thus be dated about 1427. His brief career was closely linked with that of Masolino da Panicale; the two artists collaborated on the altarpiece of *St Anne, the Virgin and Child* (perhaps previous to 1423), worked side by side in the Brancacci Chapel, and subsequently arranged to work together in Rome, in the Church of San Clemente. According to Vasari, Masaccio studied under Masolino, his compatriot and twenty years his senior. But it seems clear that Masolino's teaching was confined to matters of technique and that Masaccio's art was shaped by contacts with quite another milieu, that of the "modernizing" artists whose leader was Brunelleschi.

Masolino was in fact a man of a very different stamp. Progressive, like Ghiberti, in a moderate way and open to new ideas, he was particularly interested in perspective and in exploring its possibilities. The expressive power of the younger man's art was a revelation to Masolino and there is no question that he asked nothing better than to enrich, renovate and reform the old art tradition. But he neither could nor would break with it definitively, fearing that if he parted company with that trusted guide, as Vasari puts it, "he might lapse into excesses." Masaccio on the other hand was so convinced of the necessity for cutting loose from tradition that he sought his masters outside the field of painting—which proves that he regarded art more as a matter of general culture than one of technical accomplishment.

Early in his career he became friendly with the great architect Brunelleschi and, as was to be expected, given their difference of age, came under his influence. In the massive folds of the drapery in Masaccio's painting there is something of the plastic vigor of the great stone ribs in Brunelleschi's architecture; and there can be no doubt that the unusual disposition of space—in the form of a cross—in one of Masaccio's most impressive scenes (*The Trinity* in the Church of Santa Maria Novella, Florence) was inspired by the Barbadori Chapel in the Church of Santa Felicità. It is easy to see why this painter was better qualified than any of his contemporaries to appreciate the plastic, architectonic values of Brunelleschi's art; but it is quite possible that the architect, too, learnt something from the painter. Round about 1430 so radical a change makes itself felt in Brunelleschi's style that it has led L. H. Heydenreich to surmise that the architect's first visit to Rome took place at this time, and that not till then did he become acquainted with the relics of classical antiquity. An attractive theory, but hardly tenable, since the architect's earliest works, even the dome of Santa Maria del Fiore, show quite clearly that he must have seen and studied ancient edifices. In the Church of San Lorenzo, Florence, his concept of space as issuing from relations of perspective planes contains in embryo that vision of a space built up by the interplay of voids and masses which determined the structure of Santo Spirito church in Florence. Doubtless Masaccio's painting, not the sight of ancient edifices, led Brunelleschi towards these new spatial conceptions. Finally, it is a suggestive point that when Leon Battista Alberti, shortly before 1435, set out to elucidate Brunelleschi's theory of perspective, the book he wrote dealt not with architecture but with painting. In it he worked out at some length the logical conclusions to be drawn from the new conception of space and applied them to the representation of figures and human action. That round about 1430 there was an unmistakable shift of interest from architecture to painting was certainly due to the overriding influence of Masaccio's art. Yet it cannot be said that he consciously worked to any specific art theory or program, or that he rigorously followed Brunelleschi's postulates as regards perspective; indeed one might almost say that he showed less interest in natural appearances than in the last manifestations of International Gothic. He fully realized that if the latest discoveries and the new approach to reality were to take full effect, it was imperative to move on to a new conception of man; in other words, to create a new moral attitude. In fact his aim was to throw light on the ultimate significance of human personality, to discover the moral message implicit in the data of history. And, alongside the intellectualism of Brunelleschi's art and Donatello's bold reconstructions of historic events, the essentially moral outlook of Masaccio was likewise basic to Renaissance culture.

Opinions differ as to Masaccio's share in the *St Anne, the Virgin and Child* altarpiece. Almost all the angels are ascribed to Masolino, as is the execution, if not the original conception, of the figure of St Anne. However, the Virgin and Child are unquestionably by Masaccio. From contemporary records we learn that Brunelleschi upbraided Donatello for having used a peasant as his model for the figure of Christ Crucified. But no one could have blamed Masaccio for placing on the throne a peasant woman, even if his Madonna was at a far remove from the elegant Madonnas of courtly Gothic art.

We almost get the impression that the artist gave little thought to his figures *qua* figures. In their presentation we find no striving for elegance or grace; what he aims at and achieves is an effect of massive power and architecturally ordered composition. Neither attitudes nor faces conform to any traditional standard of beauty; on the other hand, the folds of the mantle have the solidity, the sustaining force, of the ribs of a cathedral dome, while the curves of the Virgin's mouth and eyeballs stress the effect of plastic volume. This effect of a solid mass, whose weight is "taken up" by the soaring movement of its very structure, is a transposition into terms of the human figure of the ideal lines of force in Brunelleschi's dome. The broad, low, plainly decorated throne, so different from the elaborately ornate thrones of Gothic art, serves the sole

purpose of defining spatial limits, the disposition of the masses. In this uncompromising starkness there may well have been a polemical intent, inspired by Brunelleschi—the artist is reminding us that the surface appearance of things matters little; what counts is their value, their integral structure. For Brunelleschi space was the projection of a logical construction of the intellect; for Masaccio, a modality of the human spirit as a whole, embracing all reality within itself.

We are of course concerned with a religious effigy, that of the Virgin; but this religious effigy is endowed with high moral significance and becomes a representation of human virtue at its holiest. It has been pointed out that Masaccio deliberately turned his back on the art of the late 14th century and linked up with Giotto. And it is not to be denied that Masaccio's sense of moral responsibility and the significance of history had been anticipated by Giotto. But we must not lose sight of the fact that the dramatic element in Giotto's art involved a transposition of the human situation on to the heavenly plane; for, like Dante, Giotto presupposed the certitude of man's salvation. Masaccio, on the other hand, deeply religious though he was, located his themes on earth, in the heart of reality. And to his thinking the sole warranty of a man's salvation was his knowledge of himself, his personal adhesion to a moral law and, thereby, awareness and acceptance of his responsibilities.

The Virgin of the Pisa altarpiece (now in the National Gallery, London) is still further removed from our traditional ideal of beauty and has not a trace of Gothic charm. Her massive form is organically related to the elaborate structure of the throne. The artist has been so little concerned with locating the figure in space that he has deliberately retained the traditional gold background. But here the gold no longer produces the effect of radiant light stretching out into illimitable distance; on the contrary it is a backdrop, a flat surface. In a small panel, giving a perspective view of the Baptistery, Brunelleschi had made a mirror-like expanse of polished silver do duty for the sky. Its purpose there was merely demonstrative, but Masaccio may well have taken over from this early work of Brunelleschi (it was produced at the beginning of the century) the notion of a gold ground as signifying *not-being* in contrast to the *being* of the volumes. In any case we have here an opposition between a background which is the negation of space and a figure suggesting absolute, primordial space, still without form.

Hostile to the graceful rhythms of Gothic art, Masaccio was equally averse from following the lead of Brunelleschi and Donatello and turning towards the art of classical antiquity. He was seeking to discover basic, prototypal values, those of the dawn of human life, and intuitively realized that a return to the "classics" might well frustrate this quest. It was not enough to investigate the past, however rich in noble achievements; he wished to strike down to the very roots, the beginnings of man's awareness of himself as a moral being and of his place in history. This is why he refrained from portraying the human situation under its dramatic aspects; since the mere fact of depicting these localized them in recorded time. He preferred action *in posse* to action *in esse;* action, that is, in its dormant, potential state, when it is germinating in the mind and will, and being evaluated in the light of moral responsibility.

XV 45

MASACCIO (1401-CA. 1428). THE TRIBUTE MONEY, 1426-1427. (8 ft. 4 inches × 19 ft. 6 inches)

FRESCO, BRANCACCI CHAPEL, SANTA MARIA DEL CARMINE, FLORENCE.

MASACCIO (1401-CA. 1428). THE TRIBUTE MONEY, 1426-1427. DETAIL: HEAD OF THE PUBLICAN. FRESCO, BRANCACCI CHAPEL, SANTA MARIA DEL CARMINE, FLORENCE.

MASACCIO (1401-CA. 1428). ADAM AND EVE CAST OUT OF PARADISE (DETAIL), 1426-1427.
FRESCO, BRANCACCI CHAPEL, SANTA MARIA DEL CARMINE, FLORENCE.

The Pisa altarpiece has been dispersed and of the saints that figured in it the St Paul is in Pisa, St Andrew in Vienna, while the others are in the Kaiser Friedrich Museum, Berlin. These figures are like leaden statues, ponderous and motionless, telling out in high relief on the gold background and almost seeming to project beyond the confines of the panels. Nevertheless the flicker of eyes under the heavy brows, subtle movements of the hands, a sort of pent-up tension in the bodies show that the minds are alert; this is a momentary calm preceding action and for all their massive immobility, these figures have a secret life vibrant beneath the surface. The light emanating from the forms themselves is always stronger than the sheen of the gold grounds; it does not come from any extraneous source, nor is it arbitrarily directed to certain areas. The luminosity of the zones of light is solely due to a contrast with the areas in shadow, and the latter seem dark by contrast with the light, not because light has failed to strike them. What we have here, in short, is rather contrasts of position than variations of intensity—and in fact the difference of actual illumination between the darkest and the brightest passages is comparatively small. Thus form is created, as in Brunelleschi's architecture, by a system of proportions; it does not represent an object or objects located in a pre-determined space, but is in itself the figuration of space at the exact moment when it comes into being and makes its presence known to the beholder. Here it is the human figure alone that calls space into being—reiterating the first act of the Creator calling forth light "out of the darkness that was on the face of the deep."

When, from the act *in posse*, Masaccio passes to the act itself, it seems to spring forth abruptly, untrammelled by the conscious mind. The gesture, in fact, is performed before the person making it realizes what he or she is doing; it emerges from the latent state instinctively. Illustrations of such gestures are St Peter taking the coin from the fish's mouth in *The Tribute Money*, and Mary Magdalen flinging herself down at the foot of the Cross (in the Pisa polyptych); in a gesture almost startling in its passionate abandon she seems to be tearing at the flat gold background as if to open up depths of infinite space behind it. The shrill red of her garment, the wildly outspread arms express human grief at its most poignant, but hallowed in this context by its participation in the divine tragedy, the crucifixion of the Son of God. Here we can see how different was Masaccio's attitude from Giotto's. Giotto saw in the divine tragedy an archetype of the human, by grace of which man could sublimate the calamities of the human predicament. But Masaccio saw it as at once the historical antecedent and, on the moral plane, the *raison d'être* of the strivings and sufferings that are the common lot of man. The same theme is treated, more fully, in the Santa Maria Novella frescos. There the depiction of the Trinity, for all its hieratic symbolism, is infused with an intensely human significance, owing to the fact that it is given an architectural setting, that is to say confined in a man-made space (symbol of human reality), and thereby links up with the idea of death, most tragic of all motifs.

All art historians are now in agreement as to the respective shares of Masaccio and Masolino in the frescos in the Brancacci Chapel. They were painted in 1426 and 1427 and subsequently completed by Filippino Lippi. Before these frescos Masaccio had already painted a *St Paul* which figured in a niche of the same church and also, in the cloister, a picture of a procession in the Piazza del Carmine. Both are lost, but from all accounts the *Procession* was reminiscent of Brunelleschi's perspective studies, while the *St Paul* was probably the prototype of those hierophantic figures, resembling painted statues, which recur so often in works of a slightly later period.

Needless to say, it was not the painters who chose the theme of the decorations in the Brancacci Chapel or decided on the arrangement of the frescos. But the new religious conceptions they vouch for makes it clear that commissions were given to artists belonging to the humanistic milieu. The leading theme is the life of St Peter. Two of the frescos, however (*The Temptation of Adam and Eve* by Masolino and *Adam and Eve cast out of Paradise* by Masaccio), prove that the sequence was intended also to celebrate the history of the Church, as the chosen instrument of man's salvation. These two scenes clearly relate to "Man's first disobedience," source of all our woes, that original sin which necessitated the Incarnation, and likewise to the role allotted the Church in the redemption of mankind. Though Masolino does not seem to take account of the new ideological implications of the theme—in *The Temptation* he keeps to the allegoric-naturalistic methods of the 14th century—Masaccio, on the other hand, was quick to perceive the symbolical and ultimate significance of the biblical narrative. Breaking with the past, he gives us not the mere illustration of a tale, but a revelation of the religious origin of man's moral instinct, impelling him to acts that further his salvation. Moreover, the picture is not merely organized but constructed by perspective, which being a creation of the thinking mind, adumbrates the fusion of the human and the divine. In other words, perspective is no longer the framework within which events take place; it is at once the very essence of the scene depicted and a manifestation of that universal order which is the ideal pattern of all human activity. Whereas Masolino's *Temptation* gives us a graceful illustration of the Bible story, Masaccio's *Adam and Eve* is charged with moral intimations; it is in fact a graphic meditation on the Fall of Man and his sense of guilt. Below the angel carrying out God's behest, Adam is cowering, hiding his face with his hands, Eve gasping out her anguish like a wounded animal. Yet they are advancing with measured strides, their feet solidly planted on the ground; no longer mythical, these are historical figures, the primogenitors of mankind. This explains one of Masaccio's new departures, his emphasis on volumes, the massiveness of these primeval figures, cumbrous as blocks of granite. For he is depicting humanity still rough-hewn and as yet but faintly animated by the breath of the Creator. Not yet fully differentiated, these figures cannot be precisely located in space; only action can give them definition, and they have the purity, the uncouthness, the strong yet hesitant movements of beings in process of formation. Their gestures, timid replicas perforce of the initial gesture of their Creator, are likewise creative in so far as they separate and distinguish, because Will involves the use of Reason, and Reason, which involves distinguishing, is basic to creation. In short the very presence of these figures, in itself, distinguishes and differentiates; it distinguishes their mass from a void that has not yet become space and is merely non-existence; light from a darkness that is merely opacity, an unfathomable limbo; action from inertia, good from evil. That is why no smiling landscape environs the first man; nature has not yet taken form in human awareness, and round these archaic, elemental figures (as in *The Tribute Money*) there can only be the wilderness.

True, the fresco of *The Tribute Money* depicts an historic scene; but the narrative element (split up into three parts) is distinctly secondary. In the centre of the fresco we see Christ surrounded by the apostles from whom the tax-collector is demanding the tribute money; on the left St Peter is taking the coin from the fish's mouth, and on the right, in the foreground, he gives it to the official. There is no narrative continuity in the presentation; following the outstretched arms of Christ and St Peter, the beholder's

MASACCIO (1401-CA. 1428). ST PETER HEALING THE SICK WITH HIS SHADOW (DETAIL), 1426-1427.
FRESCO, BRANCACCI CHAPEL, SANTA MARIA DEL CARMINE, FLORENCE.

gaze is led towards the finding of the money in the fish's mouth; then, abruptly, it is brought back to the scene in the foreground, the handing over of the coin. Thus the final incident of the narrative is placed nearest us in time as well as in space. Whereas the scene—presented as a brief, sharp fragment—in which St Peter bends to take the coin, is located on the margin of the composition, at a point on the horizon where space ceases to function and any plastic development of the visual data is ruled out. Time and space become a single entity, or, to put it more precisely, the time elements in the narrative are stated in terms of perspective. These frescos were painted with an eye to being viewed from the same level as the figures and this procedure, too, derives from Brunelleschi's theory of perspective. Obviously Masaccio had no wish to make the natural setting "picturesque"; his aim was to create a symmetrical design with an axis on which the plastic values pivoted. The grouped figures form a circle centering on that of Christ, starting-off point of several transversal planes which ramify into the barren landscape of the background. This is the same spatial arrangement as that

MASACCIO (1401-CA. 1428). THE TRIBUTE MONEY, 1426-1427. DETAIL: ST PETER TAKING THE PIECE OF MONEY FROM THE FISH'S MOUTH. FRESCO, BRANCACCI CHAPEL, SANTA MARIA DEL CARMINE, FLORENCE.

used by Brunelleschi for the lantern-turret of his dome, to prevent its being merely an object located in space and to make of it, instead, a form of space, a spatial entity in its own right. Masaccio saw in space a paradigm of history and this explains the desolation of the background. For Man's heritage of sin, expiable only by strict observance of the moral law, ruled out any conception of the world of nature as being a realm of bliss, that earthly paradise which the Late Gothics, men like Pisanello and Gentile da Fabriano, thought they had at last regained.

The same awareness of man's onus of responsibility and the moral values implicit in his acts can be seen also in the other frescos: *St Peter Baptizing, St Peter healing the Sick with his Shadow, St Peter and St John distributing Alms* and (except for the passages subsequently painted by Filippino Lippi) in *The Resurrection of the Son of the King of Antioch* and *St Peter seated on the Episcopal Throne*. These too are figurations of history, though for the most part given contemporary settings, the streets and public squares of Florence—as though to remind the beholder that the spiritual significance of those acts remote in time is timeless, constantly renewed in every Christian's daily life. Indeed this conception of the momentous import of every act, its ineluctable finality, fraught with salvation or perdition for the doer, is basic to Masaccio's art; also its social or (as Coluccio Salutati would have put it) "civil" implications. For, more than Brunelleschi or Donatello, Masaccio was aware that a new social order was in the making, a social order ultimately stemming from the hinterlands of history and the very dawn of human life. And with his exaltation of moral values he brought about a fusion of deep religious faith and the humanistic appraisal of life in terms of history.

FRA ANGELICO

It is easy to understand why Fra Angelico's art, with its graceful forms, bright colors and simple, poetic charm, seemed to contemporary observers the exact antithesis of Masaccio's. A century after the painter's death a legend (for which Vasari is largely responsible) grew up around his personality, the legend of an artist in a state of ecstasy, "with tears streaming down his cheeks," seeking to body forth his visions of celestial beauty. The facts, however, were rather different.

In 1407, when he was twenty, Angelico entered the Dominican convent at Fiesole, where he became a predicant friar, favorite pupil of the Blessed Fra Dominici (a guiding spirit of the Observant Dominican movement) and a friend of St Antoninus, a monk of outstanding erudition, energy and enterprise. That laudatory title "the Angelic" (previously bestowed on the great St Thomas Aquinas) was given him by his fellow monks, impressed by his exalted piety. Such indeed was his renown that the Pope, so we are told, was minded to offer him the archbishopric of Florence. In any case he summoned him to Rome to decorate the Chapel of Nicholas V in the Vatican. After being absent for three years, during which he was Prior of the Convent of San Marco at Florence, the painter returned to Rome, shortly before his death (in 1455). He was one of the leading lights of the Dominican Order at a time when the Dominicans exercised an immense influence on the religious and political life of Italy. Painting was for him a medium of edification, prescribed and governed by a well-defined program

—in other words by a corpus of religious doctrines to which he faithfully subscribed. As a matter of fact he did not take up painting till late in life; anyhow his earliest known work is dated round about 1430, by which time Masaccio's brief but brilliant career was over. Fra Angelico was a great admirer of Masaccio and though the influence of the latter on his art may not be apparent at first sight, it is unmistakable beneath the surface. Indeed all Fra Angelico's work shows how closely he kept in touch with the new ideas that were making headway in the world of art, and even adopted them—but needless to say within the limits imposed by his personal religious views and Thomist doctrine. For the idea of accepting any aesthetic theory as valid in its own right conflicted with his religious principles, according to which art was primarily, indeed exclusively, the handmaid of religion. To Fra Angelico's thinking, Nature provided the only path by which earthbound man could hope to arrive at an understanding of her divine Creator. Since this quest, involving as it did an inference from visible effect to the first cause, was an intellectual process, perspective was not ruled out *a priori*, for the good reason that perspective was one of the means by which the human intellect can explore the world of Nature and reveal the omnipresent order, established by Divine Providence, behind the veil of appearances. Nevertheless the new ideas (as formulated notably by Alberti) tended to give art a definitely intellectual bias and to divert it from its traditional religious vocation. Fra Angelico could not approve of this; what he aimed at was to uphold that tradition—and yet at the same time to create a "modern" religious art.

His chief objections to the humanistic program turned on the new conceptions of space and history; both, as we have seen, of prime importance in that program. From the Thomist viewpoint space did not exist or, rather, was an intellectual abstraction; God had created light and all existing things, both being emanations of "the heavenly bodies." As for history, there were lessons to be learnt from it because it was a factual account of past events, but we should not lose sight of the fact that all human acts are governed by Divine Providence. Thus history can never be an end, only a means. Fra Angelico's approach to these problems (anyhow in his early phase) was much the same as Dominici's in his controversy with Coluccio Salutati. It was also the position taken up by the Observants (the Dominican group in which the strictest rule was observed) as against the humanists.

In the Cortona *Annunciation* (ca. 1430) the composition is built up around a loggia rendered in perspective, in the Brunelleschi manner. A line of arches in recession links up the foreground where the Annunciation is taking place with the scene of Adam and Eve being expelled from Eden, which occupies the background. Thus here perspective indicates the logical progression from the remote cause (the Fall) to its effect (Christ's Incarnation). Now it is clear that if perspective is regarded as a logical, abstract creation of the mind, it cannot *per se* build up a new system of forms, that is to say it is not constructive, though it may help to raise each element of a composition to its maximum perfection. This is why Angelico's line is all a rhythm of exquisitely graceful curves, while colors are steeped in a celestial radiance and tonal relations expressed in terms of this all-pervading luminosity.

FRA ANGELICO (1387?-1455). THE ANNUNCIATION, DETAIL. FRESCO, AFTER 1437.
CELL, CONVENT OF SAN MARCO, FLORENCE.

FRA ANGELICO (1387?-1455). THE LAMENTATION OVER THE DEAD CHRIST, 1440-1445. (42 ½ × 64 ¾″)
MUSEO DI SAN MARCO, FLORENCE.

It is interesting to study the various scenes in the predella of *The Annunciation* with reference to the perspective-light relationship. The lighting varies with the changes of perspective—for the good reason that perspective is not treated as an end in itself or the abstract rendering of an ideal space. It serves at once for the representation of the outer world, for an analytic study of the immanent perfection of all created things and for the diffusion of universal, not incidental, light. Thus Fra Angelico was the first artist to assign a metaphysical basis to naturalistic art.

The Linaiuoli Triptych (1433) is the first of his works that can be exactly dated. The marble frame, with which the composition structurally links up, was made after Ghiberti's designs. Conceived as a new form of celebrating the glory of the Virgin, this painting contains some rhetorical effects which reveal the artist's leanings towards the literary aesthetic of the humanists. Virgin and saints alike are so many "statues" in the humanistic application of the word, that is to say in accordance with the views of Ghiberti and, a little later, Donatello. In this work we feel the undercurrent of history, but history in a limited sense, without episodes or narrative; it has more in common with a sermon or a panegyric. And here, as in a sermon, what counts most is elocution, well-rounded periods, formal continuity and clarity of diction—in a word, the Art of Rhetoric so highly prized by the Ancients. Petrarch indeed regarded Rhetoric as the most precious of the legacies of Antiquity and saw in it the type-form of all spiritual activities. However the predella scenes, inspired like so many previous works by tales from the *Golden Legend*, strike a different note; in them history is presented as a sequence of real events, meaningful and in the best sense spectacular.

Henceforth the religious ideal and the aesthetic ideal coalesce; the artist is seeking to recapture the perfect forms of all things as they were in the beginning, the forms God intended them to have and which can be discerned only by the pure in heart, by those who gaze at Nature with the desire to discover the *primum mobile* beneath the flux of appearances. When Nature is thus restored to her primordial state all contrasts are ruled out, harmony reigns everywhere, and the forms of things cease to be in conflict with the play of light. For perfect form, form which fully expresses the identification of the intellectual with the spiritual ideal, is indistinguishable from *absolute* light. In the Perugia altarpiece (1437) and the series of works previous to *The Deposition* in the Museo di San Marco, Florence, we find a striving towards the perfect fusion of form and light and shimmering, translucent color. And it is easy to imagine how this well-nigh miraculous equilibrium of form and light must have impressed and influenced Piero della Francesca, who in the same period was working at Florence, in collaboration with Domenico Veneziano.

The gap between Fra Angelico and the humanists was steadily diminishing, as is clearly proved not only by the increasingly courtly, almost worldly elegance of his *sacre conversazioni* but by the pomp and circumstance of his famous *Coronation of the Virgin* in the Louvre.

The Deposition in the Museo di San Marco—it was painted about 1440 for Santa Trinità, Florence—is one of the painter's key works. In it he demonstrated that the religious ideal of the Observants could be reconciled with the intellectual ideal of the humanists. On the right of the picture some bystanders—recognizable as humanists by the garments they are wearing—are quietly conversing, while one of them holds up the Crown of Thorns and the Nails, symbols of the Passion. Obviously these philosophers pay no heed to the realistic aspects of the event that is taking place before them; only its symbolic values interest them. Religion for them is essentially a matter of the intellect, *docta pietas*. But on the left we see the holy women praying, making ready to wrap the shroud around Christ's body, with loving reverence; and here we have *caritas*, the piety of simple souls, a religion of the heart. Between the two groups Christ's body describes a bow-like curve while in the background is a landscape extending as far as eye can reach, bathed in the tranquil light of a spring day—the most delightful landscape Fra Angelico ever painted, indeed the first true landscape in all Italian Quattrocento art. Flooded with silvery light, Christ's body has, despite its scars, a serene beauty, enhanced by the faint smile playing on His lips. Symbol of man's devotion to the God who died for him, this *Deposition* is almost like a second coming on earth, a renaissance of human *pietas* towards the Savior. No other picture better illustrates the theory advanced by Burdach who saw in the Renaissance a re-awakening of the soul, when man was "born again" in the Christian sense of the term. In this work what may be described as Fra Angelico's religious naturalism is carried to its highest pitch; for the first time in history a Christian "myth" takes concrete form.

Yet at almost the same time Fra Angelico was planning and executing the decorations in the Convent of San Marco and none of the frescos he painted in each cell bears any trace of religious naturalism. The function of these pictures was to provide the monks with themes of meditation. For while the revelation of the manifold perfections of God's creation may be of spiritual help to those whose lot is cast in the world of ordinary men, the monk, who has renounced the world, seeks a more immediate contact with God, by way of prayers and ascetic disciplines. When he was preaching to laymen Fra Angelico could take the beauties of nature for his theme and extol them with his brush, but when he addressed himself to men who had taken the vow, he replaced naturalism with symbolism. On these occasions he imparted to his painting an immaterial quality, that of the Idea in all its purity, and since his aim was not didactic or sociological but exclusively religious, he was drawn unconsciously towards that form of Platonism which, latent in humanist thought from the outset, found full expression in the philosophy of Marcilio Ficino.

In the San Marco frescos, now that he had turned his back on naturalism, Fra Angelico took thought once more of Space, but Space of a special kind, regarded as an ideal, purely geometrical concept, an abstract counterpoint of lines and planes. Light is treated as an imaginary dimension and, ceasing to be localized or limited in scope, becomes absolute, an omnipresent, transcendent radiance. This was the time when Fra Angelico's was in the fullest sense a dedicated art; when he achieved a perfect fusion between philosophic and religious modes of thought, between Reason and Faith.

After this phase of exaltation, *amor dei intellectualis*, he went (in 1447) to Rome to paint, with the assistance of Benozzo Gozzoli, the six great frescos in the Chapel of Nicholas V at the Vatican, depicting episodes in the lives of St Stephen and St Lawrence. With the accession of Nicholas V to the pontificate the Church gave official recognition to the new humanism and when Fra Angelico started work under the aegis of the new Pope he was plunged into a milieu of philosophers and men of letters, amongst whom was Leon Battista Alberti whose rationalistic views he had combated some twenty years before. Schisms were at an end; the papacy had now regained its ancient primacy and made good its œcumenical authority as against the separatist movements of the national churches. The clouds had lifted and once again the Catholic Church could proudly glorify her long historic past, inseparable from that of Rome. Thus the humanist interpretation of history no longer ran counter to the religious ideal but served, rather, to reinforce the prestige of the Church. This is why we now find Fra Angelico turning to scenes from the history of the early Church, the lives of the first

FRA ANGELICO (1387?-1455). ST LAWRENCE DISTRIBUTING ALMS, 1447-1455.
FRESCO, CHAPEL OF NICHOLAS V, VATICAN.

martyrs and confessors. Also for this reason, the architectural settings he gives these scenes tend to fall in line with the new classicism—which, at this very time, Alberti was advocating in his treatise on architecture.

The Vatican frescos may be described as Fra Angelico's "Latin" works, conceived and executed in the language of Romanizing humanism at its purest. The plenitude of forms, the directness of statement, the feeling for history and human dignity show that the artist was reverting in his old age to the conceptions of Masaccio. But whereas in Masaccio's art the historical factor was present in a latent state, and in the work of Andrea del Castagno and Pollaiuolo was limited to the representation of a brief, solitary act, in the art of Fra Angelico we always have a "story," in the loftiest sense of the term. With Fra Angelico (with Benozzo Gozzoli acting as intermediary) begins the lineage of the great Florentine story-tellers of the 15th century; they took over from him his interest in all things great and small, his pious naturalism and at the same time his basic Thomism.

These frescos may justly be regarded as the terminal point of his artistic evolution. The one and only important work that can be dated to the time when he was Prior of the Convent of San Marco is the sequence of scenes from the life of Christ which he made to decorate the doors of a silver-chest in the Church of the Santissima Annunziata. These panels, too, are in a narrative vein, but with a frankly popular appeal. It would seem that after a life spent in meditation Fra Angelico felt a need to hark back to the primal verities, the simple, elementary facts on which Christian faith is founded. In a different medium these works may be said to forestall Savonarola's hymns and "Lauds" —but, needless to say, they have nothing of that great reformer's savage indignation. Familiar themes, naïve rhythms and idioms are skillfully interwoven into the pattern of a highly cultured, deeply religious art, and the painter seems to take pleasure in a studied archaism, in which however the smooth flow of the narrative is abruptly broken here and there by unexpected accents, flashes of witty byplay. When we look at *The Flight into Egypt* or *The Massacre of the Innocents* we cannot help wondering if at the close of his life the artist did not decide—once again and for the last time—to give a new directive to his painting, which had seemed intended to appeal exclusively to the élite. Perhaps, indeed, when Fra Angelico sought to combine aesthetic values with popular appeal, he was but reverting to an aim he had set himself in earlier days: that of restoring to painting its traditional religious function and checking the current tendency towards the secularization of art.

If this was so, it follows that this great artist, whom an age-old tradition persists in calling a mystic, detached from worldly interests, was a shrewd observer of his times as well as a pious monk. Better than any of his contemporaries he perceived the significance, and diagnosed the perils, of the new culture that was coming to birth. Discreetly but with unflagging zeal he applied himself to creating a style of art that was in the highest sense exemplary; and surely the fact that this great painter was more than a dreamer of ecstatic dreams and sought to convey a message of "practical morality" should not detract in any way from our admiration of his unique genius.

SIENESE PAINTING

The trend of pictorial art in the other towns of central Italy should not be regarded as "backward" in comparison with that of Florence. No doubt it was eccentric in the exact meaning of the word—that is to say divergent from the central stream—but it was far from being merely provincial, as becomes evident when we turn to the achievement of the Sienese, some of whom, though they showed no direct interest in art theory and research, rank high among 15th-century painters. In his *Quattrocentisti senesi* (Milan 1949) Cesare Brandi proves the injustice of the view that Sienese Quattrocento painting did no more than slavishly copy the art forms of the preceding century. In fact the legend of the charming, childlike naïvety of these so-called Primitives does not hold water; and in any case, as Pierre Francastel has pointed out, true Primitives, far from being traditionalists, are always great inventors of new forms.

SASSETTA (1392-1451). THE JOURNEY OF THE MAGI. (8½×11½")
METROPOLITAN MUSEUM OF ART, NEW YORK.

GIOVANNI DI PAOLO (ACTIVE CA. 1423-1482). ST NICHOLAS OF TOLENTINO SAVING A VESSEL FROM SHIPWRECK, 1455-1460. (20 ½ × 16 ¾") JOHNSON COLLECTION, MUSEUM OF ART, PHILADELPHIA.

From the beginning of the century onward, there was a constant give-and-take between Florentine and Sienese art. However, we should not lose sight of the fact that humanism—the common measure between men of letters and philosophers such as Salutati and Bruni on the one hand and, on the other, such artists as Brunelleschi, Donatello and Masaccio—reflected a typically Florentine turn of mind and ways of thinking that were bound to be distasteful to the Sienese, given their religious and artistic background and the traditions of their ancient aristocracy. Moreover such painters as Sassetta and Giovanni di Paolo were out of sympathy with late 14th-century art and far more closely allied to the great masters of the early Trecento, to Simone Martini and the Lorenzettis. If we consider only their constructive innovations—a general enrichment of the picture surface with an ever subtler interplay of line and color—it might be said that Sienese art often progressed on much the same lines as Florentine art and sometimes even took the lead. But what was absent in Siena was an interest in the theoretical side of art, the habit of regarding its problems as bound up with those of science, philosophy and history; all, in fact, that made Florentine art not merely a new aesthetic, but the revelation of a new awareness of the world and man's relation to it. Siena clung to a legacy of the past that Florence had the courage to reject. This is why all the formal innovations transmitted by Florence to Siena in the early years of the century served solely to replenish a cultural tradition to which Form was never basic. It was in Florence that the problem of form was seriously tackled for the first time; Sienese art culture, as Cesare Brandi puts it, was and remained *una cultura dell' immágine.* Since these artists did not attach any ideological values to lines and colors, or to art the function of enlarging knowledge; and since space, for them, had no relation to reality but was merely the place occupied by the painted image, they could indulge in an almost infinite range of variations on any given theme. In 1423, when Masaccio was beginning to make his name in Florence, Sassetta painted an altarpiece for the Arte della Lana (wool-makers' guild). Here the number and intersections of the different planes, the crossings of the perspective projections and some bold foreshortenings create an abstract depth, not giving any illusion of reality. This abstract, not to say illogical, space enabled the artist to elicit unexpected harmonies in the relations between colors and, while projecting the narrative into an imaginary yet singularly convincing ambiance, to impart to figures physical unsubstantiality but undoubted effectiveness *qua* pictorial elements. As for Giovanni di Paolo, "he sensed intuitively that the value of perspective lies not in the creation of illusive distance but in rhythm" (Brandi, *op. cit.*) and in fact his perspective projections lead on to impossible horizons and the whole composition gives an impression of extreme fragility—almost as if it could fall to pieces at a touch. This imparts a curious vibrancy to the images, a sort of nervous tension, subtle and all-pervasive. But it was only later, when Florentine "form" and the Sienese "image" confronted each other, that the difference between the constructive vigor of the former and the languid grace of the latter became so marked; between an art which addressed itself to the intellect and one that aimed at being no more than painting.

PAOLO UCCELLO (1397-1475). THE ROUT OF SAN ROMANO (DETAIL), 1456-1460.
BY COURTESY OF THE TRUSTEES, NATIONAL GALLERY, LONDON.

Paolo Uccello would have been a great master—this in effect is Vasari's summing-up of his place in 15th-century art—had not his "eccentric, over-intellectual" approach to painting led him to regard perspective not as a means but as an end. And Donatello often reproached him for his "dry style full of profiles." Making as he did a cult of history, he disapproved of Uccello's art theories, since they left historical research out of account. What, he asked, was the use of theories which led neither to the discovery of the classical sources nor to a constructive vision of reality?

There is a picture by Uccello in the Louvre (unfortunately in very poor condition) in which he painted the portraits of the five "inventors" of perspective. The inscription at the foot of the picture was added later and the order in which the names are written does not tally with that of the figures. But it is interesting to find that Giotto is included and Masaccio left out. Ghiberti had seen in Giotto the originator of the "new painting" and it is known that at the age of ten, in 1407, Uccello was sent to work in Ghiberti's *bottega*. As for Masaccio, though Uccello admired him as an artist, he thought nothing of him as a theoretician—which indeed is easily understandable. In the Louvre picture he assigns to himself the role of the inventor of perspective in painting and, alongside famous representatives of the other arts, he places a mathematician, Antonio Manetti. He was convinced that if the new art (which started with Giotto) was to be carried to its logical conclusion, perspective was the *sine qua non*, since it was of the nature of an exact science and, as such, not a mere aid to painting but fundamental to it.

Uccello went to Venice in 1425 and it was only on his return (ca. 1431) that he was able to see Masaccio's frescos in the Carmine Church. He promptly espoused the new ideas with all the zeal of a neophyte; but the monumental effigy of Sir John Hawkwood ("Johannes Acutus" in the inscription) shows that as early as 1436 he had taken to interpreting Masaccio's art in terms of the humanistic theories that Alberti was advocating just at this time. Fra Angelico on the other hand stood out against them and made a cautious use of perspective, which he regarded as no more than a means of intellectualizing sensory data. Uccello deliberately rejected Fra Angelico's naturalism; to his thinking, the whole structure of form was bound up with perspective; just as, to Brunelleschi's mind, perspective was an integral part of architectural design. Feeling as he did about perspective, Uccello inevitably turned his back on naturalism and even his colors, low-keyed with a smooth enamel finish, are completely different from Fra Angelico's luminous tonalities.

True, a large number of his works—for example, the Holy Fathers at San Miniato al Monte, the prophets in the clock-face of Santa Maria del Fiore and the biblical scenes in the Green Cloister of Santa Maria Novella—reveal Masaccio's influence in no uncertain manner. Nevertheless the essentially moral implications of Masaccio's art are so to speak intellectualized; everything is re-arranged in terms of that scientifically calculated perspective which was Uccello's ruling passion and led him to create a mythology of his own and a fanciful, heraldic world—a world of the "Quaternary period" as Roberto Longhi has described it. Whereas Masaccio depicted Man with all the attributes of humanity, Uccello located him in an unreal Space and Time,

PAOLO UCCELLO (1397-1475). THE ROUT OF SAN ROMANO, 1456-1460. (72×125")
BY COURTESY OF THE TRUSTEES, NATIONAL GALLERY, LONDON.

a purely imaginary context. To this world belonged, no doubt, *The Giants* (now destroyed), a work Uccello painted round about 1445 in the Casa Vitaliani, at Padua.

The three versions of *The Rout of San Romano* (Uffizi, Louvre, National Gallery, London) were painted, it would seem, between 1456 and 1460; that is to say shortly after Piero della Francesca had completed the Arezzo frescos depicting the victories of Constantine and Heraclius. Uccello grafted his perspective methods on to Piero's mode of seeing, as in the Green Cloister he had applied them to Masaccio's. Piero, like Masaccio, did not use perspective to determine the lay-out of the scene depicted, but to crystallize it—in other words, to immobilize it in Space and isolate it from the flux of Time. And in Piero's work we find a monumental grandeur, a moral conviction of the truth and the permanence of history, quite outside the range of Uccello's wayward temperament. For Uccello Space was no less unreal, no less hypothetical than Time. His perspective is an ingenious mechanism that actuates men and horses, strewing the ground with dead or wounded combatants in terms of a carefully planned schema and a division of the picture surface into pre-determined compartments. Moreover, since every geometrical form can be adequately represented on a flat surface, he feels no need to have recourse to depth or to impart movement to figures. Once it ceases to be

PAOLO UCCELLO (1397-1475). THE ROUT OF SAN ROMANO, 1456-1460. (71 ¼ × 124 ¾″)
LOUVRE, PARIS.

concerned with either the moral implications of history or visual responses to the forms of nature, the use of perspective as an intellectual device ends up as an exercise of pure imagination; and, well before Pulci's heroi-comic epic *Morgante Maggiore*, Uccello's battlepieces drew attention to the element of romantic make-believe in the popular ideas of chivalry. Since, given these premises, depth is no more than a theoretical dimension of Space, everything becomes two-dimensional, reduced to profiles, a counterpoint of tracts of color bound in well-marked contour-lines. There is a rich play of surface effect, the colors being at once vivid and absolutely pure, though we find variations in their quality and intensity. If (as Vasari observed with shocked surprise) meadows come out blue and horses red, this curious transformation is not due to light or atmosphere; it stresses the gulf between the optical and the spatial images, the cleavage between the image in depth and that on the picture surface.

It is neither in the biblical scenes, inspired by Masaccio, nor in the battlepieces, inspired by Piero, that the poetic quality of Uccello's art reveals itself at its delightful best. For this we must turn to his more fanciful scenes, without historical pretensions: *A Hunt* (Ashmolean Museum, Oxford) and *The Story of the Jew and the Host* (Galleria Nazionale, Urbino). In these the artist is not striving for a form of expression that demonstrates to best advantage his theory of art; instead, he lets it function on simple, natural lines, as a means of evoking and recording, with amazing lucidity and vivacity, the visions of his free-ranging imagination.

Uccello's intellectual extremism (like all types of extremism) had both progressive and reactionary trends. When we recall the antithesis between Alberti's view, that painting is solely the representation of things seen, and Cennini's, that painting is the revelation of what the eye does *not* perceive, it becomes obvious that Uccello's art, which aimed at bringing to light the underlying spatial structure of the universe, adapted Alberti's ideas to those of Cennini. True, the science of perspective was a wholly secular science, but no less than religion it involved a "dogma," and in fact there was much in common between its rationalist dogmatism and the ascetic rigorism of Lorenzo Monaco. The dogma we have in mind was that of every *a priori* concept which does not stem from actual sensory experience—and indeed devalorizes it. An illustration of this point is Uccello's reluctance to make use of natural sunlight and his use of an illumination seemingly nocturnal, in which colors owe their brightness not to the impact of light but to their physical properties, the luster inherent in them. His perspective is, strictly speaking, neither schematic nor purely scientific; it is, rather, a painterly technique suggested by his researches in this field. Pressing to their logical conclusion the theories of Alberti, who aspired to a vision *ab omni materia separata*, divorced from all material things, Uccello sublimated the ancient conception of the painter as an artisan and painting as a craft on to the highest metaphysical plane. As a result of this intellectualization of art, even color was given an almost abstract beauty, owing nothing to the appearances of nature. For only thus could its intrinsic value be made perceptible and, thanks to the new science of perspective, this value was both formal and material, provided the *materia* in question was—paradoxically enough—"divorced from all material things." For these reasons we should do well to revise the opinions formerly, and persistently, held regarding Uccello and his art; he was not an artist obsessed with theories who made a fetish of perspective. It was *form* that fascinated him, we might even say he made a cult of it. He did not regard perspective as the controlling factor of the artist's vision or a means of constructing space within the picture; for him, perspective was an instrument enabling the artist, by the exercise of his intellect, to build up form and give it absolute, autonomous value. If Uccello's attitude to art has a metaphysical bias, this is not because, like Fra Angelico, he put his art to the service of a religious ideal or, like Masaccio, idealized the human element; it is because his way of seeing was guided by an inner logic and an abstract architectonic concept. Thus, indifferent to factual verisimilitude, he envisaged form as an ideal projection of the structure of the human mind.

Obviously, under these circumstances, Uccello's art, product of an essentially secular imagination, left out of account many of the problems preoccupying the more religious-minded artists; amongst them the historical significance and ethical values of human behavior and modes of thought. In the work of Andrea del Castagno, on the other hand, these specifically humanistic criteria were to play a leading part.

PAOLO UCCELLO (1397-1475). A HUNT (DETAIL).
ASHMOLEAN MUSEUM, OXFORD.

DOMENICO VENEZIANO

One of the key problems of Florentine painting in the decade 1440-1450 was that of the relations between perspective and light; in other words, between the application of a scientific structural formula and the illumination which is the prime condition of all visual experience. Filippo Lippi solved the problem empirically, by means of a compromise; whereas Piero della Francesca's solution was of a purely *a priori*, i.e. theoretical, nature. However, we should not overlook the fact that two other painters, before them, had faced up to this problem: Andrea del Castagno and, even more conspicuously, Domenico Veneziano.

In a letter written in 1438 from Perugia to Piero de' Medici, Domenico described Fra Angelico and Filippo Lippi as the two best painters in Florence. He himself had very probably worked there before 1439, the year in which he painted the famous Sant'Egidio frescos with the assistance of Piero della Francesca, then a youth. As to the nature and range of Domenico's activities during his first stay in Florence, little is known for certain, and owing to the destruction of the Sant'Egidio paintings, we have only his Santa Lucia altarpiece in the Uffizi (1445-1448) to go on. The arrangement of this picture of the Madonna with attendant saints owed much to Fra Angelico, who

PAOLO UCCELLO (1397-1475). THE STORY OF THE JEW AND THE HOST (FRAGMENT).
GALLERIA NAZIONALE DELLE MARCHE, URBINO.

DOMENICO VENEZIANO (1400/1410-1461). THE MARTYRDOM OF SANTA LUCIA. (9¾×11¼″)
PREDELLA SCENE FROM THE ALTARPIECE OF SANTA LUCIA DE' MAGNOLI. KAISER FRIEDRICH MUSEUM, BERLIN.

had by now completed his frescos in the Convent of San Marco and, abandoning the religious naturalism of which we have spoken, had employed in them a transcendental, otherworldly light that seemed to absorb into itself all spatial values. While taking over from Angelico the general conception of his Madonna Enthroned, he combined it with a lay-out in staggered planes: an elaborate recession of loggias, pillars, alcoves. The joint effect of these motifs is to dissolve the light into a silvery haze criss-crossed by sudden gleams, almost kaleidoscopic in their bright profusion.

In this altarpiece (and even more so in the predella scenes) we have an impression that the light is as it were a reflection or a by-product of the structural clarity of the perspective representation of space. It is a light deriving from relations between colored planes, their distance from each other and their balanced distribution, and is thus identical with form. Our point here, needless to say, is not that light is indispensable for the perception of form, but that in Domenico Veneziano's art light *is* form and has a special quality enabling it to reconcile all quantitative differences. Being of this nature, it does not depend on an opposition of light-and-shade for its realization. It steps up colors to the maximum brightness permitted by their quality and, seeping freely into volumes, gives them an almost geometrical regularity. In this respect Domenico takes the opposite path to Lippi's; he intellectualizes Angelico's "theological light," whereas Lippi humanizes it, bringing it back to the plane of empirical naturalism.

ANDREA DEL CASTAGNO

Born in 1423, Andrea del Castagno had already made his name as an artist in Florence by the time he was seventeen; two years later, in 1442, we find him working in the Church of San Zaccaria in Venice. As was to be expected, these early productions reveal the influence of Masaccio and his ethic. But whereas Masaccio's message was bound up with the origins of the human race, the events described in Genesis, Andrea del Castagno transposed it into a relatively "modern" setting; he viewed history as a process of transition from the primeval to the contemporary human situation. Thus he tended to side with Donatello, who so vigorously maintained that ancient history, if its lessons were to serve a moral purpose, must be presented in terms of the present and made to come to life. Both men intuitively sensed the affinities, not to say the blood tie, between the great men of Antiquity and the Tuscan people. Indeed from the humanist viewpoint, the whole value of history derived from the fact that the outstanding qualities of individuals were transmitted to future generations and "reincarnated" in due course in the *Zeitgeist* of the group. Also, like Donatello, Andrea del Castagno was at once a classicist and a realist; ancient history, as he saw it, lived again and produced its full dramatic effect only when it was presented in terms of real life, with its inevitable train of violence and passions.

In his depictions of religious themes Andrea del Castagno, though personally far from a religious-minded man, achieved an admirable fusion between the historical ideal and his cult of realism. But when—as in his frescos of *Famous Men*—he turned to illustrating frankly humanist motifs, he whittled down the historical ideal to a sort of homily, adapted to the taste of his public, and his realism amounted to little more than the use of a vernacular idiom.

Andrea del Castagno set much store on the statuesque as illustrated in the work of Donatello, the "statue" being presented as an isolated figure, though it gives the impression of having been extracted from a bas-relief (i.e. a group, with an historical frame of reference). Interesting in *The Crucifixion*, painted some time between 1445 and 1450 for the Brotherhood of Sant'Apollonia, is the difference between the figure of Christ, treated in the manner of a free-standing statue, and the group of holy women, which brings to mind a bas-relief. His procedure is the opposite of Uccello's; instead of building up an architecturally ordered space, he seeks to "register" a specific gesture, a detail or an accent. The place and the moment of time in which he locates his figures are as near as possible to the beholder, since this enables them to have the most immediate emotional appeal and maximum vitality. But these tactile qualities of his figures call for a representation of depth (in space and time) to balance them, and this cannot be adequately rendered by linear perspective with its mathematically

FILIPPO LIPPI (CA. 1406-1469). THE BANQUET OF HERODIAS (DETAIL), 1452-1468.
FRESCO, PRATO CATHEDRAL.

calculated limits. Hence Castagno's use of backgrounds which are either smooth colored surfaces, as in the "Brotherhood" frescos at Sant'Apollonia and the *Famous Men*, or else a limitless expanse of shimmering light, as in *The Crucifixion*, *The Descent from the Cross* and *The Resurrection*. The function of the contour-line circumscribing each figure is not to isolate it as an object existing in infinite space, but to bring out at once its form and spatial environment, its movement and the factors conditioning it. For Andrea del Castagno, as for Pollaiuolo after him, line was not a mental abstraction, an "idea," but the motive force behind the image. While far from rejecting the physical realities of light and color, he aimed above all at a clarity of definition that realized his vision instantly and completely. In his pictures perspective plays the part of design; instead of being used for creating the effect of space it is used for constructing forms and figures in movement, its chosen vehicle being foreshortening. This is, in fact, the special virtue of foreshortening, that it condenses the maximum space within the smallest compass and gives line its utmost potential dynamism, ready to issue in action at a moment's notice. It is this tension, the energy dormant in the line, that, for example, enables Castagno's angels to halt abruptly in mid-flight and likewise imparts to the brief, emphatic gestures of his figures not merely local but distant repercussions. Here lies the difference between Uccello's foreshortenings and Castagno's; the former visualizes figures in terms of the over-all perspective schema, whereas the latter concentrates all space in the movement paths of the scene.

This new plastic form owes nothing to the varying incidence of light on bodies; on the contrary, it derives wholly from within them and need no longer be expressed by alternating zones of light and shade. True, space and light are here identical—one may say space *is* light—, but since the former is constructed and determined by the figures and their movements, this light is quite other than the common light of day. It is an all-pervading medium or essence which remains invisible, in a latent state, until human presences and human action summon it to radiant life. This is why in Andrea del Castagno's art light has no clear source or well-defined locus of reflection. Sometimes it stresses and brings out forms by hardening colors; sometimes it glances lightly over planes and sometimes it strikes through them, as though they were transparent. This curiously "dry," inconsistent light, conditioned by the tensions of the line, serves as the unifying principle between infinite space and the human element. In this respect it anticipates that intellectual conception of light and its perfect identification with form which may rank as Piero della Francesca's supreme discovery.

FILIPPO LIPPI

In his *Lives* Vasari has a habit of relating each artist's work to his personal character; thus, in order to explain the *terribilità* of Castagno's painting, he accuses him of being a murderer and of having killed Domenico Veneziano—an obvious impossibility since Castagno died before his alleged "victim"! Similarly, in order to account for the sweetness, the gentle, human warmth pervading Filippo Lippi's art, he explains that Filippo was of a sensual and sentimental disposition. Be this as it may (and anyhow it has little real importance), Filippo Lippi's chief distinction is that he was the first artist to establish a real connection between sensory experience and pictorial representation. For, while Andrea del Castagno saw in nature no more than a field of activity for human action and emotion, Filippo Lippi sought to discover an underlying harmony between the human condition and nature and, moreover, to interpret those promptings of the soul which do not necessarily issue in an act or leave any mark on "history." His world is a world of feelings; volition, purposive action, have no place in it. He was in his early twenties and a member of the Carmelite convent when Masaccio was painting the frescos in the Brancacci Chapel and there can be no doubt it was the sight of Masaccio's frescos that gave him the idea of taking to painting. All the same his favorite master was not Masaccio but Fra Angelico.

Angelico's Thomist nominalism with its emphasis on the primacy of all created things—and therefore light, the first created thing—over Space, the "void" primordial, served Lippi as a theoretical basis and justification for his interest in nature. He regarded perspective as a means, not an end; as a purely optical means, moreover, and not (like Fra Angelico) as an intellectual instrument. Perspective enabled him to space out objects and figures in depth, to fill interstices with interesting details, giving them perfect visibility and crisp definition right up to the horizon line. Whereas Benozzo Gozzoli, when taking over Angelico's narrative elements and carrying them a stage further, aimed not at illustrating a page of history or a parable, but at "telling a story" to the best effect, Lippi, while employing the same elements, conjured up lively, colorful scenes, at the farthest possible remove from any metaphysical intent, and meant simply to give pleasure to the eye. Thus both painters, each in his own way, converted Angelico's ideal art into a lay art, eliminating from it any homiletic or religious bias and that theological, conceptual tone which was now becoming more and more outmoded. Though the public they were catering for was still that Florentine middle class to which Angelico and the humanists (though with different ends in view) had wished their art to appeal, these two painters fell in line with the trend of the times. For painting was gradually abandoning the lofty and austere ideal which had been the lodestar of the early humanists and turning more and more towards "accidentals," the manifold beauties of the world. Compared with Angelico's religious naturalism and its constant quest of tokens of the Creator's perfection in that of his creation, Filippo Lippi's art strikes us as being at once secular and pious. From his earliest works on, he refashions nature in a sort of eclectic mosaic of elements borrowed from Fra Angelico, Gentile da Fabriano and Ghiberti, and builds up an edifying picture of the boons conferred by Divine Providence on mankind.

Like Castagno, Filippo Lippi had his eyes turned on Donatello, but he left out of account the classical accent and the historical import of his sculpture. What attracted Lippi was the wonderful plasticity of Donatello's forms and the living, vibrating quality of surfaces modeled and vitalized by light and atmosphere. For, surprisingly enough, it was sculpture that inspired the Florentine painters with that interest in the problem of light which, round about 1450, became their chief preoccupation. This is not so paradoxical as it might seem, since the work of sculpture normally occupies a place where it is exposed to natural light, with the result that it modifies the light, adapting it by means of modeling to the given form of the subject portrayed, and thus transforms natural into "formal" light. We may be sure that Lippi was quite indifferent to the historical and dramatic implications of Donatello's work; he confined himself to studying the sculptor's technical procedures and handling of form. His contours all in sweeping curves, his practice of keeping the plastic roundings of bodies as low as possible (in the manner of Donatello's "flattened relief") and his fluent light that skims the surfaces of objects (e.g. in the Tarquinia *Madonna* of 1437) show that when he thus reproduces in his painting Donatello's technique of keeping his relief as low as possible, his object was to create a physical continuum between figures and their environment. Such was his desire for homogeneity that he even was at pains to prevent the "action" of the picture from diverting attention from the minutely detailed background, since only thus could the natural world be portrayed in all its plenitude.

For a theologically minded painter like Fra Angelico, light was the very essence of space, since without it not only would nothing be visible but there would be nothing there to edify the Christian soul. Pious no doubt but nothing of a theologian, Lippi

ANDREA DEL CASTAGNO (1423-1457). THE LAST SUPPER. DETAIL: THE APOSTLE JOHN.
FRESCO, CENACOLO DI SANT'APOLLONIA, FLORENCE.

took a very different view; for him the relation between light and the world of things was of a physical, not a metaphysical order. And so he applied himself to making an inventory as it were of all that physically occupies space and gives it substance. Thus the architectural elements, hitherto treated as mere perspective vistas or settings, become real buildings, architectonic elements of the composition; they have pillars, loggias, walled terraces and arcades opening on distant gardens. Landscapes are filled with tree trunks and branches, ruins and jagged rocks, above which float small, trailing clouds twisted like skeins of wool. In his art light is no longer regarded as a precondition of visibility but as a material entity integrating the elements of the picture; it is inherent in objects not as isolated units but as elements co-existing, interacting on each other and constituting, as an ensemble, the space dimension. Since each detail is circumscribed by a clean-cut contour-line and has its own chiaroscuro and relief, the effect of all these little islands of light and shade is to set up a luminous vibration throughout the picture surface. This vibration can be transmitted only by some physical medium, in this case atmosphere (which has the same origin as light) and Lippi was the first to make it perceptible, a real presence in the picture. In the same way as the interplay of bright and dark tones generates light, so an interplay of full and empty spaces creates the illusion of atmosphere. In other words, we may say that Lippi's naturalism derives from a logical application of Fra Angelico's theory of "metaphysical light." Thus we need not be surprised if his *Coronation of the Virgin*, though only slightly later than Fra Angelico's and obviously inspired by it, has no longer any ritual character and is more like some scene of gay rejoicings in an Italian town. Pierre Francastel has very rightly stressed the fondness of Italian Quattrocento artists for scenes of festal pageantry but Lippi was the first to treat them not as mere decorative details but as vital elements of the composition.

Light, in fact, ceases to have any spatial function and, instead of being shed from above upon the surfaces of things, it emanates from them. Lippi sees light as atmospheric vibration, that faint, incessant tremor which permeates the entire phenomenal world. Thus it is not the vehicle of any transcendental vision but the means of access to an ever richer diversity of visual experience. No longer does light hover over colors like a shining film; inherent in the texture of objects, it issues when they are juxtaposed. In Filippo Lippi's art the problem of the contradiction between geometric space and perceived space is, for the first time, satisfactorily resolved—on "quantitative" lines, by the use of chiaroscuro. The color-scheme is kept deliberately in a low key; when a blue or a red might, otherwise, tell out strongly, the painter makes haste to submerge it in subtly broken and blended greys and browns. Thus a new kind of perspective is created; no longer acting as a frame of reference within which pictorial elements are dovetailed together, Lippi's perspective is, rather, of the nature of an infiltration of depth among the various objects, a sort of mobile space, and it leads the beholder's gaze towards the background by way of interesting, arresting fragments that serve as stepping-stones. Here nature is not presented as the panoramic view seen through Alberti's "window," but in deep recession, full of colorful details that pleasurably stir our senses; landscape, in short, provides a setting not so much for scenes of action as for the play of feeling. The frescos in Prato Cathedral (1452-1468) were conceived in this spirit, and what holds our interest is not the action represented but the general atmosphere. There is no hint of stress or strain, everything moves to a languid rhythm, all in gentle modulations, sinuous curves and subtle cadences.

PIERO DELLA FRANCESCA

Most philosophically minded of all 15th-century painters, Piero della Francesca brought to perfection a fully integrated system of knowledge and proved himself a profound thinker as well as a very great artist. When in his early twenties he was working at Florence with Domenico Veneziano, he had an opportunity of evaluating the two great artistic ideologies of the day. One of these, sponsored by Masaccio and the theories of Alberti, assigned to art an historical and moral function; while characteristic of the other, that of Fra Angelico, was its emphasis on religion carried to the highest pitch of asceticism and other-worldliness. Piero della Francesca may well have realized that the process of transmuting intellectual truth into religious truth, however noble its aim, could only result in bringing painting to a standstill (this, in fact, was what befell Angelico himself). But he also realized, intuitively, that a synthesis was possible—and essential: that synthesis between revealed religion and science, that transmutation of dogma into the idea, which was basic to Ficino's Platonism. What Piero had in mind was something new: neither reality nor a vision of transcendence but a higher truth embracing both, and that supreme truth as he conceived it was *form*. One of Uccello's aims in his passionate researches into all the possibilities of perspective had been to arrive at an ideal form, not that of any specific object but that of space and reality as a whole. Likewise, to Piero's thinking, there could not exist—in fact there was not—any distinction between form and space, since the latter made itself perceptible, *qua* structure, only by means of form. Indeed this held good for all direct experience of reality, which in the last analysis is apprehensible only as form—essential form stripped of accidentals—existing in space. Here we can see the two parallel trends prevailing in Florence at the beginning of the century: that of the Aristotelians who proceeded from the observation of particulars to the inference of general laws and that of the Platonists who regarded the universal, the "idea," as the starting-off point for an understanding of particulars.

Piero kept abreast of all that was most advanced in the culture of his day and not without reason did his contemporaries regard him as the "philosopher artist" *par excellence*. He was well aware that in deflecting art from its traditional aim, the promotion of religious faith, he was, inevitably, venturing into the field of pure aesthetics. If any polemical intent is to be discerned in his unflagging quest of formal perfection, it reveals itself as a reaction against Lippi's naturalism, the light-hearted anecdotal art of Gozzoli and, perhaps, against Baldovinetti's elegant but somewhat shallow formalism.

Theories of art interested Piero hardly less than its practice and he set forth his views in two important treatises: *De prospectiva pingendi* and *De quinque corporibus regularibus*. These works have not the humanistic bias of Alberti's writings on the

PIERO DELLA FRANCESCA (1410/1420-1492). THE DISCOVERY OF THE TRUE CROSS (DETAIL).
THE STORY OF THE TRUE CROSS, FRESCO, 1452-1466. CHURCH OF SAN FRANCESCO, AREZZO.

PIERO DELLA FRANCESCA (1410/1420-1492). THE DISCOVERY OF THE TRUE CROSS, LEFT SIDE.
THE STORY OF THE TRUE CROSS, FRESCO, 1452-1466. CHURCH OF SAN FRANCESCO, AREZZO.

subject; they expound a strictly scientific theory of form in art. In the first-named work perspective is no longer treated as a general theory of space but as a specific means of building up the pictorial image; in other words, space exists, for Piero, only in so far as it reveals itself in forms. Unlike his predecessors he does not regard space as having an objective existence in its own right; on the contrary, it is painting

PIERO DELLA FRANCESCA (1410/1420-1492). THE DISCOVERY OF THE TRUE CROSS, RIGHT SIDE. THE STORY OF THE TRUE CROSS, FRESCO, 1452-1466. CHURCH OF SAN FRANCESCO, AREZZO.

that determines space and reveals it through the agency of form. Thus painting is regarded by him as one of the speculative sciences, an intellectual activity whose conscious aim is to formulate absolute truth, and in so far as it builds up space in terms of perspective projection involves a geometrical construction of bodies, regularly shaped forms. However, the fact that these are geometrical does not mean they are constructions of the mind alone or purely *a priori* concepts. They derive from visual experience and a transposition of the particular occurrences of history into the world of universal "ideas." Under such conditions the form-idea does not part company with visual experience but, on the contrary, reinforces it. There is no question here of a special mode of knowledge due to some mysterious, transcendental revelation; rather of an exact science with its own methods of research. And in Piero's forms, hovering though they always are on the brink of abstraction, we find all the elements of the real world: movement, color, light, the familiar concrete aspects of existing things. There is something in common between Piero's approach to art and Angelico's poetic Thomism, but the basic difference of their temperaments is evident in their renderings of light. Piero's has not the dazzling effulgence of a celestial vision but the crystalline clarity of the light of reason. In his art he rules out all that in the work of other artists reveals an interest in human passions and activities, in history as a chronicle of spectacular events, and in scenes of nature as a pasture for the eyes and for the thinking mind. "Let us begin by saying," Lionello Venturi writes, "that he does not concern himself with expressing love or hatred, indeed we might almost suspect him of a certain emotional frigidity. Whereas Masaccio created a monumental œuvre inspired by a high moral purpose, in which the Son of God and His disciples confirm their sacred mission by the miracles they perform, Piero's art stems from the contemplation of a world in which time flows so slowly that it seems to merge into eternity, and even life and death appear to coalesce on some supramundane plane."

Monumentality and immobility are, in fact, basic to Piero's vision; he tends to exclude anything in the nature of a specific event and to arrest the flow of time in an eternal moment, within a space that is static, purely formal. All the same it cannot be said that Piero's large-scale works are altogether devoid of movement. In the Arezzo frescos, for example, each scene "tells a story" and, what is more, there are two battle-pieces. So it would perhaps be truer to say that Piero aims at producing not a wholly static image but one that is in the course of becoming stabilized.

Unlike his predecessors Piero does not use perspective as a means of constructing a cage-like spatial frame for the "action" of the picture. What he does is to employ the system of proportions given by perspective as a determinant of the proportions of *form*. Sometimes, for example, such typically perspective elements as walls and pillars are aligned on a plane at right angles to the picture surface, and even blot each other out. Elsewhere, aligned on a plane parallel to the foreground, they form a chromatic background against which variously colored figures stand out. And, yet again, there are times when perspective relations are treated as it were elusively, or altogether omitted, so as to enable light to range freely over the whole scene, creating a remarkably brilliant open-air effect. In *The Dream of Constantine* the conical tent might well serve as a demonstration of the way in which geometrical regularity of form can suffice in itself to determine the quality of light and, in this particular case, to give a universal value to the light in a specific scene. Though some have thought otherwise, the cause of this geometrization of forms is not that the lighting is that of midday,

PIERO DELLA FRANCESCA (1410/1420-1492). THE ANNUNCIATION, DETAIL OF THE VIRGIN.
THE STORY OF THE TRUE CROSS, FRESCO, 1452-1466. CHURCH OF SAN FRANCESCO, AREZZO.

PIERO DELLA FRANCESCA (1410/1420-1492). ALLEGORICAL SCENE, AFTER 1472. (18½×13″) BACK OF THE RIGHT WING OF THE DIPTYCH OF FEDERIGO DA MONTEFELTRO AND BATTISTA SFORZA. UFFIZI, FLORENCE.

when the sun is directly overhead. In his earliest known work, the Misericordia polyptych, Piero retained the traditional gold background (and this as late as 1445 or thereabouts); but this did not in any way necessitate his departing from the "solid geometry" and stereometric images characteristic of his art. It is obvious that, in associating geometrical structures with the conventional gold ground, Piero had in mind Masaccio's procedures in the Pisa polyptych. But he solved the problem of light by transferring it on to the plane of form; in other words, by demonstrating that light, when it emanates from a regularly proportioned form, can, thanks to its schematic distribution, harmonize with the abstract, indefinite luminosity of a gold ground. For while there may also be a symbolic meaning in the gold ground, it is inevitably associated in the mind of the beholder with the physical properties that give it its distinctive luster. Not a trace of linear perspective can be found in *The Baptism of Christ*; the foreground is built up entirely by columniform tree-trunks and figures which, too, seem built on the lines of classical pillars, while the landscape is a freely rendered expanse of small luminous patches of color, mounds of greyish sand, brown clumps of brushwood.

Here we find an identification of light and color and a method of *suggesting* space by color-contrasts that inevitably call to mind Fra Angelico, perspective also being handled quite in the manner of Angelico—improbable though this may seem in the case of a painter so mathematically minded and so scientific in his approach to art as Piero. But none was better qualified than he to appreciate Angelico's subtle interpretation of perspective in the Cortona *Annunciation*, where it is treated as a symbolic form, like the logical relation between cause and effect. It will be remembered that Angelico used a foreshortened portico to link up the distant scene of Adam and Eve cast out of Paradise with the close-up view of *The Annunciation*. This may throw light on *The Flagellation of Christ*, whose exact significance has long been something of a puzzle to art historians. Whether the scene depicts Oddantonio da Montefeltro in the company of his evil counsellors or, as Sir Kenneth Clark has recently suggested, the tribulations of the Church after the fall of Constantinople in 1453, there is no question that perspective is here intended to serve as a liaison between two scenes, which, historically unrelated, have only an ideological association. This perspective does not correspond to any development in space or time; the central colonnade is so strongly foreshortened that the pillars seem to rest one upon the other. Thus there is no longer any question of a perspective representation of space, even geometrically planned space, and the artist's sole purpose is to bring out the symbolical and ideological relationship, the identity of *form* between the two episodes in question: the flagellation of Christ and the conversation between Oddantonio and Sigismondo Malatesta's perfidious emissaries.

The great fresco cycle (1452-1466) in the church of San Francesco at Arezzo recounts the following episodes in the Story of the True Cross: *The Death of Adam, The Queen of Sheba's Visit to King Solomon, The Burying of the Wood of the Cross, The Dream of Constantine, Constantine's Victory over Maxentius, The Torture of Judas, The Discovery and Proof of the True Cross, The Victory of Heraclius over Chosroes, Heraclius restoring the Cross to Jerusalem*. Besides the "True Cross" cycle proper there are two representations of saints and an *Annunciation*. What we have here is the history of a symbol—in other words of a "form." The Cross is not merely a symbol of the Passion but also the token of a great historical event which ushered in the dawn of a new cultural era, a momentous change in the destinies of mankind, a new conception of the relations between God, man and nature. Already Fra Angelico had sensed this intuitively, when he transformed the figure of Christ into a cross in the San Marco frescos; so had Masaccio when he painted the Trinity in Santa Maria Novella, and Brunelleschi when he based his perspective arrangement of space on an intersection of lines meeting at right angles.

The whole Arezzo cycle may be regarded as a demonstration of the proposition: Form=Space=God. The figures, too, are exalted into symbols of a race of men immune from the vicissitudes of history; witnesses or observers rather than actors in the great drama of man's life on earth, they have a proud aloofness, a more than human dignity. Rapt in frozen calm, they express their historical and moral significance not by way of any form of action but in an intense and lucid awareness of their inmost selves. And, being located in an "unreal" space, a construction of the thinking mind, they do not need the distortions Uccello gave his figures. Indeed their very presence creates a world apart, with its own spatial frame of reference, a world that no extraneous element can ever modify; and, similarly, they emanate a pure, ideal light that no ray from without can intensify and no shadow dim. In Piero's art form and light have the same metaphysical quality and thus can neither conflict nor contrast with each other. Light permeates all forms because these forms *are* space, and space *is* light.

Piero's literary source was *The Golden Legend*, which Fra Angelico had already drawn on for his homiletic scenes. The idea of presenting these themes as dramatically emotive fragments had never even crossed the latter's mind. Piero, for his part, looked beyond their dramatic possibilities, since his purpose was to achieve a total synthesis between pure space and form. In Masaccio's art man's place in history was determined by the exigencies of the human predicament, his responsibility for the guilt of his progenitors. Man, in Piero's art, has crossed the frontier, so to speak, of the human situation and definitively achieved salvation—but a "salvation" that has none of the theological significance Fra Angelico ascribed to it. For, more than any of his contemporaries, Piero seems to rule out any eschatological considerations. Salvation, as he understands it, is not to be found in heaven, but in the human consciousness; not in moral conduct, but in man's self-awareness, his feeling for the innate, inviolable dignity of his own "form." Thus the preoccupation with moral conduct which led Masaccio to depict scenes of action or dramatic situations, is transposed by Piero on to the plane of self-knowledge, of the reasoning faculty and the spirit of enquiry into first causes. Obviously this is a purely intellectual solution of the problem; yet we cannot fail to see its similarity to the religious doctrine that knowledge of God is at the base of all morality. This is, in fact, the essential difference between Piero's approach to art and the uneasy skepticism of his Florentine contemporaries, who reduced history to the level of the myth and regarded the pursuit of formal certainties or any all-embracing system as a hopeless quest.

The avenues Piero had thus opened up were carried on in several directions. These lie outside the scope of the present volume, concerning as they do the subsequent

PIERO DELLA FRANCESCA (1410/1420-1492). THE NATIVITY. (49 × 48 ¼″)
BY COURTESY OF THE TRUSTEES, NATIONAL GALLERY, LONDON.

Roman phase of the Italian Renaissance, that second flowering of humanism when attempts were no longer made to reconcile, by recourse to historical or philosophical analogies, the Christian revelation with the heritage of classical antiquity, and when the Church triumphant was regarded, rather, as a reincarnation of the glory and the wisdom of the ancients, sponsoring a rebirth of the entire system of knowledge that had passed away with the downfall of the Roman Empire.

ANTONIO POLLAIUOLO

Seen from a certain angle, the close relationship between painting and sculpture that prevailed during the first half of the 15th century proved that artists were already trying to reconcile the concept of history as the supreme value with the data of immediate visual experience. This tendency becomes more marked in the work of two artists who were both sculptors and painters: Antonio Pollaiuolo and Andrea del Verrocchio. While adopting Andrea del Castagno's vigorous design and well-nigh brutal directness of statement, Pollaiuolo failed to achieve either his majestic effects (of a somewhat literary order) or, on the other hand, his unflinching, slightly plebeian realism. On the contrary he expresses himself with a studied, almost nervous elegance and his restless line, constantly broken off and picked up again, and steeped in vibrant light, flashes across the surface of his compositions, from the figures to the far horizon. This fine-spun line, stretched almost to the breaking-point, does not define or demarcate; it is, rather, the expression of a feverish impulse, directed to no specific end. Thus the gestures and movements of figures seem to be prolonged indefinitely up to the farthest confines of the landscape and transformed into ripples of air spreading out in all directions. This flight into space corresponds to a flight into the uncharted realms of ancient myth, to the beginnings of life when both men and nature were in a state of flux, forms continually changing and any metamorphosis was possible. Indeed we are justified in reading into his *Apollo and Daphne* (National Gallery, London) a symbolic value; since it shows how, in the throes of passionate emotion, man becomes at one with the world of nature. Pollaiuolo was the first artist to give expression to his humanistic culture in a steady flow of pictures having mythological subjects: *The Rape of Dejanira*, *The Twelve Labors of Hercules* and so forth. Mythology—especially as it figures in Ovid's *Metamorphoses*—was the meeting-point, beyond space and time, between history and nature; it enabled the artist to break with the established order of space (perspective) and that of recorded time (the march of history). Hence his ability to impart to gestures a new immediacy and to the aspects of nature an unprecedented vividness. Thus the *terribilità* which the early humanists had imparted to their moral and historical ideal now gave place to what Marsilio Ficino called a *furor malinconicus*, and whereas the former had led to a total break with nature, the latter brought about a fusion between man and the natural world. And it was the concept of this fusion—signified in Verrocchio's art by a gentle, over-all vibration of the picture surface—that subsequently prompted Leonardo to reject all pre-determined systems, to aim at a direct participation in the functional life of nature, and at revealing the unalterable laws governing the cosmos, in the rhythms of a constant "becoming," the blood-stream of the universe.

ANTONIO POLLAIUOLO (1429-1498). APOLLO AND DAPHNE, SHORTLY AFTER 1475. (11 5/8 × 7 7/8")
BY COURTESY OF THE TRUSTEES, NATIONAL GALLERY, LONDON.

SANDRO BOTTICELLI (1445-1510). PRIMAVERA (DETAIL), CA. 1478. UFFIZI, FLORENCE.

SANDRO BOTTICELLI

At the opposite pole from Piero's intellectualism and his Platonic attempt to identify the Good with the Beautiful, Botticelli shows both a total unconcern with any sort of "system" and an equally complete disregard of visual actuality. In his work we find a curious intermingling of skepticism and the religious sentiment; of almost unbridled sensuality and the promptings of the moral sense. According to Vasari, it was Botticelli with his sophisticated art who gave a new direction to the painting of the age, abruptly diverting it from the task assigned to it by the early 15th-century masters, that of deepening man's knowledge of the world. Stress is often laid on his close contacts with the Florentine élite during the second half of the century, and in particular on his intimacy with Poliziano and Lorenzo the Magnificent. Actually, however, the explanation of his art would seem to lie rather in the political and moral unrest then prevailing in Florence, which came to a head in Savonarola's fiery denunciations of the existing order and led to the catastrophic downfall of the republic. For seventy years' subjection to the tyrannical rule of the Medici had ended up by destroying not only that ideal of civic freedom which had meant so much in earlier days, but also the first fine rapture of the humanist rediscovery of history, Brunelleschi's grandiose conceptions, Donatello's realistic classicism and Masaccio's moral earnestness. No longer accepted as an historical reality, antiquity was now regarded as a bygone world of myths and legends, an agreeable playground for those who realized the futility, not to say inanity, of any form of action. History, in short, was transmuted into poetry, and it is significant that little by little the humanists now turned away from philosophical disquisitions towards poems, from historical fact to fables.

Deliberately Botticelli set up a world of poetic fantasy, strange enchantments and imagined beauty, against the factual, solidly constructed world of history. It was no easy venture he embarked on: that of presenting a vision of the human situation charged with moral and religious intimations, by means of images of an ethereal lightness in which even the tragedies of life move to the rhythm of an ideal beauty. Nothing remains of the intellectual preoccupations of the early humanists, and Botticelli's lyricism is all a wild regret, a *furor malinconicus* as Marsilio Ficino called it. Data of classical antiquity are seen by him not as historical events, but as myths—as they were seen by Pollaiuolo and later (still more overtly) by Piero di Cosimo and Filippino Lippi. In Botticelli's art, however, the myth is converted, as in his *Calumny*, into an allegory. Henceforth a smiling, carefree philosophy of life could no longer satisfy the Christian soul; consciousness of the Fall and the necessity of Redemption had set up an insuperable barrier between man and nature. Nor could there be any talk of the value or goal of life, since it was now a question of God's predestination of some men to salvation and others to perdition, salvation being a matter of grace, not of acts. Thus the human situation was viewed from the angle of an Epicureanism tinged with melancholy. For these men who dreamed their lives away in wistful contemplation of a beauty that, being but a mirage of the imagination, was for ever out of reach, were haunted by the thought of being foreordained to eternal bliss or doom, according to God's will —a presage of the "personal religion" preached some years later by the Reformers.

SANDRO BOTTICELLI (1445-1510). GIOVANNA DEGLI ALBIZZI AND THE THREE GRACES. FRESCO, CA. 1486. LOUVRE, PARIS.

It must not, however, be thought that Botticelli's art was merely "escapist," a retreat into a world of dreams, or that his attitude was one of mournful resignation. It would be truer to say that he reacted strongly against the conceptions of history and action which had been given such vigorous expression by his predecessors. There is no question that Filippo Lippi and Pollaiuolo played a considerable part in the shaping of his taste. But it was Lippi's late works that interested him most and in particular the Prato frescos in which emotion did not necessarily lead to action and operated, rather, as a form of latent energy, a subjacent rhythm. Pollaiuolo expressed emotion by a line drawn taut as a steel spring, suddenly, savagely, flashing into action; Botticelli by an all-pervading tension. And whereas the former floods the scene with luminous

SANDRO BOTTICELLI (1445-1510). LORENZO TORNABUONI AND THE LIBERAL ARTS. FRESCO, CA. 1486. LOUVRE, PARIS.

vibrations, repercussions as it were of the gestures and movements of the figures, Botticelli's architectural backgrounds and ruins seem quite unreal, "the fabric of a vision." Flowers and foliage create a frankly artificial, exquisitely wrought landscape, and indeed look more like symbols than objects existing in nature. While Leonardo (who accused Botticelli of being unable to paint landscape) was the first painter to realize that nature is not to be conceived of as something stable and unchanging but as a tantalizing enigma, Botticelli was the first to have an inkling of the mystery of the human soul and indeed of life itself.

Botticelli's melancholy was essentially temperamental, due to a hyper-sensitive personality and to the tendency of a soul, wounded by contacts with the outside world, to shrink into itself for refuge. The two small pictures illustrating the life of Judith are very early works, being dated circa 1470, but already we find in them that intensely poetic emotion which was to be a characteristic of his art. One of them represents Judith returning from Holophernes' tent. After her heroic exploit, the slaughter of Israel's arch-enemy, she is filled with sadness, a vague regret perhaps for a love that might have been and now must remain unsatisfied for ever. In the tent the warriors crowd round the headless body of Holophernes, beautiful as a Greek god's. The scene is pictured through a poet's eyes, an elegiac poet's, for in Botticelli's art we can often divine a sense of bafflement, as if the real world had played him false. And it was perhaps because he had so little faith in the value of experience and the lessons of the past that he could transmute the ancient ethic into poetry.

For him, too, painting was essentially an art of form, but in the exact sense of the term: configuration, contour without content. This view was very different from that of Piero for whom "form" meant proportion, symmetry, structural balance, absolute space. Botticelli's form is rhythm, an ebb and flow *ad infinitum*, and his art comes from a world of half-forgotten things, lingering regrets, unsatisfied desires. The beauty to which he constantly aspires derives not from life and nature, but from visions of death and inaccessible horizons. Thus he gave the myth a new significance; it was no longer relegated to the remote past, but integrated into the here-and-now, while, reciprocally, every form of human activity and aspect of the world was made to disclose its poetic content and transmuted into myth. His two most famous works, *Primavera* and *The Birth of Venus*, are in fact modern myths—of youth and love, of nature and the glimpses of loveliness enfleshed that haunt our happiest dreams.

Between *Primavera* (ca. 1478) and *The Birth of Venus* (ca. 1486) Botticelli painted three biblical episodes in the Sistine Chapel of the Vatican: *The Purification of the Leper and the Temptation of Christ*, *Scenes of the Life of Moses*, *The Punishment of Korah, Dathan and Abiram* (1481-1482). Here he selected certain passages, enlarged on them and illustrated them with groups of figures linked together by continuous linear rhythms within a vast expanse of space stretching out into illimitable distance. Likenesses of eminent contemporaries are intermingled with representations of great historical figures of the past; as if to convey to the beholder that the incident depicted is no more localized in time than it is in space. In the backgrounds, on the other hand, the ancient buildings, rocks and trees, however minutely rendered, produce the effect of symbols, betokening an historical past and a world of nature equally remote. This must not be taken to mean that in turning away from visual actuality and concentrating on rhythm Botticelli had recourse to vague or ambiguous delineations. On the contrary he did much to further a more penetrating, subtler insight into the secret places of the heart. His sensitive, fluent line interprets with prodigious skill the flux of emotions which, though they may not be manifested in acts or gestures located in geometric or architecturally ordered space, permeate every moment of a life, constantly modifying its rhythms and tempo. Never before had any artist so vividly recorded the wayward eddies of the affective stream. For Botticelli's line does not convey purposive intent, but the restless tides of emotion in the human heart, its impulses and vagaries. In the two frescos in the Louvre depicting *Giovanna degli Albizzi and the Three Graces* and *Lorenzo Tornabuoni and the Liberal Arts* (ca. 1486) we may see the climactic point of this tendency to spiritualize the image and to lift it beyond the confines of mundane experience. Nevertheless this spiritualization, verging on the abstract, is animated by flashes of vividly human feeling; the most intimate, spontaneous stirrings of the heart make their presence felt in the rhythm imparted to the forms.

Calumny (Uffizi) marks a turning-point in the painter's stylistic evolution. The theme is essentially humanistic, borrowed from Lucian, whose works had recently been translated (in 1472) by Bartolommeo Fontio, and in his rendering of it Botticelli represents two groups of figures set over against an austerely classical architectural background. Whereas in *Primavera* and *The Birth of Venus* the narrative element was presented in the form of a myth, here it is treated as an allegory and given a precise

SANDRO BOTTICELLI (1445-1510). CALUMNY, CA. 1494. (24¼×35¾")
UFFIZI, FLORENCE.

SANDRO BOTTICELLI (1445-1510). THE LAST COMMUNION OF ST JEROME, SHORTLY BEFORE 1503. (13½ × 10″)
METROPOLITAN MUSEUM OF ART, NEW YORK.

ethical significance. When we remember that Botticelli was the greatest of all illustrators of Dante's *Divine Comedy*, we need feel no surprise at his desire to inculcate a moral lesson, while replacing doctrinal rigor by lyrical appeal.

This change of heart synchronized with a critical period in the life of Florence. Though the Church had been ready enough to compromise with the humanists in the field of history, it was another matter when they took to the primrose path of Epicureanism, indulged in pagan fantasies and excursions into the mythology of the pre-Christian past; above all when they toyed with subtle *rapprochements* between those myths and the truths of Christianity, between Apollo and Christ, Venus and the Madonna. Lorenzo the Magnificent died in 1492 at the time when Savonarola was thundering forth his denunciations of the abuses of the Church with ever-increasing fervor. And six years later the execution of the heroic priest coincided to all intents and purposes with the end of freedom in the Florentine republic. Botticelli was deeply moved by these tragic happenings in his native city. None the less there was no real break of continuity between his first and his second phase; there was rather a deepening and a sort of illumination of his art.

In the works of this final period—the Milan and Munich *Depositions*, the *Crucifixion* in the Fogg Art Museum and the *Nativity* in the National Gallery, London—the artist reveals in an intensely dramatic manner his new conception of the Christian life, a life no longer governed by a sense of responsibility or even any will to action. For, if salvation is a matter of grace and not of works, the moral life can be no more than an awaiting of the coming of that grace or, rather, a preparation for its advent, and the way of preparation lies through suffering, often of the cruelest kind.

In the Milan and Munich pictures the linear rhythm becomes tenser, more incisive, vibrant with emotion. Cross-hatchings and reduplications of the line heighten the tension, much as in the linear dynamism of Gothic architecture. His colors go cold and bleak, with a metallic sheen, and gleams of frigid light harden the folds of garments, sharpen the lines of features. He abandons, too, his smoothly flowing arabesque, and the broken, truncated rhythms of his line almost efface the figures it describes, with gestures that are at once symbolic and sadly true to life. Here, indeed, we have as it were an ultimate and tragic manifestation of the Gothic spirit, disciplined by the restrictions the painter imposes on his fantasy to bring it into line with his asceticism. Deliberately he adjusts the calligraphic forms of his early period to the expression of a new-found piety, unsophisticated, even popular in tone. The London *Nativity* reminds one of Savonarola's Lauds. The painter has "metrified" his composition, as if to follow the rhythm of the hymn, to reproduce the pauses between strophes, the dying fall of a ritornelle. Deliberately, too, he uses an inverted perspective recalling certain medieval or Romanesque procedures. Coming at the close of the long development of Quattrocento art on intellectual lines, this *Nativity* strikes us as a repudiation of all that humanism stood for by an artist who, despairing of the intellect, elected to return to the ingenuousness of an age of fables, of pious folklore, the simple faith of "the poor in spirit."

When studying the background of the changes that came over Florentine art in the second half of the Quattrocento, we must not leave out of account the contacts between Flemish and Florentine artists. There can be no question that the sojourn of Hugo van der Goes in Florence had far-reaching effects, yet these effects were sometimes curiously indirect. Thus Botticelli may well have been led to carry his anti-naturalism still farther in reaction against the procedures of the Flemings. In the case of Filippino Lippi, their influence is unmistakable. Filippino (1457-1504) studied under his father, Filippo Lippi, along with Botticelli, whose strong personality was not slow to dominate his fellow-pupil. In his art the practices of Flemish empiricism—keen attention to detail, meticulously precise renderings of objects—give the impression of having acted on him as a counter-irritant, leading him to make a cult of sheer bizarrerie. His aim, in fact, would seem to have been to prove that, given skillful draftsmanship, one can depict the most unlikely figments of the imagination and lend them plausibility. (Subsequently, in the 16th century, the Tuscan mannerists, with their highly elegant, if capricious, handling of forms, illustrated similar tendencies.) Finally, it may be pointed out that Piero di Cosimo availed himself of the empirical procedures of the Flemings in his lyrical and pastoral interpretations of the classical myths.

The influence of Flemish naturalism was at once more direct and more apparent in another art trend of the period which, stemming from Angelico's religious naturalism, led up to colorful narrative renderings of secular themes and ended with the creations of one of the greatest story-tellers of the Quattrocento: Domenico Ghirlandaio (1449-1494). That this painter had a quite amazing gift for vivid narration is plain to see; but it is equally obvious that he no longer concerned himself with the basic problems of art or with the researches into the problems of form which had preoccupied his great predecessors. Compared with the sublime lyricism of such an artist as Botticelli, the far-ranging imagination of Filippino Lippi, or the young Leonardo's feverish investigations of the natural world, Ghirlandaio's effusions in "plain prose" certainly strike a somewhat academic note. We might almost say he is the typical professor, one whose eclectic, unoriginal formulas may seem a little uninspiring, but whose good taste and natural finesse command respect and even admiration. Thanks to his natural facility and gift for story-telling, he was able to include in his pictures a host of incidents and objects that in principle should have been omitted from the composition as being formally incongruous; nevertheless they enrich the general effect. While Gozzoli's and Lippi's paintings provided detailed inventories as it were of scenes of nature, Ghirlandaio's also contained depictions of 15th-century social life and there is no doubt of the historical value of that lineage of painter story-tellers which, including Gozzoli and Cosimo Rosselli, ended with Ghirlandaio. They acted as a connecting link between the general aesthetic culture of the Florentine élite and the discoveries of the theoreticians. Ghirlandaio had the great merit of making the historical and religious motifs and the formal procedures of the Quattrocento masters seem natural and acceptable to his contemporaries; and, in particular, he played a large part in bringing together the source-material of Raphael's grandiose historico-religious conceptions.

As regards such Umbrian painters as Boccati and Bonfigli we must frankly admit that they were behind their time. However, during the second half of the Quattrocento there emerged two front-rank Umbrian artists: Luca Signorelli (1441-1523) and Perugino (1445-1523). They played a notable part in what might be described as the transfer of the national art center from Florence to Rome. Though both were trained in Florence, it was from Piero della Francesca that they really took their lead. Their aim, we might say, was to unravel the formal synthesis of Piero's art and to turn to account the lessons of their great precursor when composing homilies, or visual sermons, in which religious concepts were expressed in a chastened, humanistic Latin idiom. Both artists, in short, cultivated a special kind of humanism, orthodox and pietistic, not without a spice of the pedantry so often found in provincial men of letters. Perugino wished above all to illustrate a special type of feelings in representations of natural scenes and specimens of humanity no less typical. Signorelli's purpose was, rather, to encourage or deter the beholder by demonstrating the heroism of virtue and the heinousness of vice. Perugino's amiable orthodoxy was unmistakably a first step in the direction of Raphael's Christian, indeed Catholic classicism; while Signorelli's aggressive, eschatological orthodoxy pointed the way to Michelangelo's apocalyptic visions. Finally, Melozzo da Forli (1438-1494) sought, by somewhat similar methods, to convert Piero's grandiose renderings of space into effects of illusionist realism, his monumental human figures into huge, eye-filling angels, and his clarity of form into a noble pictorial rhetoric. All three artists did much to shape the course of Renaissance art at Rome in the 16th century.

SANDRO BOTTICELLI (1445-1510). THE MIRACLES OF ST ZENOBIUS, AFTER 1500. (26 ½ × 59 ¼″) PREDELLA SCENE. METROPOLITAN MUSEUM OF ART, NEW YORK.

Page 145: Dirk Bouts (1415/1420-1475). The Last Supper (detail), 1464-1467.
Central Panel of the Altarpiece of the Holy Sacrament. St Peter's, Louvain.

3

EVOLUTION OF THE FLEMISH SCHOOL

The great masters of the first half of the 15th century had prepared the ground for a total renovation of the art of painting. Not only had they come to look on man with new eyes, but their knowledge, first intuitive then scientific, of perspective had enabled them to locate him both in space and in his historical context. To the artists of the following generation fell the task of consolidating the discoveries of their predecessors—Jan van Eyck's handling of volumes and light, Rogier's emotive line, and their various technical discoveries—and of combining these with a fuller knowledge of the new conceptions of Italian humanism. This intermingling of different art streams was facilitated by the vogue for travel and by personal contacts between artists. It is a noteworthy fact that most of the painters who were the glory of Flanders in the latter half of the century were natives of Germany or Holland who had been attracted to Bruges or Louvain by the prestige of those great Flemish art centers.

The first half of the 15th century witnessed the rapid growth of the city of Louvain. In 1423 the university was founded by Duke John IV of Brabant and two years later work began on St Peter's Church. In 1448, opposite St Peter's, was laid the foundation-stone of that Gothic masterpiece of civic architecture in the Netherlands, the Louvain Town Hall, and by this time the city had become a well-known seat of learning and the home of a flourishing school of artists.

DIRK BOUTS

According to Van Mander, Dirk Bouts was born in Haarlem. It is not known where he received training as an artist, but, since the so-called School of Haarlem did not come into existence until somewhat later and the first works ascribed to him testify so clearly to Van der Weyden's influence, it has been inferred that he must have lived anyhow for a time at Brussels. However no proof of this has been forthcoming; all we know for certain is that he went to Louvain when fairly young and, while living there, married (in 1447 or 1448) Catherine van der Bruggen, by whom he had four children. Thus he may very well have seen some of the large works Rogier painted in Louvain, in particular the famous *Descent from the Cross* now in the Prado.

None of the records makes any mention of Bouts' activities between 1448 and 1457, a fact which has led Hulin de Loo to surmise that he returned to Holland during this period. This would go far to explain the many links between Flemish art and the work of such early Dutch masters as Albert van Ouwater and Geertgen tot Sint Jans.

The first works attributed to Bouts—the four panels of the Altarpiece of the Virgin (now in the Prado)—show that his style was still derivative from Rogier van der Weyden's, though markedly inferior. The scene is staged in arched recesses adorned with small sculptures in grisaille; the highly simplified setting is completely symmetrical and all the figures face towards the beholder. In fact the only original feature is the landscape, a vista of rolling hills covered with particolored trees and, in *The Visitation*, a road winding up to a group of houses built on the summit of a cliff.

These rocky crags reappear in the vast dramatic landscape of *The Descent from the Cross* (Capilla Real, Granada). Here the idiosyncrasies of Bouts' style are beginning to emerge; the monumentalism of figures is accentuated by an unwonted elongation of their torsos, while side-face presentation brings out their expressive values. In *The Entombment* (National Gallery, London) Bouts has refashioned Rogier's art and simplified his forms; the folds of garments are fuller, more fluent, and the breaks less sharply indicated. Gestures, too, are more subdued and emotion is subtly rendered by an extreme concentration of the gaze. Notable is the integration of the picture elements into space, thanks to a dexterous handling of perspective.

Four other works are definitely known to be by Bouts, and dated: *The Martyrdom of St Erasmus* and *The Last Supper* in St Peter's, Louvain, the *Portrait of a Young Man* in the National Gallery, London, and *The Justice of Emperor Otto* (Musée Royal, Brussels). The *St Erasmus* diptych (1458), if a relatively small work, shows the painter at the height of his powers. The martyrdom is taking place in a landscape bathed in a light so vivid that for the first time in art we get an impression of genuine *plein air* painting. This flooding light gives figures a volume and a plenitude, emphasized by the swelling curves of the garments, that remind us of some of the work Piero della Francesca was producing at the same time. Though the theme is cruel to a degree, it is not treated realistically, but purged of all brutal elements. Almost we have a feeling that neither the executioner nor his victim is quite in earnest; the general effect is that of a slow, stately ballet.

In the *Portrait of a Young Man*, dated 1462, where for the first time a portrait is given a landscape background, Bouts restricts himself to a quiet, brownish color-scheme faintly flushing into mauve and pink and, despite the novelty of the setting, nothing distracts attention from the linear design and the psychological implications of the face. The modeling is emphatic and the face tells out, a living presence, in a well-defined spatial environment.

DIRK BOUTS (1415/1420-1475). THE LAST SUPPER (DETAIL), 1464-1467.
CENTRAL PANEL OF THE ALTARPIECE OF THE HOLY SACRAMENT. ST PETER'S, LOUVAIN.

DIRK BOUTS (1415/1420-1475). THE LAST SUPPER, 1464-1467. (70×58″)
CENTRAL PANEL OF THE ALTARPIECE OF THE HOLY SACRAMENT. ST PETER'S, LOUVAIN.

Remarkable, too, is the unfaltering sureness of Bouts' line, sharply defining finger-joints and cheekbones, each crease and wrinkle of a face, and making every vein stand out. Nevertheless we feel that his art is dominated by considerations of another order, that this linear precision is merely incidental, and what he is seeking to express lies elsewhere; that he would have us know that the rendering, however complete, of a man's outward appearance can only bring us to the threshold of the mystery of a human personality. In his colors, too, he aims less at intensity and saturation than at creating a state of tension—between, for instance, a cold hue and a rich, warm red.

In the huge altarpiece in St Peter's, Louvain, depicting *The Last Supper*, we have one of the key works of Flemish art. Commissioned in 1464, it was completed in 1467 and the accounts of the Brotherhood of the Sacrament contain an entry in the painter's own hand, acknowledging receipt of payment. Two professors of theology had been deputed to give him all the iconographical data required for an accurate depiction of the institution of the Eucharist in the central panel, and in four lateral panels, of incidents in Old Testament history foreshadowing the Last Supper: *The Meeting between Abraham and Melchisedek*, *The Gathering of Manna*, *Elijah fed by an Angel in the Desert*, and *The Passover*. Particularly striking is the matter-of-fact rendering of the central scene; Protestantism was yet to come into being but we feel that a new conception of the Christian verities is gaining ground, stress is laid on the human aspect of the sacred figures, and on the individuality of man as an independent unit. The lay-out is strictly geometrical, its sole aim being to ensure a balanced distribution of the figures of the twelve apostles and their convergence on the central figure, that of Christ. The trapezoidal shape of the white tablecloth both gives concrete form to this underlying structural conception and holds the composition together. Faces are not diversified in all cases, those that are like each other alternating in accordance with an intricate system of correspondences. The color-scheme follows the same plan, and the darkly glowing, unrealistic hues symbolize the emotions of those participating in the first Eucharist. Gestures are arrested, the gaze of each turned inward in an atmosphere of hushed repose befitting the solemnity of the occasion. Nevertheless in the setting of this compact, well-ordered group of figures there are some rather surprising details, effects of contrast that anticipate Van der Goes; for example, the heads of the two servants framed in the kitchen hatch. Then, again, we see on the other side a narrow strip of garden, all in greys and pinks, glimpsed through a tall arched window and finally, that enigmatic figure on the extreme right, one hand resting on a sideboard. In this long face with the tight-set lips perhaps we have a likeness of the artist. His eyes seem turned towards the group around the table but the gaze is far away, almost as if he had been walking forward and some sudden thought or vision had given him pause.

The Old Testament scenes in the four side panels are of a more anecdotal order; sequences of planes in quick succession disclosing spacious, vividly green landscapes dotted with tiny figures. Only the long, stiffly built form of the prophet Elijah in the desert, over whom bends an angel with gigantic wings, has the monumental proportions of the central scene.

Bouts' last big work—the two "Examples of Justice" (Musée Royal, Brussels)—was commissioned by the Burgomaster of Louvain, who decided that pictures of this kind should figure in the Town Hall, as reminders to the judges holding court there of the two judicial virtues: much prudence and a sense of equity. Rogier van der Weyden had been given similar commissions, and Gerard David, too, depicted the cautionary tale of the corrupt judge Sisamnes. In these two pictures, which he completed shortly before his death, Bouts took as his subject the legend, recorded by the 13th-century chronicler Godfrey of Viterbo, of an incident in the life of the Emperor Otto III. Each picture contains two scenes linked up in time and space. In the first we see a Count who, accused by the Empress of having tried to seduce her, has been condemned to death; clad in a long white robe he is being led to the place of execution, accompanied by his wife. In the foreground his body is lying on the ground while the executioner holds up the severed head. The second picture shows the dead man's wife claiming redress from the Emperor; submitting to the ordeal by fire, she is clasping a bar of red-hot iron which does not burn her. And, finally, in the background we see the Empress, condemned for having falsely accused an innocent man, being burned alive.

The painter has turned to skillful account the dimensions of these exceptionally tall and narrow panels by dividing the two scenes vertically and elongating figures as if viewed in descending perspective. Thus the legs are lengthened, the effect of slenderness being heightened in the case of one of the foreground figures in the scene of the ordeal by a thin stick on which the man is leaning (Bouts had already employed this device in his depiction of the judge in *The Martyrdom of St Erasmus*). The faces of the bystanders, on the other hand, are viewed from immediately in front and given a rectangular structure with all the salient features in strong relief. In the case of some figures, for example the headsman, volume is conveyed by a special type of modeling that makes them look like statues cast in bronze. In these huge pictures whose colors have darkened with the years and, generally speaking, are in poorer condition than the altarpiece in St Peter's, the composition holds less well together; but this was only to be expected considering the shape of the panels and the number of incidents included. None the less the artist has shown much originality in his handling of expressive details and the touches of symbolism are happily conceived, for example the white flowers—symbol of innocence—that mask the gaping neck of the man who, through a miscarriage of justice, has been beheaded.

JOOS VAN GHENT
HUGO VAN DER GOES

Dirk Bouts died on May 6, 1475, a few weeks after having made his will. Though from the modern point of view his claim to immortality is based above all on the pictures of his final phase, it was the lesson of the works of his middle period that was taken over and amplified by the Ghent painters, who transmitted it to most of the contemporary European schools. Joos van Ghent and Hugo van der Goes studied together. The former, after qualifying as a master painter at Antwerp in 1460, enrolled in the Painters' Guild of Ghent in 1464, and acted as Van der Goes' guarantor when the latter was admitted to the Guild in 1467. Some years later he migrated to Italy with the help of a loan made him by his friend and he is known to have been at Urbino in 1473, attached to the court of Federigo da Montefeltro. After 1475 all trace of him is lost. Two works can be positively ascribed to him: a *Calvary* painted in or about 1464 for the Chapel of St Lawrence in St Bavo's, Ghent, and *The Communion of the Apostles* painted at Urbino for the Brotherhood of the Holy Cross. The Duke financed this work and there are records of payments made from time to time in the years 1473-1475. *The Communion* shows that Joos van Ghent's stay in Italy had little effect on his style; he kept to the technique he had learnt in Flanders. A comparison of the two works named above confirms Hulin de Loo's conclusion as to the portion of the decorations of the Palace of Urbino which can safely be attributed to Joos van Ghent. The Duke's study was decorated with representations of Saints and Doctors of the Church, and it seems clear that the upper row was entirely by Joos' hand. The figures in the bottom row, though of similar inspiration, are executed in a heavier manner and more

DIRK BOUTS (1415/1420-1475). ELIJAH FED BY AN ANGEL IN THE DESERT, 1464-1467. (34½ × 28")
UPPER RIGHT WING OF THE ALTARPIECE OF THE HOLY SACRAMENT.
ST PETER'S, LOUVAIN.

emphatically modeled; presumably they were painted (or anyhow completed) by the Spanish painter Pedro Berruguete, to whom are now ascribed the portraits of the Duke and the allegorical figures in the Palace Library.

Thus, now that its scope has been defined, we can see that Joos van Ghent's œuvre forms a uniform whole; its great and undeniable originality consists in his new handling of landscape and the stylization of his figures. In the Ghent *Calvary* the background of rolling hills and mountains is sprinkled with little groups of people, skillfully disposed one behind the other and moving in a natural manner, while colors become more and more blurred as the scene recedes. Figures are slender, elegantly built; Joos follows Bouts' method of elongating limbs and torsos but is less subservient to factual reality. He created a special type of woman, with delicately molded features, wearing a heavy headdress, bending slightly forward in a graceful curve as she makes a gesture of offering or devotion. His color, too, is peculiar to himself; he uses broken hues mixed with white; the dominants are brown, light greens, lilac mauves, bright blue and pink, arranged in new, harmonious patterns. For shadows he employs small dark hatchings.

In the Urbino *Communion of the Apostles* he does not follow Bouts' arrangement of the scene but adopts that of Fra Angelico (which he may have seen in the Vatican) and shows the disciples after they have risen from table, kneeling before Christ who occupies the center of the foreground. All the same here, too, Joos van Ghent kept to methods he had learnt in his early days. The faces of the apostles, seen in three-quarter view and curiously unsymmetrical, are depicted realistically, and in the case of one of the "outsiders" he inserts in the composition—the Venetian ambassador to the Shah of Persia, Caterino Zeno, shown beside the Duke whom he visited in 1474—he exactly reproduces the figure of the Judge in Bouts' *Martyrdom of St Erasmus.* Thus despite a slight Renaissance flavor, due to the presence of the Duke and his courtiers and to the "modern" type of architecture, this work is basically Flemish.

Though Joos, probably the elder of the two, was Hugo van der Goes' "mentor" when he was admitted to the Painters' Guild, the younger man soon took the lead and influenced his senior's art. Headstrong, nothing if not thorough, Van der Goes had no qualms about carrying his ideas to their logical conclusion and pressing his style to its extreme limit. He seems to have assimilated more rapidly and more completely than Joos the lesson of the Italians. So much so that some have thought that he, too, may have visited Italy. There is, however, no actual proof of this, nor until some definite evidence is forthcoming can we accept Panofsky's theory, tempting though it is, that Van der Goes, who is known to have been in high favor with the Court of Burgundy, may have been one of the huge cortège accompanying the dead bodies of Duke Philip the Good and his wife Isabella of Portugal on their "translation" from Bruges to the Chartreuse de Champmol in the winter of 1473-1474. This would, however, provide a satisfactory explanation of his marked influence on French painters —notably on the Master of Moulins—in the last part of the century.

Van der Goes' key work, and indeed the only one authenticated by documentary evidence, is the Portinari altarpiece in the Uffizi. Commissioned by Tommaso Portinari,

HUGO VAN DER GOES (CA. 1440-1482). THE ADORATION OF THE SHEPHERDS, 1476-1478.
(97×119¼") CENTRAL PANEL OF THE PORTINARI TRIPTYCH. UFFIZI, FLORENCE.

agent of the Medici banking firm at Bruges, it was placed in his family chapel in Sant' Egidio, the church of the hospital of Santa Maria Nuova at Florence. Three Portinari children (born between 1471 and 1474) figure on the wings beside their parents, and this enables us to date the altarpiece to near the end of the artist's career. There is no doubt he intended this monumental work to be a complete résumé of his whole life's aspirations and achievements, his legacy to posterity. This explains why, admirable

HUGO VAN DER GOES (CA. 1440-1482). THE CHILDREN OF TOMMASO PORTINARI, DETAIL OF THE LEFT WING OF THE PORTINARI TRIPTYCH, 1476-1478. UFFIZI, FLORENCE.

as are the parts taken separately, the general effect of the whole is one of over-complexity, not to say something of a patchwork. The sacred figures are shown in attitudes of statuesque repose, whereas the shepherds excitedly rushing in on the right produce an effect that is startlingly realistic, almost cinematic. There are several large open spaces in the composition, notably the one around the Child. It would seem that, far from wishing to fill these, the painter made a point of spacing out the picture elements, to enable each to make its full effect. Thus the symbolic sheaf of wheat and the vases of flowers are given an exceptional prominence. There are two kinds of angels: some look like children aged beyond their years or, rather, ageless, hardly human at all; others are plump, with chubby cheeks and much more lifelike, though a peculiar lighting gives them an almost baroque aspect (we find the same dualism in the angels pictured by the Master of Moulins). The scenic arrangement of the composition and the prominence given to certain symbolic "properties" placed well to the fore and in full light call in mind the setting of some medieval mystery-play. And it is noteworthy that another *Nativity* by this artist (in Berlin) is staged between two curtains held up by prophets on either side of the proscenium. (Similarly in one of Fouquet's miniatures, illustrating the martyrdom of St Apollonia, the action takes place on what appears to be a trestle stage of the kind used by strolling players.)

Unique in this work is its synthesis of imagination with direct observation, the ideal with the real. Thus what Bouts had just hinted at in his Examples of Justice, following on the hieratic, rather frigid composition of *The Last Supper*, here comes to fruition. In his rendering of the shepherds Van der Goes indulges in a realism of a quite exceptional boldness; they are simple folk with typical peasant faces, rough-cast, expressive features, cropped or tousled hair, and their gnarled hands are those of men who work daylong in the fields.

In one of the earliest works attributed to Van der Goes, the Vienna diptych, we already find a dramatic contrast between the lefthand panel, representing *The Fall of Man*, and *The Lamentation*. In the former Adam and Eve and the Tempter, a curious creature with a yellow belly like a lizard's and a wizened face, are placed in a radiant, lightly wooded landscape in which the naked forms of the two First Parents seem strangely fragile, vulnerable; whereas the setting of the *Lamentation over the Dead Christ* is a bare landscape and the group of tragically emotive figures was obviously inspired by Van der Weyden, as re-interpreted by Joos van Ghent. Here the didactic purpose —the lesson of the Fall and its consequences—is evident. And in *The Death of the Virgin* (Musée Communal, Bruges) the painter's last work, the faces of the Apostles grouped round the death-bed seem magnified, as it were, by the expression of their anguish, their sense of irremediable loss, while pale cold colors stress the effect of bleak desolation, the very nadir of despair.

From the writings of the monk Gaspard Ofhuys, his intimate friend, we learn that towards the close of his life the artist's mind began to give way and he was subject to fits of acute melancholia. In these moods he despaired of the salvation of his soul and kept repeating that he was damned eternally. The Father Superior of the priory he had entered as a lay brother had music played to him to soothe his nerves on these occasions. To make things worse, though still in the prime of life, he foresaw the end was near and he would not live to complete the vast body of work he had dreamt of and gain the recognition of posterity. He died at the priory in 1482.

To some extent Van der Goes' forebodings were justified. Though he was far from being without honor in his own country it was in foreign lands that his remarkable discoveries and inventions had the most lasting effect. As it so happened, the most brilliant member of the School of Bruges hailed from Germany; but he became so thoroughly imbued with the art of his adopted country that he has long been regarded as the most "Flemish" of all the early Flemish masters.

HANS MEMLING

An entry in the Register of the Citizens of Bruges for the year 1465 states that Memling was born at Seligenstadt on the Main, near Frankfort. It is not known where he served his apprenticeship but the accuracy with which he depicted on the Shrine of St Ursula (in the Hôpital Saint-Jean at Bruges) some of the chief architectural features of Old Cologne suggests that he lived for some time in that city. In the same group of pictures Memling included a representation of the Brussels Town Hall and everything points to the fact of his having been a pupil of Rogier van der Weyden, who died in 1464. In many of his works he employed themes already used by his master, though treating them in his own manner. In January 1465 Memling acquired the status of a citizen of Bruges and such was his success that by 1480 he was owner of three houses and his name figured in a list of the 140 citizens who paid the highest taxes. His wife, née Anne de Valkenaere, by whom he had three sons, died in 1487. His own death took place in August 1494, and he was buried in the graveyard of St Giles's Church.

Thus after a youth spent in other cities under the auspices of other masters, he passed most of his life in Bruges, where Petrus Christus had kept the Eyckian tradition alive. And one of the most interesting features of Memling's work is that we discern in it an effort to revivify his great predecessors' art, while keeping faithful to their spirit. His output was copious and the fact that his major works have remained in the setting for which they were intended—the Hôpital Saint-Jean, in which there lingers still, miraculously immune from any aroma of modernity, the characteristic atmosphere of the Middle Ages—enables us better to understand and appraise his art than that of other artists of the period. Memling was until recently regarded as chief of the Flemish Primitives and Eugène Fromentin paid a glowing tribute to his genius in his great work *Les Maîtres d'Autrefois*. But that was eighty years ago, and now that the much earlier achievements of the Flémalle Master and Jan van Eyck have come into the limelight and attention has been drawn to the creative originality of Hugo van der Goes, a tendency has developed to accuse Memling's work of insipidity and to belittle its importance. This tendency, to our mind, is quite unjustified. For when Memling's own work is separated from that of his pupils and doubtful attributions are excluded, we find that he is not guilty of those technical shortcomings of which it is now the fashion to accuse him. The suavity and serenity of his art—not due,

HUGO VAN DER GOES (CA. 1440-1482). THE ADORATION OF THE SHEPHERDS (DETAIL), 1476-1478.
CENTRAL PANEL OF THE PORTINARI TRIPTYCH. UFFIZI, FLORENCE.

as some have thought, to any lack of driving force—point, rather, to a fully integrated conception of the painter's craft and a coherent ideology. His aim was not merely to produce eye-pleasing pictures, but also—and this was something new in art—to build up elaborate sequences arranged in a cyclically composed pattern. We see this notably in *The Passion of Christ* (Galleria Sabauda, Turin) and *The Life of the Virgin* (Alte Pinakothek, Munich) which was presented to the church of Notre-Dame, Bruges, in 1480.

Memling's masterwork, *The Mystical Marriage of St Catherine* in the Hôpital Saint-Jean at Bruges, was painted for the chapel of the hospital in the years 1475 to 1479. Its composition is the same as that of an earlier work, the triptych of Sir John Donne of Kidwelly (Chatsworth Estates Company, Chatsworth), but much elaborated and amplified—which shows how mistaken is the view that Memling's art was static, unprogressive. The strict symmetry of the lay-out does not produce an effect of monotony, but admirably serves its purpose: that of depicting in an ordered framework incidents in the lives of the two Saints John, each being separated from its neighbor by a pillar, and containing realistic excerpts from everyday life; for example a wooden crane being used for loading barrels on a quay. Each of these small scenes is executed with loving care, and its lively movement makes an effective foil to the immobility and superb indifference of the sacred figures in the foreground, clad in sumptuous garments of skillfully contrasted hues. Still more remarkable is the originality of the lateral panels, in particular that depicting St John's vision in the isle of Patmos; the fantastic landscape, with its winged horses, a wrecked ship and Death on horseback menacing a group of men who are vainly trying to hide themselves in caves, anticipates the weird imaginings of Hieronymus Bosch.

To combine convention with reality was obviously Memling's chief aim. In the St Christopher triptych (Musée Communal, Bruges), commissioned in 1485 by William Moreel and his wife Barbara de Vlaenderbergh, the donors and their numerous progeny are painted (in the lateral panels) with a suavity that makes an admirable foil to the ascetic severity of the central panel depicting St Christopher accompanied by St Maurus and St Giles. Each of these huge figures is shown in isolation with a strip of appropriate landscape annexed, and the transitions from one to the other, though wholly arbitrary, never seem in the least forced or unnatural, while an adroit use of large tracts of flat color in the costumes gives the composition a monumentally ordered structure. It is interesting to note that when Memling is dealing with small figures or "extras" the faces are unflinchingly lifelike and he makes no effort to beautify them. When, however, he depicts the Virgin or saints of high degree, he goes about it in a very different way; their faces are flawless ovals and conform to an ideal norm of beauty. Yet despite this differentiation between celestial beings and ordinary mortals, unity is safeguarded by the atmosphere charged with otherworldly intimations that envelops all alike.

HANS MEMLING (CA. 1433-1494). THE MYSTICAL MARRIAGE OF ST CATHERINE, 1479. (67½×67½") ►
CENTRAL PANEL. HÔPITAL SAINT-JEAN, BRUGES.

HANS MEMLING (CA. 1433-1494). THE BAPTISM OF CHRIST, DETAIL FROM THE BEHEADING OF ST JOHN THE BAPTIST, 1479. LEFT WING OF THE MYSTICAL MARRIAGE OF ST CATHERINE. HÔPITAL SAINT-JEAN, BRUGES.

Towards the close of his life Memling produced two works, each exceptional as to its size and each a masterpiece of craftsmanship. One is *The Shrine of St Ursula* presented in 1489 to the Hôpital Saint-Jean at Bruges; small as were the surfaces available, he succeeded in including all the incidents of the travels and martyrdom of the saint and the maidens accompanying her. This famous work has been unjustly decried; nothing could be more charming than these little scenes with their settings of pink architecture in which the artist reproduces with loving care the most picturesque buildings in Cologne. Much skill and taste has gone to the grouping of the figures, and harrowing as are so many of the scenes, cruelty is redeemed by sheer beauty. In 1491 Memling completed and signed the triptych of *The Passion*, commissioned by a banker, Henri Greverade, for the Chapel of Our Lady in Lübeck Cathedral. This gigantic work, summing-up of a lifetime's achievement, exercised an enormous influence on the painters of Northern Germany.

Memling's landscapes also struck an authentically new note. At once agreeable to the eye and admirably true to life, they show Nature under her companionable aspects, tamed by man, planted with trees at regular intervals and dotted with

HANS MEMLING (CA. 1433-1494). ST JOHN IN PATMOS (DETAIL), 1479.
RIGHT WING OF THE MYSTICAL MARRIAGE OF ST CATHERINE. HÔPITAL SAINT-JEAN, BRUGES.

HANS MEMLING (CA. 1433-1494). PORTRAIT OF THE MEDALLIST GIOVANNI CANDIDA, CA. 1478. (11×7¾″)
MUSÉE ROYAL DES BEAUX-ARTS, ANTWERP.

sunlit, unpretentious houses, reaches of still water on which swans are gliding. Nothing like this was being produced in Flanders at the time and we are reminded, rather, of Fouquet and the Master of Moulins. Memling almost always uses landscapes of this kind as the backgrounds of his portraits and he has no qualms about bringing his figures out into the open and exposing them to the full light of day.

GERARD DAVID

What makes Memling's work so attractive is its intimate poetic atmosphere, no less than the ingenuity and versatility of his craftsmanship. In Gerard David who, like Bouts, was of Dutch origin we find a more vigorous personality but a rather prosaic outlook on life and art; he had little inventiveness, his interests centered on the concrete and material and his œuvre was in a sense the swansong of the Flemish School.

He was born at Outwater about 1460 and it is thought he served his apprenticeship at Haarlem before moving to Bruges, where he was admitted as a master-painter to the Painters' Guild. His rise to fame was rapid. He received commissions from the Burgomaster in 1488, 1495 and 1498, and after Memling's death was universally regarded as the leading painter of the day. He was in close touch with the Carmelite convent of Sion to which in 1509 he presented the large *Virgin among Virgins* (now in Rouen Museum). In 1515 David enrolled in the Painters' Guild of Antwerp, which city, now that Bruges was losing her prosperity owing to the silting up of the river Zwyn, was becoming the chief commercial center of Flanders. However he continued living in Bruges and it was there he died, on August 13, 1523.

In the earliest works ascribed to him—for example the small panel of *The Jews* in Antwerp Museum and the two large "Examples of Justice" (signed and dated 1498) now in the Musée Communal at Bruges—the personages are placed side by side: thickset figures with big, squarish heads, grouped in a rough and ready manner and forthrightly depicted. We cannot help feeling that the artist gloats over scenes of cruelty, stressed by such rather crude devices as gaping mouths expressing agony and beads of sweat on the forehead of the wicked judge who has been brought to book.

In *The Virgin among Virgins* in Rouen Museum, a huge composition in which the painter with his wife and daughter figure in the background, the Virgin and her companions are symmetrically disposed, seated or kneeling, and all look very much alike; in fact the general effect is one of monotony. None the less there is an atmosphere of pleasing intimacy and a remarkable softness in the modeling, due to the use of relatively full brushstrokes and the melting of one tone into the other.

Gerard David's greatest work, the St John the Baptist altarpiece (Musée Communal, Bruges), contains two sets of wings; for the donor (Jean des Trompes, burgomaster of Bruges) and his first wife and, after her death in 1520, for his second wife, who is shown facing the Virgin. This repetition of similar subjects at some years' distance enables us to follow David's evolution towards that "purism" (if we may use a modern term) which was his leading contribution to the art of the period. In the central scene, the Baptism of Christ, the treatment of each figure and the landscape setting reveals a curious transformation of the themes employed by David's great precursors. Each is re-interpreted, made more explicit and given an immobility affecting not so much individual attitudes as the whole pictorial construction. When he depicts the naked form of Christ, the Baptist's gesture, the angel clad in bright brocade, all the elements of mystery and the rich variety of forms we find in earlier treatments of the theme have been drained away, and the landscape, too, is rendered with a sort of metallic exactitude. True, details are enlarged on, with the result that flowers and leafage tell out with a surprising clearness; but the over-all effect is one of bleak aridity—we are worlds away from Van Eyck's rich translucencies, his smoothly flowing rhythms. But now that their intrinsic interest was recognized these picture elements were given a larger place and put to new uses. David's two small panels, originally on the reverse of *The Nativity* and now in the Rijksmuseum, Amsterdam, depict country scenes, sunlit tree trunks and leafage, a dark pond with cattle grazing nearby. There are no figures and this is one of the earliest pictures in which landscape achieved emancipation and was treated, not as a mere accessory, but as a subject in its own right. True, Van Eyck had pointed the way with the big thickets of trees around the central motif of *The Adoration of the Lamb* and the dark forests in the panels of hermits and pilgrims. And looking further back, we have the landscapes of the Limbourg brothers, with which, after sixty years' more conventional handling of these motifs, David linked up to such happy effect. Perhaps we have here the manifestations of a tendency inherent in the Dutch temperament, for landscape is similarly treated by Geertgen tot Sint Jans, David's contemporary (born at Leyden in 1460), who, however, seems never to have left Holland, where he died aged thirty-five. The only difference is that Geertgen imparts more animation to his vast green landscapes, sprinkling them with animals, and indeed anticipates Bosch's famous "Paradise" scenes. Another of Geertgen's idiosyncrasies is his keen interest in light effects and his nightpieces such as *The Nativity* (National Gallery, London) rank among the best 15th-century productions in this genre.

There are grounds for believing that David may have visited Italy and stayed in Genoa, where two of his larger pictures are preserved in the Palazzo Bianco, and signs of his influence have been traced in the work of several Ligurian painters and in that of Lodovico Brea who was painting *The Vocation of the Just in Paradise* for the church of Santa Maria di Castello in Genoa at the time. Against this view is the fact that the records of the Confraternity of Our Lady of the Dry Tree at Bruges show that David paid his membership dues from 1508 to 1514 without a break; still this does not necessarily mean he never left Bruges during those years. Moreover, in the Genoa *Calvary* and the *Transfiguration* in Notre-Dame de Bruges, he seems to have been directly inspired by some of Giovanni Bellini's works, and we find him, like Bellini, trying out "variations" on the same figure posed in different attitudes. Here he sets his horizon line very low with the result that the figures, looming up against a stormy sky, assume monumental proportions. But throughout this last phase David's work was becoming ever more jejune; his was, in fact, a dying art—dying at the very time when in the young School of Antwerp Patinir was creating those vast, elemental landscapes in which the human figure seems to melt into the countryside.

GERARD DAVID (CA. 1460-1523). MADELEINE CORDIER, SECOND WIFE OF THE DONOR JEAN DES TROMPES, DETAIL. RIGHT WING OF THE ST JOHN THE BAPTIST TRIPTYCH, 1502-1507. MUSÉE COMMUNAL, BRUGES.

RUELAND FRUEAUF THE ELDER (1440/1450-1507). THE MAN OF SORROWS. (71 ½×46″)
ALTE PINAKOTHEK, MUNICH.

NEW ART FORMS IN GERMANY AND AUSTRIA

During the second half of the 15th century German painting (except in southern Germany where the local schools tended to take their lead from Italy) was wholly dominated by Flemish influences. This had not been the case with the painters of the previous generation. Though they cannot have failed to be impressed by the Europe-wide prestige of Van Eyck's art, Conrad Witz and Stephan Lochner had each followed his own bent, the former cultivating an art of expressive stylization, the latter one of elegance and languid grace. But from now on Rogier van der Weyden's rigid, brilliantly realized formulas were the order of the day. Always in close touch with Flanders, the Cologne painters fell almost effortlessly into line; theirs had always been a flexible, versatile technique, and could easily be adjusted to the new requirements. The Master of the Life of Mary—named after the large panels (now in Munich) of his Altar of the Virgin, which comprise some of the most complete and detailed depictions of life in 15th-century Germany—was a first-class draftsman, notable being the firmness of his contour-lines enclosing broad tracts of translucent color. Though he lacks Lochner's far-ranging imagination and flair for the significant detail, his elongated figures have a stately presence and hold the eye.

The Master of the St Bartholomew Altar faithfully recapitulates earlier themes, the only difference being that he stresses to an extreme degree the flamboyant elements of Gothic architecture and the fragility of his figures; their limbs are preternaturally slender, gestures expressive and elaborate. The singularity of his art, its imperviousness to the art currents of the day and the fact that his chief works were made for the local Carthusian church have led some to think this artist was a monk who worked alone, without pupils or assistants. Very different were the Master of the Holy Kinship, the Master of St Severin and the Master of the Legend of St Ursula; artists of the Flemish lineage revitalized by Memling, they aimed above all at realistic accuracy and at creating an intimate, homely atmosphere. The Master of St Ursula excelled in his renderings of secondary, anecdotal figures; faces are remarkably lifelike and their expressions natural. The colors are gay, he painted on canvas with light touches, and his work has an engaging, fragile daintiness.

Flanders was in close business relations with the Hanseatic seaports, where works by Rogier van der Weyden and Memling found a ready market and were much admired, and copied, by the local German artists. Hinrik Funhof, a Saxon painter active at Hamburg and Lüneburg between 1475 and 1485, is even said to have gone to Flanders and studied under Bouts. Like Bouts he made a point of modernizing his sacred figures, not only as regards their costumes but by making them behave like and resemble ordinary mortals. Hermen Rode, active between 1485 and 1540 at Lübeck, and Bernt Notke, a Pomeranian, who painted the famous *Mass of St Gregory* in the Marienkirche at Lübeck, displayed a similar tendency towards the omission of superfluous detail and a simplification of forms, combined with realistic observation.

MASTER OF THE LIFE OF MARY (ACTIVE CA. 1450-1480). THE VISITATION, CA. 1460.
(33½×41¼") PANEL FROM THE ALTARPIECE OF THE VIRGIN. ALTE PINAKOTHEK, MUNICH.

CASPAR ISENMANN

In the Colmar School we find strongly marked German characteristics co-existing with what is perhaps the happiest example of the acclimatization of Flemish themes in a foreign country. Colmar Museum has a number of panels by Caspar Isenmann which originally adorned the high altar of St Martin's Church. Though of quite small dimensions, these compositions contain animated, strongly expressive scenes, whose well-balanced proportions often create a grandiose effect. Particularly striking are the painter's accurate and elegant renderings of figures in movement, and the almost bestial ugliness of certain faces, portrayed with a full-blooded expressionism anticipating that of Grünewald.

CASPAR ISENMANN (?-CA. 1492). THE RESURRECTION, 1462-1464.
PANEL FROM THE HIGH ALTAR OF ST MARTIN'S CHURCH. MUSÉE UNTERLINDEN, COLMAR.

MARTIN SCHONGAUER

The program Martin Schongauer—"Handsome Martin" to his contemporaries—set himself was at once highly ambitious and admirable in its way, in spite of the fact that it led to a sort of depersonalization of art. He tried to keep under control the impulse towards over-emphatic expression which was his German heritage (he was a native of Colmar and son of an Augsburg goldsmith) and at the same time to outdo the Flemish masters whose works he obviously had studied in his youth. That these studies had been fruitful and also that he had familiarized himself with the achievements of his compatriots is proved by his engravings, but these can be fully understood only in the light of his paintings, which they helped to popularize, though often failing to convey their eloquently emotive grandeur. Schongauer worked chiefly at Colmar, where the sixteen scenes of the Passion and the Life of the Virgin which once figured on the high altar of the Dominican Church are now preserved in the Unterlinden Museum. Among his favorite themes were the Nativity, the Holy Family, the Adoration of the Shepherds. But for him the theme counted less than the manner of handling it; he reduced the human figure to a system of graceful curves, expressive in their own right, while breaks and angles in the line sufficed to suggest recession and relations of planes. In his prints he applied himself to discovering new ornamental motifs, meaningful arabesques. In doing this he took to pieces, so to speak, the human body, animal and vegetable forms, and studied each part separately, so as to include in his paintings only the essential elements, stressing these with accents inserted at the most telling places. And by this economy of means he effortlessly achieved an effect of monumentality, however small the picture. The outer coat of paint has been badly rubbed on the exterior panels of the Dominican high altar, thus we now can see its ground-plan—stylized and synthetic, with a fine precision in the design. Schongauer, so an early 16th-century writer tells us, "was so excellent an artist that his paintings were carried to Italy, Spain, France and England and other parts of the world." And his admirable prints anticipated Dürer's.

MICHAEL PACHER
RUELAND FRUEAUF

South German and Austrian painters confined themselves to researches of a purely plastic order. The ancient tradition of the sculptor-painter still prevailed and the architectural elements of Italian art, which these painters obviously studied, encouraged the production of huge altarpieces in which the two media, sculpture and painting, were integrated to spectacular effect. The leading figure of the age was Michael Pacher (active from 1467 to 1498) who made the large St Wolfgang altarpiece still in the church of the Upper Austrian lakeside town of this name; the altarpiece of the Fathers of the Church (1483), now in the Alte Pinakothek, Munich, for the convent of Neustift; and the altarpiece at Gries near Bolzano (1471-1475). Pacher goes about his painting in the manner of an expert wood-carver, expressing movement by his sinuous, dynamic line. Thus he builds up a world of mobile, fluctuating forms; the figures, shown in oddly strained postures and clad in billowing drapery that defies the law of gravity, seem struggling to align themselves to the architectural complex in which they are located, to its intricate traceries and vaultings. Creation of a dreamer of strange dreams and propagandist in intent, Michael Pacher's œuvre brilliantly anticipates Baroque.

MARTIN SCHONGAUER (?-1491). NOLI ME TANGERE. (44¾ × 32¼″)
PANEL FROM THE HIGH ALTAR OF THE DOMINICAN CHURCH. MUSÉE UNTERLINDEN, COLMAR.

MICHAEL PACHER (CA. 1435-1498). ST AUGUSTINE, DETAIL OF THE CENTRAL PANEL OF THE FATHERS OF THE CHURCH ALTARPIECE, 1483. ALTE PINAKOTHEK, MUNICH.

Taking its lead from this great artist, a whole school developed in Upper Austria and the Tyrol, particularly in the region between Passau, Salzburg and the Mondsee. Marx Reichlich revivified that familiar theme of The Life of the Virgin, placing his amply molded figures in deep architectural vistas or mountain landscapes echeloned in rising planes, while the Master of Mondsee and the Master of Grossgmain effected a curious stylization of the Flemish prototypes. Finally, Rueland Frueauf the Elder, who worked at Salzburg from 1478 on and died in 1507 at Passau, proved himself a master of structural organization in his big *Crucifixion* (Vienna) and his *Man of Sorrows* (Munich), in which the form of Christ tells out magnificently in a setting rendered with a fine economy of means.

The Nuremberg School was represented by Hans Pleydenwurff and, after him, by Michael Wolgemut (Dürer's much-revered master). They took from Flemish art only what served their purpose, that of stressing and elaborating the frenzied rhythms of their almost brutally realistic compositions.

Last of the German Primitives, Hans Holbein the Elder, who was born at Augsburg, had glimpses of the ideal his more famous son and Albrecht Dürer were so powerfully to realize. His pencil sketches show him to have been an excellent draftsman but his pictures, lit though they are by flashes of inspiration, do not hold together; his means were inadequate and he was also hampered by his allegiance to traditional forms. Indeed his work already seemed outmoded as against that which Dürer, only a few years his junior, was now producing. Thanks to the knowledge and experience he had acquired in the course of his travels in Germany and Italy, Dürer was able to achieve that ideal beauty and balanced composition these German painters had so long been striving for. With him began the German Renaissance and there was nothing left for the elder Holbein but disconsolately to watch the triumph of this new art for which he had unwittingly prepared the way.

PAINTING IN SPAIN AND PORTUGAL

The visits of an artist of such genius and renown as Jan van Eyck could not fail to affect the course of art in the Iberian peninsula. Soon after the coming of the Burgundian embassy, the King of Aragon decided to send some local artists to Flanders, amongst whom was the Valencian painter Luis Dalmau. It seems probable that he was working in Jan van Eyck's studio at the time when Jan was giving the final touches to the Ghent altarpiece. For when on his return to Barcelona some years later Dalmau was commissioned to paint *The Virgin and the Councillors,* he produced what is in effect one of the most curious re-interpretations of a Flemish prototype. As in Van Eyck's compositions the Virgin is seated on a throne with her dress billowing out in front of her. The scene is staged in the choir of a Gothic cathedral, glimpses of distant buildings can be seen across the transept windows, and the Virgin is attended by groups of singing angels, their fair hair rippling over big, richly embroidered mantles. There can be no doubt whence Dalmau drew inspiration for these figures and for those of the patron saints, posted on either side, who are commending the councillors to Our Lady. The large round, strongly individualized heads of these officials and their sumptuous red robes are reminiscent, if at a long remove, of Van Eyck's Canon van der Paele. Thanks to a recent restoration the colors have regained the density and luster peculiar to the oil medium. But these innovations had no sequel in Barcelona for many years to come.

JAIME HUGUET

Thus the leading Catalan artist of the second half of the century, Jaime Huguet, continued painting in tempera, and in his sensitive, exquisitely wrought early works —such as *St George and the Princess* (Barcelona Museum) and the small altarpiece of the Epiphany (Vich Museum)—kept to the methods current in the ateliers of Luis Borrassa and Bernardo Martorell. Before long, however, he broke with the past, broadened his composition and also the structure of his figures. Moreover, when depicting members of the lower classes, he added touches of direct observation and a healthy, forthright realism. Huguet was not only a superb technician who never scamped his work, but exceptionally prolific; from 1455 on he produced a number of large retables in quick succession: the St Anthony Abbot altar (which was destroyed by fire in 1909), Sts Sennen and Abdon (in Santa Maria, Tarrassa), St Vincent (Barcelona Museum), the Constable (Santa Agueda Palace), St Bernardino and the Guardian Angel (Barcelona Cathedral), St Augustine (Barcelona Museum). His art is essentially graphic; its expressive power derives uniquely from the drawing, while the colors are thin and lusterless, merely illustrative. The glittering splendor of these retables is due to the superadded decoration, a lavish use of painted and gilded reliefs, carvings and inlays of precious metals. The actual painting is merely part of a majestic whole, so richly ornamented as often to give an impression of overloading; indeed it is something of an effort to discern the artist's message amid this gorgeous profusion of craftsmen's work.

BARTOLOMÉ BERMEJO

The cosmopolitan School of Valencia, with its colorful expressionism, was equally slow to break with the old procedures. Its leading painters, Jacomart and Reixach (and their many satellites) produced altarpieces more and more crowded with scenes of small dimensions, in which they aimed at giving figures solidity and volume; but they owed little or nothing to the "new ideas." Still, Jacomart visited Naples several times in the course of the King of Aragon's campaigns, and possibly it was he who prepared the way for the exchange of ideas between the Valencian School and Italy, whence the new developments of Spanish painting in the late 15th century certainly derived, though how this came about is a moot point. The fact remains that Rodrigo de Osona the Elder and Bartolomé Bermejo, though trained on essentially Flemish lines, came subsequently under the influence of the schools of Padua and Ferrara.

Without question Bermejo is the greatest 15th-century Spanish artist. Though a considerable part of his oeuvre has been identified, next to nothing is known about his life. His real name was Bartolomé de Cárdenas (Bermejo, meaning "red," was an allusion to his red hair) and he was a native of Cordova. But he cannot be assigned to any local school or group, and seems to have been one of those international-minded 15th-century painters, free-lances of art, who traveled widely. Some of his works have been discovered in Italy—but it does not follow that he ever lived there. Others—for example *Santa Engracia* (Isabella Stewart Gardner Museum, Boston), *St Michael* (Lady Ludlow's Collection)—were originally in churches in the neighborhood of Valencia and it seems fairly certain that he resided, anyhow for a while, in this part of Spain.

While in his big figures of saints, Bermejo retains something of the ultra-lavish decoration characteristic of the Valencian school, he adjusts his forms to a well-marked arabesque, while large tracts of dark flat color and the white of draperies strike broad contrasts, creating an effect of monumental space. In later works such as *The Resurrection* and *The Descent into Limbo* (Barcelona Museum) and the *Pietà of Canon Despla* (Barcelona Cathedral) which he completed in 1490, he stages the scenes in vast, eye-filling landscapes bathed in the glow of sunset. The background of this Pietà is divided into two parts, both remarkably impressive: on one side we see a welter of greenish clouds tinging with eerie light some rocky hills dotted with houses and windmills; on the other a roseate sky strewing glints of ruddy gold upon an Eastern city. Bermejo's *Virgin and Child* in Acqui Cathedral (Italy) is equally effective. Both the central figure and the steeply rising landscape, with its high cliffs crowned with houses seem reminiscent of Mantegna. Moreover several motifs as well as the general arrangement of the scene are so similar to those of Rodrigo de Osona's *Crucifixion* (Valencia) that it seems likely both these artists took their lead from Italy.

FERNANDO GALLEGO

Meanwhile in Cantabrian Spain, Andalusia and Portugal there had been developing a busy oversea trade with Flanders, then at the height of its commercial prosperity. Hitherto the schools of painting in this part of the peninsula had been backward and relatively sterile. But the combined effect of economic progress and political changes did much to remedy this state of affairs. When the Catholic monarchs re-united the kingdoms of Castile and Aragon they gave Spain as it were a new center of gravity. In Andalusia the regions occupied by the Moors were definitively liberated, while for the Portuguese began the heroic age of expeditions into Africa and great sea ventures. As was to be expected, the courts and the élite kept open house to the art that had made its name throughout the West, and encouraged local artists to adopt the Flemish style. The Netherlandish "Primitives" became immensely popular and Queen Isabella built up a collection of Flemish paintings (now in the Royal Chapel of Granada), in which figured Van der Weyden's earliest triptychs and one of the major works of Dirk Bouts' early days. Indigenous painters were quick to catch up with the new techniques and there soon developed what was in effect a Hispano-Flemish school. But—if we leave out of account the admirable portraits of the Marquis of Santillana and his wife by Jorge Inglès (whose name suggests that he was of foreign extraction)—these works were somewhat rustic, not to say uncouth, though some have a pleasant, earthy savor; for example *The Nativity* (1475) by the Master of Avila, an echo at a long remove of the Flémalle Master's rendering of the same subject. Most original of these artists was Fernando Gallego who made several big altarpieces (Zamora Cathedral, the New Cathedral of Salamanca and the Weibel Collection, Madrid). His stylistic innovations, showing a tendency towards distortion, have much in common with the practice of Conrad Witz: prominent eyes, fleshy, expressive lips, contorted gestures. Here, too, we have what seems like a belated echo of the art of the North, and there is every reason to believe that Gallego had seen and studied Schongauer's engravings.

Younger by a generation, Pedro Berruguete realized that the methods of the past had had their day and must now be superseded, and it was to Italy that he turned for guidance. Born in Paredes de Nava near Palencia, a region in which Gallego often worked, he may well have acquired from

BARTOLOMÉ BERMEJO (ACTIVE BETWEEN 1470 AND 1498). SANTA ENGRACIA, CA. 1477. (64¼×28½")
ISABELLA STEWART GARDNER MUSEUM, BOSTON.

JAIME HUGUET (?-1492). THE MASS OF ST AUGUSTINE (DETAIL), 1486.
CENTRAL PANEL OF THE ST AUGUSTINE ALTARPIECE. MUSEUM OF CATALAN ART, BARCELONA.

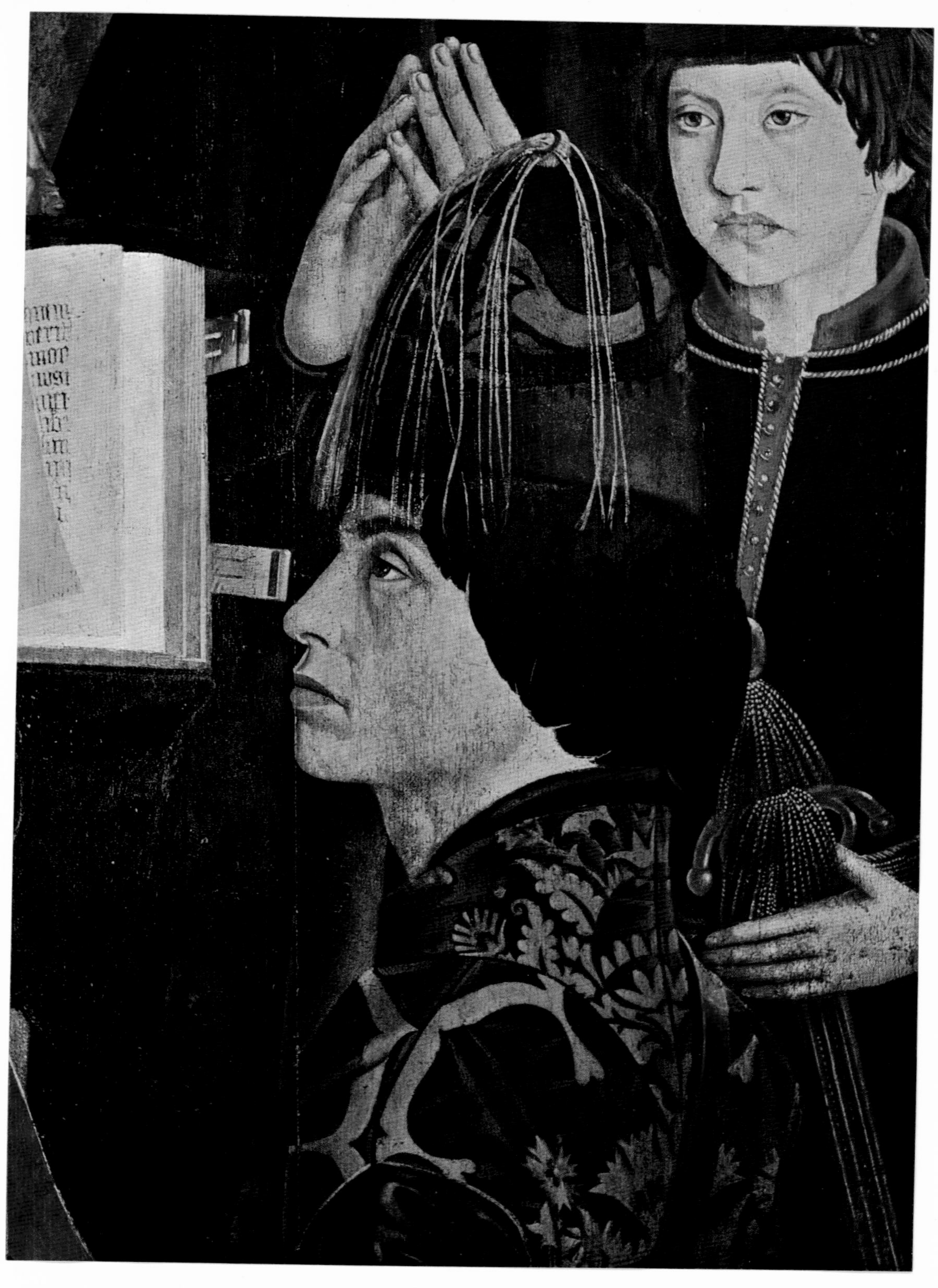

NUÑO GONÇALVES (?-1471). KING ALFONSO V AND PRINCE JOHN, DETAIL FROM THE LEFT PANEL OF THE ST VINCENT POLYPTYCH, CA. 1470. NATIONAL MUSEUM OF ANTIQUE ART, LISBON.

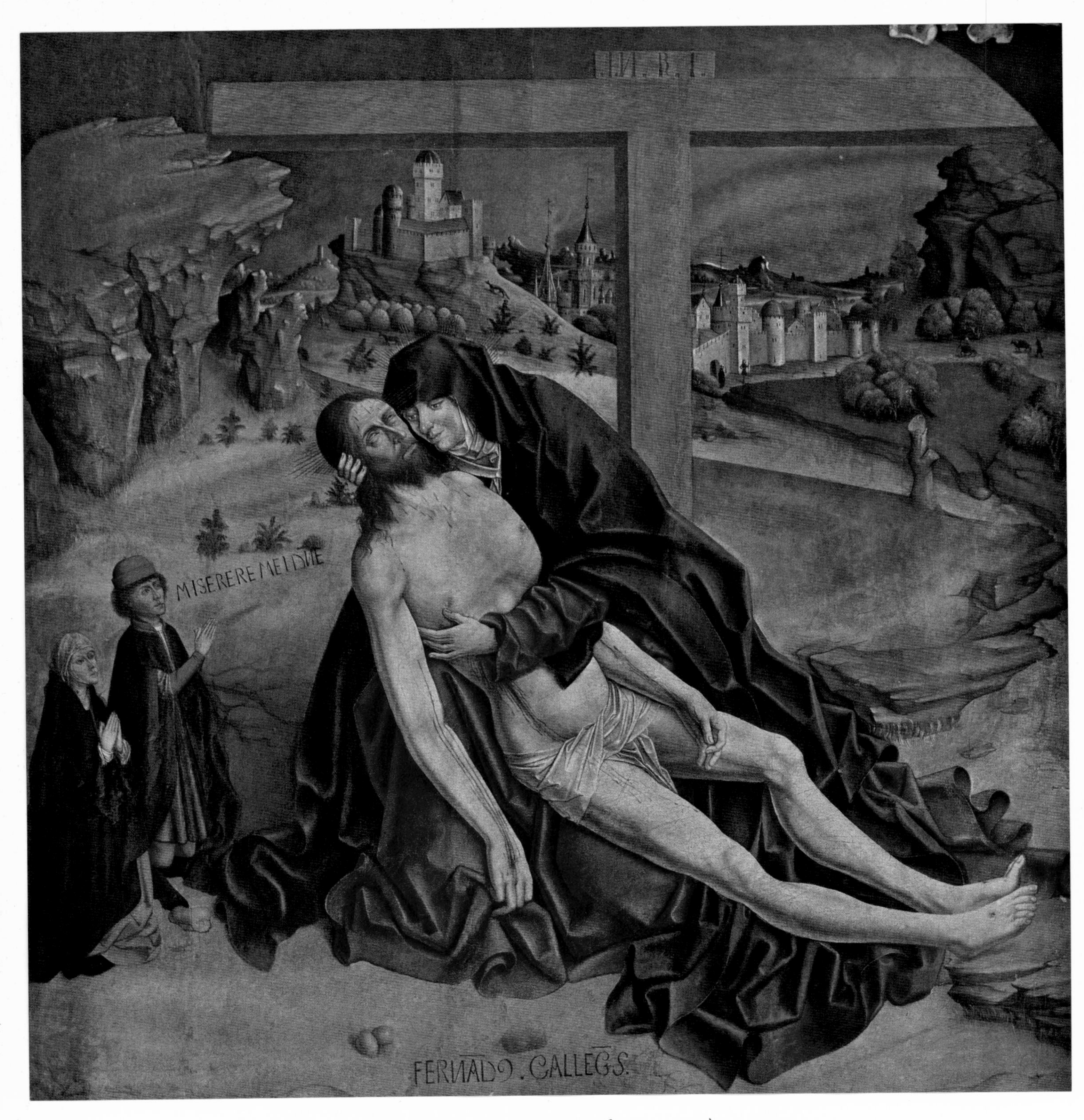

FERNANDO GALLEGO (ACTIVE BETWEEN 1467 AND 1507). CALVARY.
PANEL FROM AN ALTARPIECE NOW DISPERSED. WEIBEL COLLECTION, MADRID.

that master a thorough grounding in the procedures of the Flemings. Hulin de Loo believes that he rounded off this training with a stay in Naples. Anyhow, when Berruguete made his appearance at the court of Federigo da Montefeltro in Urbino (his presence there in 1477 is documented), he was evidently a highly accomplished artist, since he was commissioned to paint the Duke's rather large, strongly expressive hands, in Piero della Francesca's picture of Federigo kneeling before the Virgin. He was also called on to complete and continue Joos van Ghent's frescos in the Duke's study. His style became more and more Italianized and it was he who painted the figures of the Liberal Arts in the ducal library. Finally, the portraits of Federigo and his son seem to be by Berruguete's hand. Allegorical figures, buildings aligned in geometrical perspective, settings inspired by antiquity, bodies rendered with strict regard to anatomical proportions—all these characteristics reappear in the works produced by Berruguete after his return to Spain in 1483, in spite of the fact that he was obliged to keep to the traditional religious themes. Even in the big altarpiece at Avila, depicting the lives of St Thomas and St Peter—and still more in the pictures he painted in the churches of his native province—Berruguete included in the predellas large symbolic and allegorical figures, Jewish kings, Doctors and Fathers of the Church, treated in his Urbino manner.

NUÑO GONÇALVES

Not until the middle of the century did an independent Portuguese school of painting emerge, and this was largely due to the patronage of the "Navigator Kings" and the appearance of a painter of high originality, Nuño Gonçalves, cited by Francisco de Hollanda a century later in his repertory of "eminent painters." But he remained in relative obscurity until, at the beginning of the present century, J. de Figueiredo drew attention to his work, with the result that his St Vincent polyptych is now the pride of the National Museum of Antique Art at Lisbon. Gonçalves was King Alfonso's favorite painter between 1451 and 1467; he drew a handsome salary and made cartoons for tapestries which were executed at Tournai. The Altarpiece of the Veneration of St Vincent consists of two symmetrical triptychs showing members of the royal family and Portuguese grandees doing homage to their country's patron saint. The leading figure in each central panel is St Vincent who is portrayed as a good-looking youth. In one he is accompanied by Henry the Navigator, Alfonso V and the young Infante John; in the other by the Archbishop of Lisbon and military and naval officers in full uniform. On the other panels are compact rows of figures: members of the nobility, monks, fishermen and representatives of the foreign colonies in Lisbon, a Moor, a Jew. With the exception of the King all are shown full face or in three-quarter view, symmetrically disposed in a half-circle around the saint. There is no landscape or architecture, and perspective is indicated solely by the tiled floor. This crowded composition of life size figures produces almost the effect of tapestry. The very real genius of this artist reveals itself both in accurate, synthetic draftsmanship and in his masterly arrangements of broad tracts of color. While taking the principles of Flemish art as his starting-point, Gonçalves re-interpreted them on new lines and proved himself one of the most powerful creative spirits of the 15th century.

THE PAINTERS OF PROVENCE AND LE BOURBONNAIS

SITUATED at one of the great crossroads of Western Europe, where the trade route between Burgundy and Flanders and that of Spain and Italy intersected, and benefiting by the presence and protection of the Pope and the opulence of the papal court, Avignon was an oasis of peace even in the most troubled years of this eventful 15th century and a favorite resort of artists from all over France. Though in its early days the School of Avignon had been under the domination of Italian artists, and during the pontificate of the Antipope Benedict XIII (the Aragonese, Pedro de Luna), of Catalans and Spaniards, these foreign influences had long ceased to operate; all the names of painters figuring in the records from the year 1430 onwards are typically Provençal or have a French ring. In the lists he has compiled after many years of painstaking research, Labande includes no less than five hundred large altarpieces mentioned in documents of the period as having been made in this part of France alone. The orders for them were given by convents, merchants and corporations as well as by members of princely houses. In fact a taste for works of art was steadily gaining ground in all classes of the population throughout the country. Donors kept a close eye on the works for which they gave commissions; they insisted on their portraits' being good likenesses, done from the life, and even specified the number of sittings in some cases. Contracts were drawn up before a notary, precisely stipulating the subject or subjects to be treated, the colors to be used, the quality of the wood (deal or walnut) and the date on which delivery was to be made.

THE MASTER OF THE VILLENEUVE PIETÀ

It was in this deeply religious Provençal milieu that one of the century's most poignantly emotive works of art, the Villeneuve *Pietà* (Louvre), was painted by a great artist whose name we shall probably never know for certain. As in the Rohan Hours, but here in a full-size picture in which the donor plays a direct part in the divine tragedy, we find huge, monumental figures, imbued with passionate but restrained emotion, placed in a very simple setting consisting only of a few symbolic elements. There is no need, as some have done, to talk of Portuguese or Spanish influences; on the contrary, the kinship is unmistakable between this *Pietà* and other works produced in Provence at the time. One of them is the Boulbon altarpiece, originally in Saint-Marcellin's church at Boulbon which was annexed in 1457 to the parish of the Church of Saint-Agricol of Avignon. Almost identical in these two altarpieces is the figure of the donor with his gnarled hands with strongly marked veins, the rectangular face with its high cheekbones, receding nose and deeply sunken eyes. We find the same cranial structure, rendered in less austere colors, in many of Charonton's figures. Also the diapered borders in the *Pietà* are the same as those in *The Coronation of the Virgin* and the Chantilly *Virgin of Mercy*. This has led several authorities, amongst them Canon Requin, to suggest that the Villeneuve *Pietà*, clearly a later work, should be ascribed not to Charonton himself but to Pierre Villatte, his young assistant.

MASTER OF THE VILLENEUVE PIETÀ. PIETÀ, CA. 1460. (63 ½ × 85 ¾")
LOUVRE, PARIS.

It would seem that, following a trend of the times, the works of the Avignon School were then in process of becoming at once more rustic and more realistic. The Boulbon altarpiece reveals this tendency when we compare it with the Aix *Annunciation*, to which, however, it is clearly affiliated. Notable is the resemblance between the figures of God the Father in these two works. The majestic God of the Boulbon altarpiece has the same features as His Son, though the appearance of the latter after His sufferings, whose instruments figure on the right of the composition—the lamp used during the early hours of the Passion, the hammer, the pincers, the scourge, the rods, the hand that buffeted Him, the spear, the reed and sponge, the pillar and the rope—is both younger and bears the marks of the ordeal He has undergone. In Enguerrand Charonton's

Coronation of the Virgin, on the other hand, where the scene is laid in Heaven, the faces of Father and Son have a wonderful serenity, the sublime aloofness of immortals.

Some details in the Boulbon altarpiece are surprisingly realistic; for example, the pebble that keeps the cover of the tomb from slipping. But this picture is unfortunately in a very poor state; the colors have faded almost out of recognition and little more than the bare bones of the design are left. In the *Pietà*, however, painstakingly restored, the colors have been stabilized and we can admire their warm, soft luster and full-bodied density. Here, too, the artist's personality makes itself better felt, notably

MASTER OF THE VILLENEUVE PIETÀ. PIETÀ (DETAIL), CA. 1460. LOUVRE, PARIS.

his gift for transmuting elements of visual actuality into grandiose symbols and of making each face reveal the secrets of the heart, irradiated by an inner light. The Virgin's, for example, is not that of a woman yielding to despair; she is ennobled, sublimated by her grief, and her set face, carved one would think in wood or stone, has an ethereal pallor; whereas the faces of Mary Magdalen and St John, bathed in the brilliant sunlight that also plays upon the distant domes of "Jerusalem the Golden," have the soft plenitude of living flesh. His economy of means, his rejection of all extraneous, unessential elements, enabled the Master of the Villeneuve *Pietà* to create a work that was in the truest sense epoch-making. Like the Rohan Master vis-à-vis the Flemish illuminators, he provided an epitome of all that was best in the art of a great contemporary school, taking from it only what was vital.

NICOLAS FROMENT

In the work of Nicolas Froment and King René's artists the art of the Provençal School undergoes a change; here the influence of royal patronage is making itself felt, with the result that there is closer intercourse with the French schools of other courts (at Tours and Moulins) and with foreign art-centers. After the ill-starred Sicilian venture and his captivity in Burgundy, King René relished more than ever the amenities of his beloved Provence. He owned a number of handsome residences in this part of France, amongst them the châteaux of Tarascon, Gardanne, Vallobre, Peyrolles and Pertuis. At Aix, not content with his palace, he took over a stately mansion, the Hôtel de Viviers, in which he made many improvements with the aid of the best artists available. Some of them were recruited locally, others were foreigners; thus two Netherlanders, Coppin Delf and Barthelemy de Clerc were personae gratae at the royal court. Himself a writer, the King had his books illustrated with the splendid miniatures to which his *Traité sur les Tournois* and his *Livre du Cœur d'Amour Epris* (Book of the Lovelorn Heart) owe their renown. The illustrations of the former, pen and wash drawings, are perhaps by the King's own hand. In *The Lovelorn Heart* the art is subtler, volumes are fully rendered and the artist has tackled problems of lighting calling for much finesse; for example, effects of early sunrise and the half-light in a room lit by a flickering candle. In the scene of "Love taking away the Sick King's Heart to give it to Desire" the conical tent, the vigorously modeled forms and chiaroscuro cannot fail to remind us of the famous *Dream of Constantine* in Piero della Francesca's Arezzo frescos. (The two works were almost contemporary.) A little later we find the Dutch painter Geertgen tot Sint Jans producing somewhat similar work; hence the theory some have put forward that this artist was one of the Netherlandish painters called in by King René. It is, moreover, to these northern influences that certain characteristics of the art of Nicolas Froment are commonly attributed.

Fairly copious information regarding Froment's life and works is available, and we can get a good idea of his personality. He was born at Uzès about 1425 and mention is made of his presence in the records of this city for the years 1465 and 1467, that is to say several years after he had signed the triptych entitled *The Resurrection of Lazarus* now at Florence, in the Uffizi. On February 12, 1468, he rented a house in the Place

NICOLAS FROMENT (CA. 1425-CA. 1483). THE BURNING BUSH, 1476. (161 × 119¾″)
CATHEDRAL OF SAINT-SAUVEUR, AIX-EN-PROVENCE.

du Puits-aux-Bœufs at Avignon, near the Palace of the Popes; it was there that the festivities greeting the arrival of legates and important visitors usually took place. In 1474 Froment purchased the house in which he was living and two nearby houses as well. Six years later Catherine Spiefami, widow of an Aix merchant, commissioned him to make an altarpiece depicting *The Death of the Virgin*. Two other contracts make mention of Froment's activities in the City of the Popes; when in 1473 the papal legate Cardinal de Bourbon made his state entrance into Avignon, Froment was called on to decorate the triumphal arch with historical scenes, while in 1476, and again in 1481, he painted oriflammes for the reception of Cardinal Giuliano della Rovere, subsequently Pope Julius II. But most interesting of all the contracts given this painter is that relating to the triptych of *The Burning Bush*, painted to the order of King René for the altar of the Grands Carmes of Aix, which is now in Aix Cathedral. Froment also played a leading part, from 1476 on, in the decoration of the king's private residence, the Hôtel de Viviers. In 1482 he made his Will, and an entry dated December 1484 in the royal archives refers to him as "the late Nicolas Froment."

There is no reliable evidence that he traveled in Italy and France. Probably his first signed picture *The Resurrection of Lazarus* (1461) found its way to Florence only after the Revolution; in any case, there is no trace of Italian influence in it. Froment did not come into really close touch with King René's court until the aging king had settled for good in Provence, where he died in 1480. He may well have found frequent reminiscences of Van der Goes and Van Ouwater in paintings made by the Dutch artists in the king's entourage. But such influences took effect, it seems, only belatedly; anyhow they are more evident in *The Burning Bush* than in *The Resurrection of Lazarus*. For we must not be misled by the fact that the theme of the latter was also that of one of Van Ouwater's major works and was employed by several Dutch painters of the time; Froment's handling of it is different, at once quite original and technically rather gauche. In one of the wings he depicts the inner garden of a castle; it is laid out in the typically French manner and in it we see small figures in court costumes playing chess. This is obviously a work of his youth; he has not yet learnt to integrate the various elements of the composition into a balanced unity; there is something undisciplined, indeed awkward, in his presentation of the scene. Particularly striking is the contrast between the mystical exaltation of the sacred figures and the coarseness of the others. With their pendulous noses, flaccid chins, goggle eyes and grotesque headgear, they look more like caricatures of humanity than ordinary mortals.

But in *The Burning Bush* (1476) we have a work of Froment's maturity, when he had purged his art of these incongruities. The theme is interpreted in an unusual and highly interesting manner. Instead of God the Father it is the Virgin who appears to Moses, nor is it the young Moses who figures here, but a wrinkled, benevolent-looking old man who has been taken unawares in the act of removing his shoes and is holding up his hand to shield his eyes from the blinding celestial light. Beside him is a shepherd's scrip and a keg of wine, and sheep are grazing (this was perhaps a tactful tribute to King René's pastoral propensities; he liked playing at being a shepherd). But most original of all is the serried clump of oak-trees with slender tongues of flame issuing from the leafage. The landscape, on the other hand, is rather tedious, crowded with buildings of various kinds and styles which lack the purity and precision of Charonton's landscape vistas, or even those in the Les Perussis altarpiece (by an unknown artist) in which are depicted the Avignon plain and Saint Bénézet's bridge. Most attractive in the *Burning Bush* triptych is the impression it gives of orderly arrangement, its restfulness, and this effect is heightened by the figures in the wing-panels showing the king and his wife Jeanne de Laval, attended by their patron saints, kneeling at praying-desks under big crimson curtains, their faces turned towards the central scene. Both portraits seem remarkably true to life; the artist has not attempted to idealize the king's heavy jowl, flat nose and bulging chin, or the queen's long, pale, unattractive face. Yet for all their lifelikeness these faces are deliberately stylized, formally constructed. It is noteworthy that the painter of the Moulins triptych obviously imitated Froment's composition, though he handled it with more amenity and his forms are graceful, more smoothly modeled. Thus Froment's contribution to the evolution of the French portrait, which proceeded without a break from Fouquet to the Master of Moulins and Clouet, was of considerable importance.

THE MASTER OF MOULINS

That famous illuminated manuscript, *The Lovelorn Heart*, was dedicated to Jean II, Duke of Bourbon. During the second half of the 15th century Cardinal de Bourbon often visited Avignon and there was a constant interchange of ideas between Provence and the cities of Lyons and Moulins where, under the patronage of the Court, a highly refined art was taking form. Charles I, Duke of Bourbon from 1434 to 1456, had married a princess of the House of Burgundy and when he decided to have his mausoleum built in the new chapel of the Souvigny basilica, he called in Sluter's best pupil, Jacques Morel of Avignon. The forty-four alabaster Mourners and the kneeling angels which figured in the niches of the pedestal are gone, but the recumbent effigies, massive, supremely tranquil forms rendered with a fine simplicity, still are wonderfully impressive, despite the scars of time. Charles I's three sons succeeded him one after the other: from 1456 to 1488, Jean II who married Catherine d'Armagnac; in 1488 Charles II, Archbishop of Lyons (who had been made Cardinal in 1477); and finally, from 1488 to 1503, Pierre II, Sire de Beaujeu, who had married Louis XI's daughter Anne de France, "Madame la Grande," regent of the kingdom during the minority of King Charles VIII.

Jean II, who had called in the famous sculptor Michel Colombe to work for him, presented the Collegiate Church (later Cathedral) of Moulins with the altar of the Conception, adorned with the magnificent stained-glass window depicting the Virgin in Glory enthroned in a golden blaze of light, crowned with twelve stars and with the crescent moon beneath her feet. Pierre II and Anne de France were nothing if not house-proud; their château at Chantelle and palace at Moulins were by far the finest residences of the period, while Duchess Anne's charming "lodge" may be said to usher in the Renaissance in France. In front of the palace, on the slopes leading down to the river Allier, were extensive gardens full of exotic trees, mazes and artificial

MASTER OF MOULINS (ACTIVE BETWEEN 1480 AND 1500). NATIVITY WITH CARDINAL JEAN ROLIN, CA. 1480.
($21\frac{1}{2} \times 28\frac{3}{4}$″) MUSÉE D'AUTUN.

grottoes in the Italian manner. In the Duke's window there figured, alongside St Catherine, Jean II and Catherine d'Armagnac, the Cardinal de Bourbon, Pierre II and Anne, with their children, all escorted by their patron saints. Executed with remarkable precision, these figures are presented in a setting of sumptuous fabrics worked in oriental patterns, perhaps the Lucca textiles which were so popular at Lyons at the time. But the crowning glory of the Collegiate Church was the triptych commissioned by the Duke, representing *The Virgin and Child accompanied by Angels*. In the lateral panels the rulers are shown in all their regal pomp and power, and there is a striking difference between these figures and the homely simplicity of the portraits in the stained-glass window and an older double portrait now in the Louvre.

MASTER OF MOULINS (ACTIVE BETWEEN 1480 AND 1500). PORTRAIT OF A YOUNG PRINCESS. (12 ½ × 9″)
ROBERT LEHMAN COLLECTION, NEW YORK.

Around this key work by the Master of Moulins have been grouped a large number of pictures clearly by the same hand, ranging from the Autun *Nativity* (ca. 1480), the *Annunciation* in the Art Institute of Chicago and the Brussels *Virgin and Child*, to the portraits of a donatrix with Mary Magdalen in the Louvre; of Cardinal de Bourbon (Alte Pinakothek, Munich); of a young princess (more probably Margaret of Austria, betrothed to Charles VIII, than Suzanne de Bourbon who figures beside her mother in the Moulins triptych) in the Lehman Collection, New York; of a donor with St Maurice or St Victor in the Glasgow Art Gallery. Also to the Moulins Master are usually ascribed the touching portraits of those sickly young princes, the dauphins Charles-Orland and Charles VIII's son Charles (in the Louvre). All these pictures have clearly marked characteristics distinguishing them from contemporary Flemish works, notably from those of Van der Goes, to whom they were once attributed. They are more in the tradition of Fouquet, though showing an advance on it. The portraits are simple and forthright, conscientious and admirably objective. Where there is ugliness the artist records it frankly, but with none of Froment's over-emphasis and harshness. He created a special type of womanhood, with a broad prominent forehead, strongly molded features, clean-cut lips, a face at once expressive and intelligent. No less characteristic are his countrysides of rolling hills, groves of oak or walnut trees among which sometimes rises a church steeple or a house mirrored in a lake. He has obvious affinities with Memling, but his light is softer, more natural. The treatment of architecture is somewhat soberer than in Gerard David's work and indeed foreshadows the Renaissance. Finally, the brushwork is nothing short of superb; it has a fine velvety quality, a translucence and sometimes a density unknown, or all but unknown, since the days of Van Eyck. It combines the delicate perfection of the miniature with the rich glow of the stained-glass window.

The Moulins triptych celebrates a theme already employed in a window of the Collegiate Church, and loosely paraphrases a passage of the Apocalypse. "Here is she whose praises are hymned in the sacred book. Robed in the sun, she hath the moon beneath her feet, and hath been deemed worthy to be crowned with twelve stars." The symbolism is easy to interpret. The Virgin and Child are encircled by the radiant, ever-changing colors of the rainbow, signifying the illumination of the soul pondering on the divine mystery. Everything points to the fact that the maker of this triptych was a member of the group of artists employed by the Bourbon court, who provided the Collegiate Church with its wonderful stained-glass windows, finest of all 15th-century windows according to Prosper Mérimée. This familiarity with the technique of the glass-worker obviously played a large part in his artistic formation, and accounts for the lustrous, translucent sheen he imparted to his color.

The names of the principal artists at the Bourbon Court are known to us. They were Pietre, surname of Charlot du Moustier (active between 1484 and 1499), who was perhaps an ancestor of the family of 16th-century portrait-painters of that name; Claude and Jean Avisart; Etienne Saulnier (died 1503), chief glass-painter to Anne de France; Jean Richier d'Orléans, born at Beaugency, trained in Provence, known to have been at Carpentras in 1491, whose marriage took place at Avignon in 1493, and who shortly after settled at Moulins; and, finally, Jean Prévost, often referred to as "Jean the Painter," artist and glass-painter to Cardinal de Bourbon at Lyons, a successful rival of Jean Perréal, who was bidden several times to Moulins. However, despite much research-work the eminent archivist of the Allier Department, Paul Dupieux, has failed to find any direct evidence in support of his theory that the central panel of the triptych was painted by Jean Prévost and that Jean Richier made the portraits of the Duke and Duchess in the wings. All the same he has definitely proved that the identification of the Master of Moulins with Jean Perréal was an error, due to a confusion between the latter and a "Jehan de Paris" who at a much earlier time had held a menial post in the household of the Dukes of Bourbon. Thus the problem of the authorship of the great Moulins triptych still awaits solution.

In the Autun *Nativity* which is dated about 1480—its donor Cardinal Rolin, son of the famous Chancellor of Burgundy, died in 1483—we find an interesting and original interpretation of themes employed by Van der Goes. There is here no striving for expressionist effects in the representation of the shepherds who, like St Joseph and the donor, are gazing with rapt attention but without any show of emotion at the scene before them. The Child Jesus and the little angels are winsomely human figures, indeed only the Virgin strikes an otherworldly note with the ethereal delicacy of her features, her face as white as its linen headdress and the cool harmony of colors in her garment of light and dark blue. The simplicity and naturalness of this *Nativity* are quite exceptional. Twenty years later in the *Annunciation* in grisaille on the back of the volets of the Moulins triptych the artist showed once more his bold originality in the way he treated what was by then a hackneyed subject. Here we have not, as in so many grisailles, simulated statues—for one thing the pedestals have completely disappeared—but supple figures, full of life: the angel of the Annunciation rising through the air, the kneeling Virgin making a charming little gesture of surprise and awe, the gracefully built angels hovering around. No other artist ever embroidered on this familiar theme such exquisite, gossamer-light arabesques.

This unnamed master was the last of the great Primitives in the lands north of the Alps. We can appreciate his genius all the better when we turn to the work of an artist temperamentally akin who worked at Avignon and Marseilles. This is the painter (almost certainly Josse Lieferinxe, born in the diocese of Cambrai) who made the St Sebastian altarpiece, now dismembered (Brussels, Avignon, Baltimore and Philadelphia). Its style is definitely archaic and provincial; the statue-like figures clad in hieratic garments with straight-falling folds are placed in architectural settings of the new kind inspired by Italy, but over-simplified and paltry. Similarly the northern French schools made no progress beyond the first pictures of the School of Amiens, Simon Marmion's painstaking depictions (Marmion is thought to have painted the *Scenes from the Life of St Bertin* now in the Kaiser Friedrich Museum, Berlin), and the minutely detailed renderings of landscape and Parisian edifices in the works of the Master of Saint-Gilles.

MASTER OF MOULINS (ACTIVE BETWEEN 1480 AND 1500). VIRGIN AND CHILD WITH ANGELS, DETAIL FROM THE CENTRAL PANEL OF THE MOULINS TRIPTYCH, 1498-1499. MOULINS CATHEDRAL.

Page 193: Antonello da Messina (1430?-1479). St Jerome in his Study (detail). National Gallery, London.

4

PAINTING IN NORTHERN ITALY

Owing to its geographical position northern Italy was more accessible than any other part of the country to the culture of the lands beyond the Alps and it was there that the courtly-social naturalism of Late Gothic took firmest root, and soon had its most perfect flowering in the work of Pisanello and Jacopo Bellini. Distinctive of this art are its delicately precise handling of details, line that at once defines the picture elements and holds them together, and the use of colors that, while specifying objects, integrates them into an elegantly balanced whole. Though artists of this persuasion were fascinated by the beauties of the visible world, they were not in the least interested in discovering its laws or underlying structure. To their thinking beauty could be seen in everything, down to the smallest details of visual experience: flower petals, birds' feathers, butterflies' wings. They were on the best of terms with the world around them and saw in nature a large-scale replica of human society; in which every object and every living being had a twofold value—in itself and as part of an harmonious whole. However, the pleasure they found in the contemporary scene did not prevent them from casting backward glances at antiquity; on the contrary all that won their admiration in the former was associated with more or less chimerical visions of the legendary past. But Pisanello and Jacopo Bellini, like Gentile da Fabriano, Ghiberti and Masolino, visualized history in the light of a vast recessional perspective reaching out into infinity which, instead of enlarging things and events, made them seem progressively smaller.

Very different was the program of the Florentine artists working in Venetia: Donatello, Uccello, Andrea del Castagno, Filippo Lippi. They gave objective reality to events by means of the dual perspective of Time and Space, and did not believe in continuity of rhythm but in the permanence of fixed proportional relations. Hence there arose a new, profoundly historical way of seeing, in line with the exegeses of antiquity that the men of letters and Aristotelian philosophers at the University of Padua were producing in large numbers at the time. There was much talk about the ties of blood with ancient Rome, emphasis being laid on the fact that Livy was born at Padua and Virgil at Mantua. Also much labor was devoted to determining the exact meaning of the classical texts, but chiefly from a philological angle and not, as at Florence, with an eye to the civic and moral lessons inculcated by them. Though the works of art produced by Squarcione were sadly uninspired, his school was a great center of humanist culture and in close touch with Donatello, who lived for many years at Padua. This was evident in the decorations in the Ovetari Chapel of the Church of the Eremitani in Padua (destroyed in the bombardments of March 1944); they were made between 1448 and 1452 by a group of painters headed by Mantegna.

MANTEGNA

If in the field of art Piero may be described as the century's supreme philosopher, Mantegna was its chief philologist. Needless to say, this term should be interpreted in its loftiest sense; no other artist showed such zeal in his quest of historical sources or carried his analysis of the "linguistics" of forms in painting to such lengths.

It was from Donatello that Mantegna learnt the value of history and the significance of antiquity. We should, however, note that what he saw in the latter was neither formal perfection nor an ideal beauty—nature glorified—but a testimony to certain eternal values, the personalities of great men and their deeds. When he depicts an historical event he does not exploit its dramatic possibilities, or try to make it live before our eyes. Yet even in his early works he reveals an intensity of expression far exceeding the dramatic effects of Donatello. Mantegna does not aim at the dramatic in this sense; it would be truer to say that a work by him is a tragedy in the classical, Aristotelian application of the word. The tragic sense of life is there, and he brings it home to us, but he seeks its origin in the depths of time. And when he clothes it in an antique garb, this is in order to bring out its immutable, eternal quality.

Mantegna's art reveals a curious dualism: a will to combine contemporary figures with deliberately archaic form. And this desire to express the flux of time in rigid, timeless patterns gives the picture, paradoxically enough, a temporal aspect, that of a discourse or a "tract for the times." For he does not altogether do away with the discursive rhythm of Gothic painting; rather, he transforms it, adjusting its tempo to the logical, predestined course of history. Taking a lead from Alberti's dictum that Florentine design is an equivalent of the Platonic "idea," we might say that Mantegna's drawing corresponds to the Aristotelian logos.

Mantegna treated history and perspective as being one and the same, and though he regarded perspective as an instrument of vision, it was intellectual, not optical, vision he had in mind. For he took no interest in nature as a field of visual experience; its value was that it testified to great deeds of the past and, so to speak, authenticated them. Like everything forming part of the legacy of antiquity, nature too was in ruins, but that was only on the surface, due to the ravages of time, and did not in any way

ANDREA MANTEGNA (1431-1506). THE DEATH OF THE VIRGIN, CA. 1462. (21 ¼ × 16 ½″)
PRADO, MADRID.

ANDREA MANTEGNA (1431-1506). DECORATION FOR THE BRIDAL CHAMBER (DETAIL), 1474.
FRESCO, DUCAL PALACE, MANTUA.

impair the basic structure. Time and men could destroy appearances, but form they could not destroy, and it was history's privilege to discern the immutable reality of form behind the changeful aspects of the temporal.

Starting out from the pointers given him by Donatello's low reliefs (and from nothing else), Mantegna built up his own perspective, full of distances implied rather than expressed, and the merest hints of three-dimensional volume. His drawing does not purport to represent distance; it demarcates zones of vision in which each object, no matter where, has equal clarity and density, an equally distinct contour-line, relief and color. He did not, like the Florentines, regard the picture as a flat surface on which the illusion of depth could be created; for him it was a two-dimensional screen, shallower even than Donatello's near-flat bronze reliefs.

This explains why he gives his line the longest possible, most devious trajectory, winding its way across the picture in an endless chain of convolutions, as though to hollow out a place, a niche in which to house each object. Yet, for all its seeming vagaries, it is under strict control, governed by the thinking mind, and in fact reminds us of a chain of reasoning based on successive syllogisms. Unlike Piero's synthetic, unified form, Mantegna's is analytic, composite. Each figure, object, bit of landscape has the value of an historical record; indeed he does not so much compose as reconstruct, ensuring the unity of the picture by a logical rearrangement of fragmentary data. What he thus achieves might be described as the "restoration" of an ideal antiquity, in which history and nature bear equal part. In the altarpiece of San Zeno's at Verona (ca. 1459) we have a good example of the way in which Mantegna set about this. As a philologer and archeologist,

ANDREA MANTEGNA (1431-1506).
DECORATION FOR THE BRIDAL CHAMBER (DETAIL), 1474.
FRESCO, DUCAL PALACE, MANTUA.

he does not seek to elicit from history lessons bearing on the present day; his attitude to history, though profoundly moral in its implications, might better be described as eschatological. He regards the past as a world apart, behind the veil, to which only great minds have access; a tragic world, since it is a world of death, and it is death alone that consecrates true grandeur. These conceptions are illustrated to wonderful effect in that famous picture *The Dead Christ* (Brera, Milan), in which we see the huge dead body lying flat, revealing in immobility its superhuman structure. Painted with a realism undared by any previous artist, Christ, by way of His physical death, has entered into the historical domain.

We have already pointed out that Mantegna tended to give his works the form of discourses or visual sermons. Even the tragic implications of a scene, deriving more from the personalities of the leading figures than from anything they do, seem rather to be described than depicted. The plastic qualities of his art are not determined by any spatial referents; they do not implement a way of seeing or portraying, but one of celebrating or consecrating the value of great historical events. To Mantegna falls the credit of having revived the art of Rhetoric, in the classical (and correct) application of the term: the use of discourse governed by a logic which, in the last analysis, stems from knowledge of the law of causation—in this case historical causation.

In 1453 he married Jacopo Bellini's daughter, Nicolosia, and as a result came in close touch with his artist brother-in-law, Giovanni Bellini. Under his influence Mantegna tempered his lapidary art with milder sentiments, touches of warmer tones, and indulged in settings at once more natural and more pleasing to the eye. And this enlargement of his field of experience was accompanied by a more human, more classical appreciation of antiquity.

Stress must be laid on his contacts with the court of Mantua when we appraise the works of his maturity. It was at Mantua (and in Rome) that he came under the spell of the literary humanism whose spokesman was Leon Battista Alberti: a humanism which, based as it was on an admiration of ancient monuments and a cult of the vestiges of the Roman past, went back truly to the sources. It was between 1484 and 1492 that he painted nine scenes of *Triumphs* (now at Hampton Court) for the Court theater at Mantua. These evocations of classical antiquity combine with Mantegna's characteristic rhetorical tone a real feeling for space and a tendency towards monumental, spectacular effects reminding us of Alberti's architecture in the church of Sant'Andrea at Mantua.

In the frescos in the Bridal Chamber of the Ducal Palace of Mantua, this feeling for architectonic space harmonizes with the "modernistic" depiction of scenes of everyday life at the Gonzaga court. The ceiling decoration—an impluvium painted in *trompe-l'œil*, over which women and foreshortened *putti* are peeping down—is a bold effect of spatial illusionism, at once perspectival and atmospheric. The painter no longer needs to resort to line for indicating the relations between figures and objects, and locates the latter in a spatial context that, though reduced to essentials, is full of life and motion and suffices to create the appropriate historical climate.

It is a significant fact that the works of Mantegna's maturity, in which, abandoning the documentary presentation of history, he falls back on mythology and allegory, are those from which Correggio took a lead when, in the 16th century, setting his face against Raphael's classical composition and Michelangelo's tragically emotive idealization, he turned towards an art of delicate shades of feeling, motifs lightly touched on, hinted at rather than revealed—in a word, a thoroughly anti-classical type of art. It is easy to see why 16th-century Venetians regarded Mantegna's work as "cold and lifeless" (Dolce's description of them), and indeed their philological, antiquarian classicism was at a far remove from Giorgione's impassioned vision. Yet we must not forget that the robust exuberance and poetic classicism of Titian's art would be unthinkable had not Mantegna with his "experiment in history" prepared the way for it, and it was this historical sense that, despite the intervention of Giorgione's lyricism, Titian recaptured.

THE FERRARESE PAINTERS

That Mantegna's classicism meant more than a mere observance of academic canons is proved by the strangely composite art produced by the Ferrarese painters when they combined Mantegna's procedures with those of Piero and the Flemish school, which Rogier van der Weyden in person made known to them. It might, however, be said that the art of Ferrara was a matter of subtraction rather than addition; each of its elements was stripped of all doctrinal accretions in contact with the others and made to reveal its essential, underlying qualities. The Ferrarese had little liking for the naturalism of Flemish art or for its reliance on empirical experience in the handling of details; nor did Piero's theory of perspective and form commend itself to them. As for Mantegna, what interested them in him was less his classicism than his tragic sense of life and his human feeling.

The works of Cosimo Tura, Francesco del Cossa and Ercole da Roberti and the Palazzo Schifanoia frescos—*summa* of Ferrarese Renaissance art—reveal a clearly Nordic, medieval outlook on the world. And whenever this is directed on the historical conceptions of the Renaissance, it transforms myth and history into astrology, rationalism into sophistry, systems of knowledge into flights of fancy.

Cosimo Tura spent his formative years at Padua and his contribution to Renaissance art was a reflection of the medieval spirit at its most anti-realistic. He had no wish to express the drama in human life, the mental and moral anguish of thinking man; what he aimed at was the sudden crystallization, in an abstract, hypothetical space, of forms forever changing in the course of time. Associated as it was with a tradition that found expression solely in the form of rhythm, Piero's art gave Tura a lead—but in the opposite direction. Turning his back on balance and proportion, he broke up the even flow of the composition so as to secure the exotic effects and elegant surprises of a deftly dislocated rhythm. Almost one might say that in a spirit of defiance he practises a sort of antilogic; his line swerves off abruptly where one would expect it to adhere, forms are curiously twisted or cut short where normally they would fuse into the composition, ingenious discords enrich the color orchestration. Here form is,

FRANCESCO DEL COSSA (CA. 1435-CA. 1477) AND ASSISTANTS. ALLEGORY OF THE MONTH OF APRIL (DETAIL), CA. 1470. FRESCO, PALAZZO SCHIFANOIA, FERRARA.

and is meant to be, "absurd"; but the absurd, too, has a coherence that sophisticated minds can appreciate. The problem of form is inverted; form is no longer viewed as the product of an intellectual operation that starting out from the material datum transcends it, but as an invitation, still more subtly intellectual, to see, in this transfiguration of matter, the *nec plus ultra* of metaphysics. So we have come full circle and are back where we started, at a demonstration of the vanity of human thought. Expressions on faces and physical suffering at its most intense are still depicted, but are sublimated on to an abstract plane and contemplated with that curious aesthetic aloofness which comes of an extremity of pain and transforms its pangs into the symbolic movements of the dance.

One of the best of the painters who worked on the Schifanoia frescos, Francesco del Cossa left Ferrara in 1470 and settled at Bologna. Less subtle, less original than Tura's, his art conveys an impression of greater sensitivity. He, too, drew inspiration from those two pathfinders of Ferrarese art, Piero and Mantegna, and their joint influence shows in his clean-cut composition, the purity of his light and color, a consum-

FRANCESCO DEL COSSA (CA. 1435-CA. 1477) AND ASSISTANTS. ALLEGORY OF THE MONTH OF APRIL (DETAIL), CA. 1470. FRESCO, PALAZZO SCHIFANOIA, FERRARA.

mate harmony between rhythm and structure, movement and monumental expression. He simplifies Tura's restlessly emotional art and explores a new range of feelings, sometimes achieving vividly dramatic effects by the crystalline clarity of the contours of his forms. His perspective creates a novel kind of space, a sort of magnetic field in which, as if by magic, realism and abstraction coalesce.

Ercole da Roberti took over the procedures of Francesco del Cossa, but carried a stage further the latter's tendency towards a narrative art imbued with keen sensibility. In the altarpiece he painted in 1481 for the Church of Santa Maria in Porto near Ravenna (now in the Brera, Milan), outlines are vibrant, forms seem permeated by the ambient air, colors acquire a curiously throbbing vitality and new tonalities. As Gamba has pointed out, we here can see the gradual infiltration into Ferrarese painting—hermetic, charged with magic overtones in its earlier phase—of the warm colors and emotive accents of such painters as Giovanni Bellini. In his later work, Roberti (influenced perhaps by Melozzo da Forli) developed a monumental form of expression and a solemnity in the presentation of his themes reminiscent of Mantegna.

In the productions of Lorenzo Costa the magical element in the art of Ferrara disappears altogether. This is perhaps less apparent in his first phase when he was under Tura's influence, but is plain to see in the works produced at Mantua and Bologna. For after following a path parallel to Ercole da Roberti's, he turned aside from Ferrarese sources of inspiration towards the mellifluous rhythms of Perugino and Francia.

The first sign of a revival of art in Lombardy was the fresco cycle of *The Life of St Peter Martyr* in the Church of Sant'Eustorgio, Milan. These frescos are now by common consent attributed to Vincenzo Foppa. In his *Crucifixion* (1456), now in the Bergamo Museum, this artist pointed the way to a new treatment of plastic volumes in his dramatic accentuation of masses plunged in light. As Longhi has observed, this innovation had far-reaching effects on the evolution of 15th-century painting at Brescia. In Milan, on the other hand, the humanist art trend—illustrated both by the rough-hewn forms of Butinone and Zenale, and by those, more elegant, of Bergognone—was wholly deflected from its course by the impact of Leonardo's art.

ANTONELLO DA MESSINA

The transition from Mantegna's "cold and lifeless" painting to Titian's sensual exuberance was largely the work of those two great artists, Giovanni Bellini and Giorgione. Nevertheless, a considerable share in bringing about this change of heart must be attributed to the stay in Venice in 1475 of a Sicilian, Antonello da Messina.

In order to account for the flowering of this fine painter's art in surroundings which, if not absolutely provincial, were so far from all the great art centers, Vasari thought up a story to the effect that Antonello had visited Flanders and been initiated into the mysteries of oil painting and learnt how to give his colors their characteristic softness. Recently Longhi has seen in Piero's art the origin of the amazing plenitude of forms and volumes we find in Antonello's painting, and thus explains the obvious links between Venetian and Central Italian art.

Modern research-work (by Lauts, Bottari, and Fiocco) has ruled out the possibility of Antonello's having been to Flanders; the most that can be said is that he was trained in a milieu much influenced by Flemish art, as was then the case with Southern Italy and Naples. Nor does it seem that Piero's art had any direct influence on Antonello; it reached him at second hand, perhaps through Francesco Laurana, a sculptor who had worked at Urbino and whose perfectly proportioned forms, burnished as it were by light, show that he had studied Piero's work to good effect.

Naturalism is not an adequate explanation of Flemish art; there is certainly more, far more, to it than that. But this was an idea that was current in Florence in the second half of the Quattrocento, and Flemish naturalism was regarded as the antithesis of the Florentine art ideal. For Tuscan Renaissance art derived from intellectual research, whereas that of the Northerners was based on empirical observation. The essential difference between naturalism and intellectualism was clearly stated by Michelangelo in the *Dialogues* transcribed by Francisco de Hollanda. And though he did not share Michelangelo's views, Leonardo, too, took it for granted that the ideals of Flemish and Florentine art were incompatible.

COSIMO TURA (?-1495). ST GEORGE AND THE DRAGON (DETAIL).
FRESCO, FERRARA CATHEDRAL.

Even his earliest works show that it was not owing to any revelation, whether direct or otherwise, of Piero's art that Antonello broke with a tradition which by now had lost its driving force. There is no difference in quality, no indication of any sudden change of outlook, in the works showing signs of Flemish influence and those of his later period. All alike evince a keen interest in form and an equal sureness of execution. The setting of the Sibiu *Crucifixion* is a far-flung landscape steeped in light, stretching out towards a turquoise-blue sea that blends into the azure of the sky. In *St Jerome in his Study*, on the other hand, the scene is staged in a closed room seen through the doorway, and here the picture space is divided up into compartments, by the desk, the shelves and a portico seen in perspective. It seems clear that the painter knew nothing of the practice and principles of the Florentines as regards the architectonic ordering of space and the necessity for it to be homogeneous; that in fact he was not working to any given theory. Yet all the same he clearly realized the need for unifying the space presented in the picture, if by means of an almost physical order. Taking his lead from the Flemish painters, he treated space as a *locus*, a predetermined and restricted area, within which all the objects represented link up with one another in an elaborate network of relations.

Space for Antonello is no more than a condition of the co-existence of the various picture elements; a condition, moreover, thanks to which the painter can give all the objects he depicts, however different, equal importance and an equal value. This shows that he had grasped what was in fact the guiding principle of Flemish painting: its fondness for an enclave marked off from the outside world by well-defined boundaries, within which each thing is at once itself and everything, at once particular and universal. Here we have the metaphysical—as opposed to the naturalistic—aspect of Flemish art; that which enables it to invest each place, no matter how prosaic, with an aura of transcendence, and every object with a mystical significance.

From the start of his career Antonello concerned himself with problems of this order; he did not aim at an objective or literal representation of things but at revealing their inmost being, their undisclosed quintessence. To his mind, harmony or unity whether of space or form should naturally arise from the assemblage of the various pictorial elements, and not from the use of any *a priori* formula, however scientific. When in *The Crucifixion*, for example, he raises the horizon-line, this is not only in order to make room for the detailed depiction of a landscape background; it at once enables him to create an effective backdrop and to reveal, in terms of color, the depth of space, its *density*. Behind the three crosses in the foreground stretches a landscape seen across a transparent medium, much as the pebbly bed of a mountain stream can be seen through the clear water. We feel that the artist's chief concern here is to make us conscious of this intervening medium; that imponderable, omnipresent substance which saturates the air and envelops figures, so that we see them like twigs within a block of ice. This medium in *The Crucifixion* is flooding, dazzling light; in the *St Jerome* a warm, reposeful dusk. But both alike create a *locus conclusus* in which objects are transformed automatically into "images" without being subjected to the intellectual

ANTONELLO DA MESSINA (1430?-1479). ST JEROME IN HIS STUDY. (18 × 14 ¼″)
BY COURTESY OF THE TRUSTEES, NATIONAL GALLERY, LONDON.

process of representation. These paintings make us realize even more clearly how the Florentine artists always viewed their subjects in terms of action, and life as a "becoming," whereas Antonello sees his subjects always in terms of "being."

The Cefalù *Portrait of a Man* and the Munich *Virgin of the Annunciation* likewise illustrate this will to identify the representation of the motifs with that of space, though here there is an inversion of the procedure described above. The figures are shown in close-up and there is no indication of the setting. They create their own space, their own third dimension and frame of reference. All "accidentals" that might obtrude are suppressed, so that the image has the same depth and density throughout. Such contrasts of light and shade as exist are only in the over-all texture of the setting; both figures and the atmospheric medium are enveloped in a very gentle vibration of the picture surface, implemented in *The Virgin of the Annunciation* by a quivering of the hands, the Virgin's parted lips and quiet breathing; in the *Portrait of a Man* by his enigmatic smile and stubbly cheeks. The artist manifests his interest in detail not, as formerly, through a diversity of observed facts, but by his selection of a specific moment—characterized in the *Portrait* by the man's intriguing smile; in the picture of the Virgin by her meek, rapt gaze and a faint movement of her hands.

The San Gregorio polyptych (1473) proves beyond all doubt that Antonello must have been acquainted with Piero's art. Here he has obviously sought to portray figures monumentally and to create an equal balance between voids and masses. True, we still find the same continuity and unity of form and space, but from now on Antonello aims at creating a metrical equivalence between them, based on a relation of proportions. When we observe, for instance, the way perspective is handled in the steps of the throne, we see that he is not seeking to convey recession in depth but to geometrize their form. In the Syracuse *Annunciation* the *raison d'être* of the pillar in the foreground (a motif certainly derived from Piero) is to emphasize the softness of the chiaroscuro and the shimmering texture of the air, and also by means of the cylindrical shaft to suggest unity of volume as against the fluidity of the atmosphere. But it is clear that this dense space—almost, one might say, congealed in a crystalline translucency—is not governed by any law of symmetry; it is laid out in terms of a foreshortening that deviates, if only very slightly, from the axial line of vision. In his *Salvator Mundi* (National Gallery, London) and the Palermo *Virgin of the Annunciation* the perspective elements—the outstretched hands and the desk—are so presented as to convey an impression, just a hint, of asymmetry. Antonello does not aim solely at creating a spatial structure valid for all time and in all circumstances, but also at defining a special case, a particular spatial condition linking up with a subjective, even temporary condition. It is the outcome, on the intellectual plane, of that factual empiricism whose lesson Antonello had so well grasped—and spiritualized. Space for him was no longer a system but a fact of sensory experience and therefore under certain circumstances its substance might change, though not its value, and such was its value as an element of man's awareness of the world that it conferred on the particular the quality of the universal. This explains why Antonello ranks so high as a portrait painter and it is, in fact, in his portraits that his conceptions of form and space are most clearly indicated. For since Space is the ultimate intellectual form of human experience, it has no configuration other than that which man assigns to it. And in this respect Antonello went far beyond the anthropocentrism of the humanists.

When he was at Venice in 1475 Antonello painted the San Cassiano altarpiece. What little has survived of the work (now in Vienna) shows that here the artist turned the technical proficiency he had acquired in the course of his career to brilliant account. Renouncing once for all the intimate charm of his earlier manner, when he was under Flemish influence, he now aimed at monumental composition and liturgic majesty. The same applies to the Antwerp *Crucifixion*. Whereas in the Sibiu *Crucifixion* space was rendered by colored fragments, honey-combed as in cloisonné work, it is given in the Antwerp version a depth that is inherent in the color, in its vibrancy and translucency, the result being a muted, over-all animation and a mysterious accord with the human emotions quickened by the scene.

The influence of this phase of Antonello's art on the evolution of Venetian painting in general, and in particular on that of Giovanni Bellini, will be discussed hereafter. But the influence was reciprocal, and Antonello's *St Sebastian* (Dresden) owes something to the pioneer work that was being done by Giovanni Bellini and Mantegna during the same period. No doubt his quest of an ideal proportion in this picture is far more reminiscent of Piero than of Mantegna; yet we must not forget that, but for Mantegna's humanistic interpretation of visual experience, Antonello might well have failed to perceive the profoundly classical implications of Piero's art. The full-bodied form telling out against the crystal-clear outlines of the houses is intended not to suggest plastic values, but to calibrate space in terms of density and luminosity of color. In short, Antonello's chief contribution to the art culture of the Renaissance was this demonstration that it is possible to give the idea of Space—an eminently intellectual concept, "form" *par excellence*—without recourse to rationalism, which involves not merely critical detachment but a certain aloofness from visual actuality.

In Venetian architecture of the 14th and early 15th century we still find the linear rhythms of Gothic decoration intermingled with Byzantine color, which had lost nothing of its appeal. In painting, too, Jacobello da Fiore and Michele Giambono heightened the effect of their clean-cut linear patterns with a wealth of rich, translucent colors. But the first Venetian painters to turn to account the innovations in the handling of form which the Florentines had brought to Padua and Venice were Jacopo Bellini, who had worked as an apprentice under Gentile da Fabriano, and Antonio Vivarini. All the same they failed to grasp the full significance of the new discoveries and (for example) saw in the perspective rendering of space no more than a means of including in the picture a larger range of incidents and a greater variety of colors. Meanwhile Carlo Crivelli, who made no secret of his debt to Mantegna, demonstrated the possibilities of a new handling of that master's forms after divorcing them from their classical and ideological premisses. The effect achieved was one of decorative abstraction, uneasily united with an expressive but artificial forcefulness.

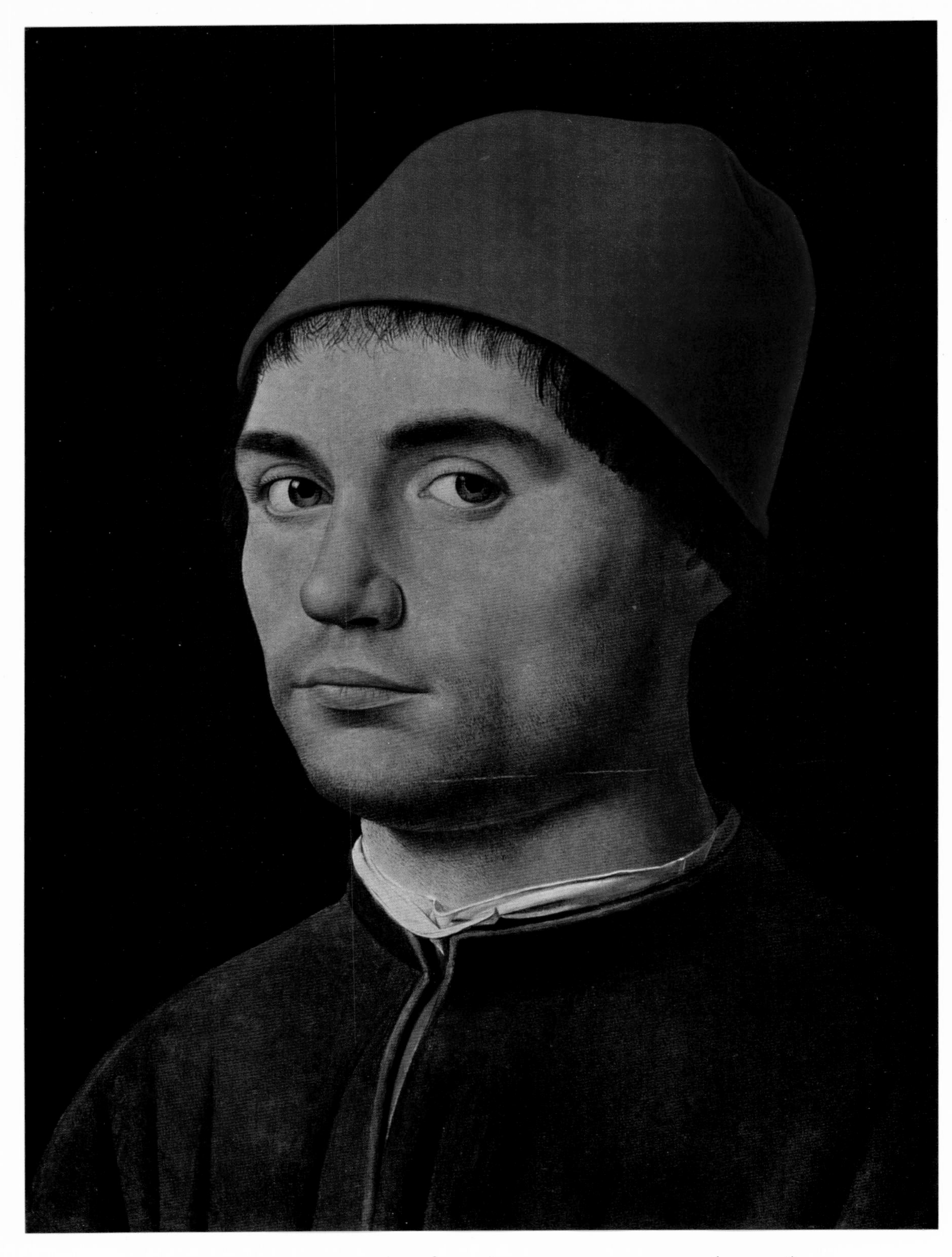

ANTONELLO DA MESSINA (1430?-1479). PORTRAIT OF A MAN. (14×10″)
BY COURTESY OF THE TRUSTEES, NATIONAL GALLERY, LONDON.

GIOVANNI BELLINI (CA. 1430-1516). PORTRAIT OF THE DOGE LEONARDO LOREDAN (FRAGMENT).
BY COURTESY OF THE TRUSTEES, NATIONAL GALLERY, LONDON.

GIOVANNI BELLINI

To Gentile and especially Giovanni Bellini, even more than to Bartolomeo Vivarini, was due the new direction given to Venetian painting at this time. Not that Gentile went deeply into the problems of perspective; all he did was, starting out from his father Jacopo's use of perspective in his vistas of idealized architecture, to apply these principles to a detailed treatment of landscape. His big pictures are crowded with tiny scenes of contemporary life, anticipating in some ways the neatly arranged landscapes, known as *vedute*, which delighted the Venetians in the next century. In his work perspective served two purposes. It provided the *veduta* with a new dimension, that of depth, thanks to which the "story" could be told more fully. And, secondly, it enabled him to harmonize light and figures in a sequence of luminous surfaces (mostly buildings) which acted at once as sources of light and as backdrops. Within this deep expanse of open space the play of light lent animation to the motley crowds thronging piazze and canals. In Gentile's predilection for the contemporary scene we have perhaps an aftermath of that taste for representations of courtly-social life which had characterized Late Gothic. Actually, however, his interest in the immediate present was far more spontaneous and alert than that of the Gothics—as is proved by his lively renderings of what he saw on his visit to Constantinople. He had no qualms about enlivening his narratives with fragments of "low life," nor had he the slightest wish to present incidents and figures *sub specie aeternitatis*; he simply wished to portray the social scene exactly as he saw it.

Gentile's brother Giovanni Bellini, on the other hand, brought the rendering of form to a perfection unmatched by any other 15th-century Venetian, and it was he who pointed the way to that "classical" painting in the grand manner which was one of the most striking achievements of Venetian art in the next century. We have already spoken of his debt to Mantegna, whose austerity and crystalline purity of form attracted him so strongly; as also did Mantegna's narrative art, at once as dignified as a Latin oration and intensely emotional. Nevertheless he was quite unimpressed by the erudition, the persistent emphasis on history, and the rigorously logical formulas in which Mantegna took such pride. Giovanni Bellini's handling of religious themes was totally different. Instead of conveying his message by way of maxims and examples culled from the past, he built up a mythology that was not classical but Christian, and sought to persuade not by logic but by an appeal to the feelings. But this "appeal to the feelings" —like naturalism and the imaging of nature—needed an historical context to sponsor it; and in fact, whether deliberately or not, Bellini conformed to the ideas of the new school of humanists who, following the lead of Almorò Barbaro, were turning away from the logic of the philosophers and the careful erudition of the schoolmen, and seeking to elicit the "glamour" of antiquity rather than its history. What interested them far more than the epic tales of legendary heroes was the intuitive understanding of nature shown by the ancients. It was in fact due to Bellini that the word "nature" came to have a positive, active meaning and ceased being regarded merely as an antithesis of "the idea" or an object of intellectual cognition. No doubt nature could be conceived of only in relation to man, but it was something more than an indispensable scene of his activities. Nature gave a ready welcome to the soul which, escaping from the prison-house of the particular, aspired to be merged into the All. There and only there the secret yearnings of the heart found a response, and a satisfying, if inexplicable, balance was achieved between the outer world and the human soul; man was at peace in an environment where, miraculously, time and space were unified.

This explains why Giovanni Bellini was eminently a contemplative, indifferent to drama and action. His religious sentiment led him to humanize his divine figures and to discover an underlying harmony between them and nature, which was illuminated and elucidated by their apparition. The humanist element in his outlook makes itself felt supremely in his ability to convert the Christian mythos into a naturalistic myth. In this respect his painting is no less classical than Mantegna's, but already in his classicism we detect a vein of profound sadness and the rankling unrest soon to be symptomatic of a certain decadence. The most characteristic work of this phase (which might be described as Bellini's elegiac period) is the Brera *Pietà* (ca. 1470). In the foreground the figures stand out behind a marble slab against the dying light,

GIOVANNI BELLINI (CA. 1430-1516). SACRED ALLEGORY, CA. 1490. (28¾×46¾") UFFIZI, FLORENCE.

a prolongation into infinite space of the unutterable sadness of the Mother giving her Son the last embrace. To this profoundly human emotion corresponds the forlorn beauty of the landscape background.

The altarpiece of *The Coronation of the Virgin* (Museo Civico, Pesaro) was given the date of 1473 by Longhi, and he sees in it a turning-point in Giovanni Bellini's artistic career. We find in it a still deeper research into the harmony between nature, *qua* myth, and space, *qua* schematic concept. When we recall the importance assigned to nature in his earlier work, we can easily see why Bellini's art developed on these lines. He did not make a geometrical conception of space his starting-point and then proceed to an empirical observation of the natural scene but, on the contrary, transformed the naturalistic myth into a spatial myth. Even later works such as the *Sacred Allegory* in the Uffizi show that by then space had come to mean to him the intellectual-allegorical form of nature. Sponsoring as it did a concord between the soul of man and the outside world, nature was interpreted by him in terms of "sympathies" of colors. Perspective, he felt, could not be indicated by line alone; it was by means of color relations that depth and spatial structure were rendered to best effect. Thus color and its mutations became the very substance, not merely the superficies, of the thing portrayed.

In the Pesaro altarpiece, the white back of the throne which frames the background landscape acts also as a luminous screen and links up the figures with space. The effect of recessive depth is suggested by color relations or, more exactly, by the quantity of light present in the quality of the colors. It would seem that Bellini was the first artist to apprehend the possibility of representing space by means of tonal relations, but—and this is distinctive of his art—he associated with the universal character of spatial form a particular tone of light, and this was always an emotive tone.

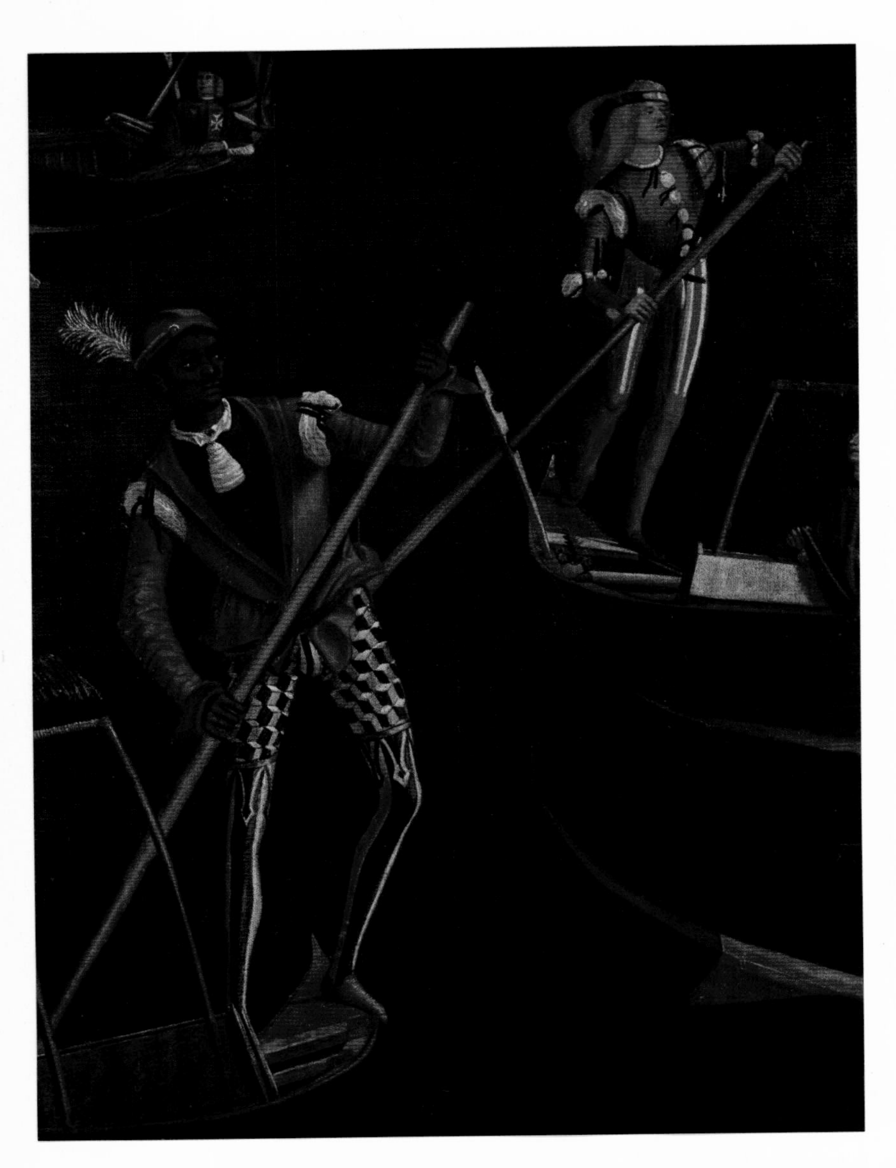

VITTORE CARPACCIO (1455?-1525).
THE MIRACLE OF THE CROSS (DETAIL).
GALLERIE DELL'ACCADEMIA, VENICE.

VITTORE CARPACCIO (1455?-1525). THE ARRIVAL OF THE AMBASSADORS,
DETAIL FROM THE LEGEND OF ST URSULA, 1491-1495. GALLERIE DELL'ACCADEMIA, VENICE.

The Naples *Transfiguration* constitutes another landmark in Bellini's art. Figures are symmetrically disposed and a skillful arrangement of clearly defined planes, refracting and reflecting one another, creates an impression that these figures are mirrored, in an almost literal sense *inter se*. No longer represented in the archaic nudity of its geological structure, the landscape is clothed with grassy fields and flowers and animated by human presences. The "tense" is changed; here the eternal past has been converted into an eternal present, in the same way as the ancient moral code, handed down from generation to generation, is superseded by a new and kindlier morality, an ethic of the heart. Masterly illustrations of Bellini's allegorical naturalism are the Uffizi *Sacred Allegory* and the Venice *Allegories*, which also stress the transition from Mantegna's historical ethic to that conception of a "natural" ethic which enabled the 16th-century masters to ascribe to sensory experience the value of a direct source of knowledge and of the intellectual apprehension of reality.

The San Giobbe altarpiece (in Venice) has much in common with Antonello's San Cassiano altarpiece, but in the former Bellini advances beyond Antonello's humanism and the exact balance between man and nature he achieved. Here Bellini aims at setting forth a new value which, making naturalism its starting-point, affirms the primacy of the human element. Thus he no longer represents a vast open expanse but stages the action in an alcove adorned with gold mosaic-work and gleaming marble. In it reigns a half-light filled with broken gleams of vivid color summoned forth by light reflected from the marble and the gold. This light enfolds figures, seeps into forms and colors, and the fusion of space and figures creates a new monumentality. Emotions, too, are given a new direction, towards a mental attitude that finds expression not in action but in contemplation.

This is the period of the Madonnas whose gaze seems so strangely remote, held by an inner vision; of those *Sacre Conversazioni* in which the intimate communion between forms and nature creates a mood of hushed repose; of portraits which already bear the stamp of that vague disquietude and sadness we associate with Giorgione's figures. It is in the big San Zaccaria altarpiece (1505) at Venice that Bellini's art comes nearest Giorgione's. Much the same as that of the San Giobbe altarpiece, its composition gives the effect of a greater spaciousness and there is a richer vibrancy in the modulations of light and atmosphere. Figures seem enveloped in a haze of golden dust, form is created by tonal relations, and ceremonial formalism superseded by poetic overtones, evoked by the all-pervading harmony between man and nature.

Bellini's later works such as the San Giovanni Crisostomo altarpiece (Venice) and the *Feast of the Gods* (Washington) painted in 1514 for Alfonso d'Este illustrate both his final compositional technique, that of painting by tonal values, and the tendency of the new humanism to discern in "the poetry of nature" what was most rewarding in the heritage of antiquity. And here we have the two chief elements of the art of Giorgione and that of Titian in his youth. There was in fact no break whatever between Mantegna's austere classicism and the emotive classicism, full of Hellenistic reminiscences, that characterized Venetian painting in the early 16th century.

Vittore Carpaccio, however, who was more in sympathy with Gentile Bellini, seems to have shut his eyes to Giovanni Bellini's formal innovations. In fact he played much the same part in Venice as Ghirlandaio played in Florence at about the same time. A keen observer and charming story-teller, Carpaccio pictured the everyday life of Venice under the aspect of a fairytale. In *The Legend of St Ursula* (1491-1495) and *Scenes of the Life of St George* he showed how the color-light employed by Bellini for his rendering of space could be applied to a lively narrative full of realistic touches. Thus he deflected Bellini's art towards a more vivacious manner of expression, more accessible to the general public and often with a frankly popular appeal. And so discarding once for all the fragile metaphysical framework of the myth, he created one of the most attractive narrative cycles of the entire Renaissance.

VITTORE CARPACCIO

VITTORE CARPACCIO (1455?-1525). KING DEONOTUS DISMISSING THE AMBASSADORS, DETAIL FROM THE LEGEND OF ST URSULA, 1491-1495. GALLERIE DELL'ACCADEMIA, VENICE.

BIBLIOGRAPHY

INDEX OF NAMES

LIST OF COLORPLATES

SELECTED BIBLIOGRAPHY

FLEMISH PAINTING

GENERAL

C. VAN MANDER, *Het Schilderboeck*, Haarlem 1604. (French translation by H. HYMANS, *Le livre des peintres*, 1884; English translation in C. VAN DE WALL, *Dutch and Flemish Painters*, New York 1936). — KRAMM, *De levens en werken der Hollandsche en Vlaamsche Kunstschilders*, Amsterdam 1856-1863. — DE BUSSCHER, *Recherches sur les peintres gantois des XIVe et XVe siècles*, Ghent 1859. — C. BLANC, *Histoire des Peintres, école flamande*, Paris 1864. — MICHIELS, *Histoire de la Peinture flamande*, 11 vols., Paris 1865-1878. — CROWE & CAVALCASELLE, *The Early Flemish Painters*, 2nd edition, London 1872. — A. WAUTERS, *La peinture flamande*, Paris 1883. — G. HULIN DE LOO, *Catalogue critique de l'exposition de Bruges*, Ghent 1902. — M. J. FRIEDLÄNDER, *Von Van Eyck bis Breughel*, Berlin 1921. — F. WINKLER, *Die altniederländische Malerei*, Berlin 1924. — M. J. FRIEDLÄNDER, *Die altniederländische Malerei*, 14 vols., Berlin-Leyden 1924-1937. — H. FIERENS-GEVAERT & P. FIERENS, *Histoire de la peinture flamande des origines jusqu'à la fin du XVe siècle*, 3 vol., Brussels 1927-1930. — R. FRY, *Flemish Art: A Critical Study*, New York 1927. — P. LAMBOTTE, *Flemish Painting before the 18th Century*, London 1927. — M. ROOSES, *Art in Flanders*, New York 1931. — WERF, *Vlaamsche Kunst en Italiaansche Renaissance*, Malines 1935. — J. LAVALLEYE & A. VERMEYLEN, in *Geschiedenis van de Vlaamsche Kunst*, Antwerp 1936-1937. — J. LAVALLEYE, *La peinture et l'enluminure des origines à la fin du XVe siècle* in *L'art en Belgique du Moyen Age à nos jours*, publié sous la direction de P. FIERENS, Brussels 1939. — J. LAVALLEYE, *Le portrait au XVe siècle*, Brussels 1945. — Martin DAVIES, National Gallery catalogues: *Early Netherlandish School*, London 1946. — P. FIERENS, *Le fantastique dans l'art flamand*, Brussels 1947. — H. B. WEHLE & M SALINGER, *Catalogue of Early Flemish, Dutch and German Paintings*, Metropolitan Museum, New York 1947. — *Dictionnaire des peintres*, preface by P. FIERENS, notices on the 15th-century painters by R. CAZIER & R. L. DELEVOY, Brussels 1950. — J. VAN DER ELST, *L'âge d'or flamand*, Paris 1951. — A. JANSSENS DE BISTHOVEN & R. A. PARMENTIER, *Le Musée Communal de Bruges*, Antwerp 1951. — J. G. LEMOINE, *Les peintres primitifs sous un aspect nouveau*, Bordeaux 1952. — C. ARU & E. DE GERADON, *Les primitifs flamands: la Galerie Sabauda de Turin*, Antwerp 1952. — E. PANOFSKY, *Early Netherlandish Painting*, Harvard University Press, Cambridge, Mass., 1953. — J. LAVALLEYE, *Répertoire des peintures flamandes des XVe et XVIe siècles: collections d'Espagne*, Antwerp 1953. — R. GENAILLE, *De Van Eyck à Bruegel*, Paris 1954. — Martin DAVIES, *Les Primitifs flamands: The National Gallery of London*, Antwerp 1954, 2 vols.

THE PROBLEM OF THE BROTHERS VAN EYCK

K. VOLL, *Die Werke des Jan van Eyck, eine kritische Studie*, Strasbourg 1900. — J. WEALE, *Hubert and John van Eyck, Their Life and Work*, London 1908. — G. HULIN DE LOO, *Les Heures de Milan*, Brussels 1911. — J. WEALE, *The Van Eycks and Their Art*, London, New York & Toronto 1912. — M. CONWAY, *The Van Eycks and Their Followers*, London 1912. — F. WINKLER, *Der Genter Altar von Hubert und Jan van Eyck*, Leipzig 1921. — M. J. FRIEDLÄNDER, *Die altniederländische Malerei*, vol. 1, Berlin 1924. — A. SCHMARSOW, *Hubert und Jan van Eyck*, Leipzig 1924. — M. DVORAK, *Das Rätsel der Kunst der Brüder van Eyck*, Munich 1925. — M. DEVIGNE, *Van Eyck*, Brussels-Paris 1926. — E. DE BRUYN, *La collaboration des frères van Eyck dans le retable de l'"Adoration de l'Agneau"*, in *Mélanges Hulin de Loo*, Brussels 1931. — P. FIERENS, *Jean van Eyck*, Brussels 1931. — L. SCHEWE, *Hubert und Jan van Eyck*, The Hague 1933. — E. RENDERS, *Hubert van Eyck, personnage de légende*, Brussels 1933; id., *Jean van Eyck, son œuvre, son style, son évolution*, Bruges 1935. — C. H. POUTHIAS, *Découverte du secret des Van Eyck*, in *L'Amour de l'Art*, June 1935. — O. KERBER, *Hubert van Eyck*, Frankfort 1937. — C. DE TOLNAY, *Le retable de l'Agneau mystique des frères Van Eyck*, Brussels 1938. — H. BEENKEN, *Hubert und Jan van Eyck*, Munich 1941. — J. DUVERGER, *Het Grafschrift van Hubert van Eyck en het Quatrain van het Gentsche Lam Gods-Retabel*, in *Verhandelingen van de Koninklijke Vlaamsche Academie voor Wetenschapen, Letteren en Schoone Kunsten*, VII, 4, Antwerp & Utrecht, 1945. — P. COREMANS & A. JANSSENS DE BISTHOVEN, *Van Eyck, l'Adoration de l'Agneau mystique*, Antwerp 1945. — L. VAN PUYVELDE, *L'Agneau mystique*, Paris 1946. — A. H. CORNETTE, *De Portretten van Jan van Eyck*, Antwerp 1947. — A. ZILOTY, *La découverte de Jean van Eyck*, Paris 1947. — S. SELZBERGER, *La Sainte Barbe de Jean van Eyck*, in *Gazette des Beaux-Arts*, 1948. — A. SJOBLOM, *Quelques réflexions sur le chœur des Anges et les citronniers du Retable de Saint-Bavon*, in *Miscellanea Leo van Puyvelde*, 1949. — E. RENDERS, *Jean van Eyck et le Polyptyque, deux problèmes résolus*, Brussels 1950. — L. BALDASS, *The Ghent Altarpiece of Hubert and Jan van Eyck*, in *Art Quarterly* XIII, 1950; id., *Jan van Eyck*, London 1952. — A. DE SCHRIJVER & R. MARIJNISSEN, *De vorspronkelijke plaats van het Lam Gods-Retabel*, Antwerp 1952. — L. COREMANS, *L'Agneau mystique au laboratoire*, Antwerp 1953. — E. PANOFSKY, *Early Netherlandish Painting*, Chap. VII-VIII, Harvard University Press, 1953. — V. DENIS, *Tutta la pittura di Jan van Eyck*, Milan 1954.

THE MASTER OF FLÉMALLE - ROGIER VAN DER WEYDEN

A. WAUTERS, *Roger van der Weyden, ses œuvres, ses élèves et ses descendants*, Brussels 1856. — A. PINCHART, *Roger de la Pasture dit Van der Weyden*, Brussels 1876. — K. VON TSCHUDI, *Der Meister von Flémalle*, in *Jahrbuch der Königlich Preussischen Kunstsammlungen*, XIX, 1898. — FIRMENICH-RICHARTZ, *Rogier van der Weyden, der Meister von Flémalle*, in *Zeitschrift für bildende Kunst*, 1898-1899. — P. LAFOND, *Roger van der Weyden*, Brussels 1912. — F. WINKLER, *Der Meister von Flémalle und Roger van der Weyden*, Strasbourg 1913. — MAETERLINCK, *Le Maître de Flémalle et l'école gantoise primitive*, in *Gazette des Beaux-Arts*, 1913. — M. HOUTART, *Quel est l'état de nos connaissances relativement à Campin, Jacques Daret et Roger van der Weyden?*, (Communication faite au XXIIIe Congrès de la Fédération archéologique), Ghent 1914. — M. J. FRIEDLÄNDER, *Die altniederländische Malerei*, vol. II, Berlin 1924, and vol. XIV, Leyden 1937. — VERHAEGEN, *Le polyptyque de Beaune*, in *Congrès archéologique de France*, XCI, 1928. — P. JAMOT, in *Gazette des Beaux-Arts* 1928. — J. DESTRÉE, *Roger de la Pasture-van der Weyden*, 2 vols., Paris and Brussels 1930. — E. RENDERS, *La solution du problème Van der Weyden-Flémalle-Campin*, 2 vols., Bruges 1931. — M. J. FRIEDLÄNDER, in *Pantheon* 1931. — P. ROLLAND, *Les Primitifs tournaisiens*, Brussels 1932. — J. LAVALLEYE, *Le problème*

Maître de Flémalle-Rogier van der Weyden, in *Revue belge de philologie et d'histoire*, XII, 1933. — HULIN DE LOO, *Roger van der Weyden*, in *Biographie Nationale de Belgique*, vol. XXVII, Brussels 1938. — C. DE TOLNAY, *Le Maître de Flémalle et les frères Van Eyck*, Brussels 1938. — P. ROLLAND, *Het drieluik der Zeven Sacramenten van Roger van der Weyden*, in *Annuaire du Musée Royal des Beaux-Arts*, Antwerp 1942-1947. — MEYER SHAPIRO, *The Symbolism of the Mérode Altarpiece*, in *Art Bulletin*, XXVII, 1945. — E. MICHEL, *Roger van der Weyden*, Paris & Berne 1945. — P. ROLLAND, *Découvertes de peintures murales à Tournai*, in *Phoebus*, No. 3-4, 1946. — T. MUSPER, *Untersuchungen zu Roger van der Weyden und Jan van Eyck*, Stuttgart 1948. — VOGELSANG, *Rogier van der Weyden, Pietà: Form and Color*, New York (1949). — P. WESCHER, *Eine unbekannte Madonna von Rogier van der Weyden*, in *Phoebus* 1949, No. 3. — F. J. SANCHEZ CANTON, *Un gran cuadro de Van der Weyden resucitado*, in *Miscellanea Leo van Puyvelde*, Brussels 1949. — J. HELD, *Ambroise Benson et le Maître de Flémalle*, in *Les Arts plastiques*, May-June 1949. — J. MAQUET-TOMBU, *Autour de la « Descente de Croix » de Roger*, in *Bulletin de la Société Royale d'Archéologie*, Brussels, July 1949; id., *Les tableaux de justice de Roger van der Weyden à l'Hôtel de Ville de Bruxelles*, in *Phoebus* 1949, No. 4. — E. PANOFSKY, *Early Netherlandish Painting*, chap. VI, IX, Harvard University Press, 1953.

PETRUS CHRISTUS

J. WEALE, *Peintres brugeois, Les Christus*, Bruges 1909. — M. J. FRIEDLÄNDER, *Die altniederländische Malerei*, vol. I, Berlin 1924; id., *The Death of the Virgin by Petrus Christus*, in *Burlington Magazine*, June 1946. — SIMONE BERGMANS, *Portrait de femme*, in *La Peinture ancienne*, 1952. — G. BAZIN, *Petrus Christus et les rapports italo-flamands*, in *Revue des Arts*, 1952.

DIRK BOUTS

A. WAUTERS, *Thierry Bouts de Haarlem et ses fils*, Brussels 1863. — VAN EVEN, *Monographie de l'ancienne école de peinture de Louvain*, in *Le Messager des Sciences historiques*, XXXIV, 1866. — A. GOFFIN, *Thierry Bouts*, Paris & Brussels 1908. — M. J. FRIEDLÄNDER, *Die altniederländische Malerei*, vol. III, Berlin 1925. — L. BALDASS, *Die Entwicklung des Dirk Bouts*, Vienna 1932. — W. SCHÖNE, *Dieric Bouts und seine Schule*, Berlin & Leipzig 1938. — L. BALDASS, *Dirk Bouts, seine Werkstatt und Schule*, in *Pantheon*, XXV, 1940.

HUGO VAN DER GOES

A. WAUTERS, *Hugues van der Goes, sa vie et son œuvre*, Brussels 1872. — J. DESTRÉE, *Hugo van der Goes*, Brussels 1914; reprinted 1926. — K. PFISTER, *Hugo van der Goes*, Basel 1923. — M. J. FRIEDLÄNDER, *Die altniederländische Malerei*, vol. IV, Berlin 1926. — F. WINKLER, *Der Meister von Moulins und Hugo van der Goes*, in *Pantheon*, X, 1932. — J. LAVALLEYE, *Juste de Gand, peintre de Frédéric de Montefeltre*, Louvain-Rome 1936. — R. REY, *Hugo van der Goes*, Paris 1945. — J. DUVERGER & A. DE GROOT, *Werk van Hugo van der Goes en van Antoon van Dyck e Brugge*, in *Miscellanea J. Gessler*, 1948. — C. DE TOLNAY, *Hugo van der Goes as a portrait painter*, in *Art Quarterly*, VII.

HANS MEMLING

J. WEALE, *Hans Memling*, Bruges 1901. — K. VOLL, *Memlinc, Des Meisters Gemälde* (Klassiker der Kunst), Stuttgart 1909. — G. HUISMAN, *Memlinc*, 1923. — A. GOFFIN, *Memlinc*, Brussels 1925. — G. HULIN DE LOO, *Chronologie de l'œuvre de Memlinc*, in *Friedländer Festschrift*, Leipzig 1927. — M. J. FRIEDLÄNDER, *Die Altniederländische Malerei*, vol. VI, Berlin 1928. — G. MARLIER, *Hans Memlinc*, Brussels 1934. — G. BAZIN, *Memlinc*, Paris 1939. — P. LAMBOTTE, *H. Memling, le maître de la châsse de Ste Ursule*, Antwerp 1939. — L. BALDASS, *Hans Memlinc*, Vienna 1942. — J. LAVALLEYE, *Les peintres flamands du XVe et l'Italie*, in *Arts plastiques*, May-June 1949. — M. J. FRIEDLANDER, *Memling*, Amsterdam 1950. — J. LAVALLEYE, *Memlinc à l'hôpital Saint-Jean*, Brussels 1953.

GERARD DAVID

E. VON BODENHAUSEN, *Gerard David und seine Schule*, Munich 1905. — M. J. FRIEDLÄNDER, *Die altniederländische Malerei*, vol. VI, Berlin 1928. — R. A. PARMENTIER, *Bronnen voor de Geschiedenis van het Brugsche schildersmilieu in de XVIe eeuw*, in *Revue belge d'archéologie et d'histoire de l'art*, 1942, I. — R. LANGTON DOUGLAS, *La Vierge à la soupe au lait by Gerard David*, in *Burlington Magazine*, December 1946. — M. J. FRIEDLÄNDER, preface to the catalogue of the Gerard David Exhibition, Bruges 1949. — S. SULZBERGER, *Gérard David a-t-il été à Venise?*, in *Kunsthistorische mededeelingen*, 1-2, The Hague 1949.

PAINTING IN THE GERMANIC COUNTRIES

GENERAL

M. MERLO, *Kölnische Künstler*, Cologne 1850. — C. BLANC, P. MANTZ, A. DEMMIN, *Histoire des peintres, Ecole allemande*, Paris 1883. — H. JANITSCHEK, *Geschichte der deutschen Malerei*, Berlin 1890. — A. MICHEL, *Histoire de l'Art*, vol. III, 1st part, Paris 1907; vol. V, 1st part, Paris 1912. — E. HEIDRICH, *Die altdeutsche Malerei*, Jena 1909; reprinted with a supplement by H. Möhle, Jena 1941. — L. RÉAU, *Les Primitifs allemands*, Paris (1910). — C. GLASER, *Zwei Jahrhunderte deutscher Malerei*, Munich 1916. — F. BURGER, H. SCHMITZ, J. BETH, *Die deutsche Malerei vom ausgehenden Mittelalter bis zum Ende der Renaissance* (Handbuch der Kunstwissenschaft), 3 vols., Berlin-Neubabelsberg 1913. — C. G. HEISE, *Norddeutsche Malerei*, Leipzig 1918. — O. H. FÖRSTER, *Die Kölnische Malerei vom Meister Wilhelm bis Stephan Lochner*, Cologne 1923. — C. GLASER, *Die altdeutsche Malerei*, Munich 1924. — H. REINERS, *Die Kölner Malerschule*, Munich 1925. — W. WORRINGER, *Die Anfänge der Tafelmalerei*, Leipzig 1924. — H. HARLINGER, *Die Kunst der Gotik* (Propyläen Kunstgeschichte), Berlin 1926. — W. VAN DER BRIELE, *Westfälische Malerei*, Dortmund 1926. — G. DEHIO, *Geschichte der deutschen Kunst*, vol. II, Leipzig & Berlin 1927. — C. GLASER, *Les Peintres primitifs allemands*, Paris 1931. — R. SEIFERT-WATTENBERG, *Deutsche Maler bis Holbein*, Munich 1933. — W. R. DEUSCH, *Deutsche Malerei des 15. Jahrhunderts*, Berlin 1936. — W. PINDER, *Vom Wesen und Werden deutscher Formen, Geschichtliche Betrachtungen*, in *Die Kunst der ersten Bürgerzeit*, vol. II, Leipzig 1937. — H. BUSCH, *Meister des Nordens*, Hamburg 1940. — F. WINKLER, *Altdeutsche Tafelmalerei*, Munich 1941. — C. LINFERT, *Alt-Kölner Meister*, Munich 1941. — O. FISCHER, *Geschichte der deutschen Malerei*, Munich 1942. — P. DU COLOMBIER, *L'Art allemand*, Paris 1946. — G. KAUN, *Deutsche Malerei des 15. und 16. Jahrhunderts*, Calw & Stuttgart 1949. — G. ROUCHÈS, *Peinture allemande, XIVe-XVIe siècle*, Paris 1949. — A. HULFTEGGER, *Evolution de la Peinture en Allemagne et dans l'Europe centrale*, Paris 1949. — A. STANGE, *La peinture allemande*, Paris 1950.

P. Ganz, *Malerei in der Schweiz*, Zurich 1924. — G. Schmidt and A. M. Cetto, *Schweizer Malerei und Zeichnung im 15. und 16. Jahrhundert*, Basel.

W. Suida, *Österreiche Malerei in der Zeit Erzh. Ernest des Eisernen und Kön. Albrechts II*, Vienna 1925. — E. Buchbeck, *Primitifs autrichiens*, Brussels & Paris 1937.

MONOGRAPHS

Waldburg Wolfegg, *Lukas Moser*, Berlin 1937. — Gerstenberg, *Hans Multscher*, Leipzig 1928. — G. Otto, *Hans Multscher*, Burg bei Magdeburg 1939. — D. Burckhardt, *Konrad Witz*, Basel 1901. — M. Escherich, *Konrad Witz*, Strasbourg 1916. — H. Graber, *Konrad Witz*, Basel 1922. — O. Fischer, *Konrad Witz*, Bremen 1938. — W. Ueberwasser, *Konrad Witz*, Basel 1938. — J. Gantner, *Konrad Witz*, Vienna 1942. — H. Wendland, *Konrad Witz*, Basel 1945. — G. Schmidt, *Conrad Witz*, Geneva 1947. — O. H. Förster, *Stephan Lochner*, Frankfort 1938. — Karl vom Rath, *Der Meister des Bartholomäus Altares*, Bonn 1941. — Bergsträsser, *Caspar Isenmann*, 1941. — F. Haack, *Friedrich Herlin*, Strasbourg 1900. — Wurzbach, *Martin Schongauer*, 1880. — Burckhardt, *Die Schule Martin Schongauers am Oberrhein*, 1888. — A. Gérodie, *Schongauer*, Paris 1912. — M. J. Friedländer, *Martin Schongauer*, Leipzig 1923. — E. Buchner, *Martin Schongauer als Maler*, Berlin 1941. — Flechsig, *Martin Schongauer*, Strasbourg 1944. — J. Baum, *Martin Schongauer*, Vienna 1948. — L. Baldass, *Konrad Laib und die beiden Rueland Frueauf*, Vienna 1946. — W. Manowsky, *Die Gemälde des Michael Pacher*, Munich 1910 — R. Stianny, *Michael Pachers Sankt Wolfganger Altar* Vienna 1919. — Hempel, *Michael Pacher*, Vienna 1931. — O. Scheurer, *Michael Pacher*, Leipzig 1940.

PAINTING IN SPAIN AND PORTUGAL

GENERAL

S. Sanpere Miquel, *Los cuatrocentistas catalanes*, 2 vols., Barcelona 1905-1906. — A. Michel (editor), *Histoire de l'art*, vols. III & IV: *La peinture en Espagne et au Portugal*, by E. Bertaux, Paris 1908 & 1911. — V. von Loga, *Die Malerei in Spanien von 14. bis 17. Jahrhundert*, Berlin 1923. — A. L. Mayer, *Historia de la pintura española*, Madrid 1923; reprinted 1942. — *Spanish Art*, Burlington Magazine Monograph II, London 1927. — A. L. Mayer, *El estilo gótico en España*, Madrid 1929. — C. R. Post, *A History of Spanish Painting*, Cambridge, Mass., 1930 etc. — Marquis of Lozoya, *Historia de l'arte hispanico*, 5 vols., Barcelona & Buenos Aires 1931-1949. — E. Tormo, *Los museos de Valencia*, 2 vols., Madrid 1932. — A. Duran y Sanpere, *La peinture catalane à la fin du moyen âge*, Paris 1933. — J. Gudiol Ricart, *La pintura gótica a Catalunya*, Barcelona 1938; id., *Spanish Painting*, Toledo (Ohio) 1941; id., *Historia de la pintura gótica en Cataluña*, Barcelona 1944. — E. Lafuente Ferrari, *Breve historia de la pintura española*, 3rd edition, Madrid 1946. — M. Serullaz, *Evolution de la peinture espagnole*, Paris 1948. — P. Guinard & J. Baticle, *Histoire de la peinture espagnole*, Paris 1950. — J. Lassaigne, *Spanish Painting*, 2 vols., Geneva 1952. — J. Gudiol Ricart, J. Ainaud de Lasarte & S. Alcolea Gil, *Cataluña*, Barcelona 1955.

Virgilio Correia, *Os pintores portugueses dos seculos XV e XVI*, Lisbon 1928. — R. dos Santos, *L'art portugais*, Paris 1938; id., *L'art portugais*, Paris 1953.

SPANISH PAINTERS

E. Tormo, *Jacomart y el arte hispano-flamenco cuatrocentista*, Madrid 1913. — F. J. Sanchez-Cantón, *Maestro Jorge Inglés, pintor y miniaturista del Marqués de Santillana*, in *Boletín de la Sociedad española de Excursiones*, 1917. — E. Tormo, *Bartolomé Bermejo*, in *Archivo español de Arte y Archeologia*, 1926. — C. Gamba, *Pietro Berruguete*, in *Dedalo*, 1927. — F. J. Sanchez-Cantón, *Tablas de Fernando Gallego en Zamora y Salamanca, in Archivo Español de Arte y Archeologia*, 1929. — E. Tormo, *Rodrigo de Osona, padre e hijo, y su escuela*, in *Archivo Español de Arte y Archeologia*, 1932-1933. — Rowland, *Jaime Huguet*, Cambridge, Mass., 1932. — R. Lainez, *Pedro Berruguete, pintor de Castilla*, Madrid 1935. — G. Hulin de Loo, *Pedro Berruguete et les portraits d'Urbin*, Brussels 1942. — D. Angulo, *Pedro Berruguete en Paredes de Nava*, Barcelona 1946. — J. Gudiol Ricart & J. Ainaud de Lasarte, *Huguet*, Barcelona 1948.

PORTUGUESE PAINTERS

J. de Figueiredo, *O pintor Nuno Gonçalvès*, Lisbon 1909. — F. J. Sanchez-Cantón, *Una gloria peninsular, las tablas de San Vicente*, 1921. — Nyron M. Jirmounsky, *Problème des primitifs portugais et Notes sur la composition des panneaux de Saint-Vincent*, 1940 & 1941. — L. Reis-Santos, *Contribuiçãos para o estudo de gran polìptico de S. Vicente de Fora*, 1943. — João Couto, *A radiografia de Santo no painel do Infante*, in *Boletim do Museu Nacional de Arte antiga*, *Lisbon* 1944. — Garcez Teixeira, *O agrupamento, o significado dos paneis de S. Vicente*, Lisbon 1944 & 1945.

FRENCH PAINTING

GENERAL

C. Blanc, *Histoire des peintres, Ecole française*, Paris 1865. — Abbé Requin, *Documents inédits sur les peintres d'Avignon*, Réunion des Sociétés des Beaux-Arts des départements, Paris 1889. — P. Mantz, *La peinture française du IXe siècle à la fin du XVIe*, Paris 1897. — C. Benoit, *La peinture française à la fin du XVe*, in *Gazette des Beaux-Arts*, Paris 1901-1902. — L. Courajod, *Leçons professées à l'école du Louvre*, Paris 1901. — Abbé Requin, *L'école avignonnaise de peinture*, in *Revue d'Art ancien et moderne*, August 1904. — H. Bouchot, *Les primitifs français*, Paris 1904; id., *La peinture en France sous les Valois*, Paris 1904. — P. Durrieu, *La peinture à l'exposition des primitifs français*, Paris 1904. — G. Hulin de Loo, *L'Exposition des Primitifs français du point de vue de l'influence des frères Van Eyck sur la peinture française et provençale*, Société d'Art et d'Archéologie de Gand, May 1904. — P. A. Lemoisne, *Notes sur l'évolution du portrait enluminé en France du XIIIe au XVIIe siècle*, Paris 1907. — A. Michel (editor), *Histoire de l'Art*, vol. III: Paul Durrieu, *La Peinture en France de Jean le Bon à la mort de Charles V. Le règne de Charles VI*, 1907; vol. IV: *La Peinture en France depuis l'avènement de Charles VII jusqu'à la fin des Valois*, 1922. — Abbé Arnaud d'Agnel, *Les comptes du roi René*, Paris 1908-1910. — J. Guiffrey & P. Marcel, *La peinture française: Les Primitifs*, Paris 1910-1912. — L. Dimier, *Les Primitifs français*, Paris 1911. — L. Maeterlinck, *L'énigme des primitifs français*, Ghent 1921. — G. Brière, *Musée du Louvre, Catalogue des peintures de l'école française*, Paris 1924. — J. Guiffrey (editor), *La*

Peinture au Musée du Louvre: P.-A. Lemoisne, *Ecole française XIVe, XVe et XVIe siècles*, Paris 1925. — E. Male, *L'art religieux de la fin du Moyen-Age en France*, Paris 1925. — L. Dimier, *Histoire de la Peinture française des origines au retour de Vouet, 1300 à 1627*, Paris & Brussels 1925. — J. Guiffrey, P. Marcel & C. Terrasse, *Les Primitifs*, 2nd series, Paris, 1926-1932. — P. Lavallée, *Le Dessin français du XIIIe au XVIe siècle*, Paris 1930. — W. R. Valentiner, *Unknown Masterpieces*, London & New York 1930. — A. Blum & P. Lauer, *La miniature française au XVe et au XVIe siècle*, Paris & Brussels 1930. — A. C. Barnes & V. de Mazia, *The French Primitives and their Forms*, Merion (Pa.,) 1931. — P.-A. Lemoisne, *La Peinture française à l'époque gothique, XIVe et XVe siècles*, Leipzig 1931. — L. H. Labande, *Les Primitifs français; peintres et peintres-verriers de la Provence occidentale*, 2 vols., Marseilles 1932. — G. Hulin de Loo, *L'exposition d'art français à Londres en 1932; Notes sur quelques tableaux du XVe siècle*, in *Bulletin de l'Académie royale de Belgique*, Brussels 1932. — R. Schneider & G. Cohen, *La formation du génie moderne dans l'art de l'Occident*, Paris 1936. — J. Dupont, *Les Primitifs français (1350-1500)*, Paris 1937. — G. Bazin, *La Peinture française des origines au XVIe siècle*, Paris 1937. — G. Jedlicka, *Französische Malerei, Ausgewählte Meisterwerke aus 5 Jahrhunderten*, Zurich 1938. — C. Sterling, *La Peinture française: Les Primitifs*, Paris 1938. — L. Gillet, *Les Primitifs français*, Marseilles 1941. — C. Jacques (Sterling), *Les Peintres du moyen âge. La peinture française*, Paris 1941. — Martin Davies, National Gallery Catalogues: Early French School, London 1946. — J. L. Vaudoyer, *Les peintres provençaux*, Paris 1947. — G. Ring, *A Century of French Painting, 1400-1500*, London 1949. — C. Sterling, *Les peintres primitifs* (toutes les écoles des XIVe et XVe siècles), Paris 1949.

PAINTERS OF THE LOIRE AND THE BOURBONNAIS
ROHAN MASTER

P. Durrieu, *Le Maître des Grandes Heures de Rohan et les Lescuier d'Angers*, in *Revue des Arts*, 1912. — A. Heimann, *Der Meister der Grandes Heures de Rohan und seine Werkstatt*, in *Staedel Jahrbuch*, Frankfort 1932. — J. Porcher, *Les Grandes Heures de Rohan*, Geneva 1943; id., *Les Grandes Heures de Rohan*, in *Journal of the Warburg and Courtauld Institutes*, 1945.

JEAN FOUQUET

Curmer, *L'œuvre de Jehan Fouquet*, 2 vols., Paris 1866. — Burty, *Les Heures d'Etienne Chevalier, les Antiquités judaïques*, in *Gazette des Beaux-Arts*, 1868. — Bouchot, *Jean Foucquet*, in *Gazette des Beaux-Arts*, 1892. — Friedländer, *Die Votivtafel des Etienne Chevaliers von Fouquet*, in *Jahrbuch der Königlich Preussischen Kunstsammlungen*, 1896. — Gruyer, *Les quarante Fouquet de Chantilly*, Paris 1897. — Leprieur, *Jean Fouquet*, in *Revue de l'art ancien et moderne*, April-November 1904. — Thompson, H. Yates, *Facsimile of Two Histories by Jean Fouquet from vol. I and II of the Ancienneté des Juifs...*, London 1903. — P. Durrieu, *La question des œuvres de jeunesse de Jean Fouquet*, Paris 1904. — Marquet de Vasselot, *Deux émaux de Jean Fouquet*, in *Gazette des Beaux-Arts*, August 1904. — G. Lafenestre, *Jehan Fouquet*, Paris 1905. — H. Omon, *Antiquités et guerres des Juifs*, Paris 1906; id., *Grandes Chroniques de France illuminées par Jean Fouquet*, Paris 1908. — Durrieu, *Les Antiquités judaïques et le peintre Jean Fouquet*, Paris 1908; id., *Le Boccace de Munich*, Munich 1909. — T. Cox, *Jehan Foucquet, Native of Tours*, London 1931. — R. Vitry, *La Pietà de Nouans*, in *Gazette des Beaux-Arts*, April 1932. — H. Focillon, *Le style monumental dans l'art de Jean Fouquet*, in *Gazette des Beaux-Arts*, January 1936. — Y. de Raulin, *Jean Fouquet, peintre de l'archevêque Jean de Bernard*, in *Gazette des Beaux-Arts*, June 1936. — O. Pacht, *Jean Fouquet, A Study of his Style*, in *Journal of the Warburg and Courtauld Institutes*, 1940-1941. — K. G. Perls, *Jean Fouquet*, Paris 1940. — G. Cohen, *The Influence of the Mysteries on Art in the Middle Ages*, in *Gazette des Beaux-Arts*, 1943. — P. Wescher, *Jean Fouquet und seine Zeit*, Basel 1945. — C. Sterling, *Jean Fouquet*, in *Art Bulletin*, June 1946.

MASTER OF MOULINS

Maulde de la Clavière, *Jean Perreal, dit Jean de Paris, sa vie et son œuvre*, in *Gazette des Beaux-Arts*, 1895 & 1896. — R. Dupieux, *Les maîtres de Moulins*, Moulins 1946; id., *Arts et artistes en Bourbonnais*, in *Bulletin de la Société d'émulation du Bourbonnais*, Moulins 1948. — H. Goldblatt, *Le Maître de Moulins*, in *The Connoisseur*, June 1948. — A. Guy, *La Cathédrale de Moulins*, Moulins 1950.

PAINTERS OF PROVENCE
MASTER OF THE AIX ANNUNCIATION

C. Aru, *Colantonio ovvero il Maestro dell' Annunziazione di Aix*, in *Dedalo*, XI, 1931. — L. Demonts, *Le Maître de l'Annonciation d'Aix et Colantonio*, in *Mélanges Hulin de Loo*, Brussels 1931; id., *Le Maître de l'Annonciation d'Aix et Colantonio*, in *Revue de l'Art ancien et moderne*, LXVI, 1934. — A. Liebreich, *L'Annonciation d'Aix-en-Provence*, in *Gazette des Beaux-Arts*, February 1938. — J. Boyer, *L'Annonciation d'Aix*, in *Arts*, March 19, 1948.

ENGUERRAND CHARONTON

Abbé Requin, *Un tableau du roi René au Musée de Villeneuve-lès-Avignon*, Paris 1890. — P. Durrieu, *La Vierge de Miséricorde d'Enguerrand Charonton et Pierre Villatte au Musée Condé*, in *Gazette des Beaux-Arts*, July 1904. — L. Demonts, *Une sainte Vierge en oraison d'Enguerrand Charonton*, in *Revue de l'Art ancien et moderne*, 1927 & 1935. — M. Marignane, *Enguerrand Charonton*, Paris 1938. — C. Sterling, *Le Couronnement de la Vierge par Enguerrand Quarton*, Paris 1939. — L. H. Labande, *L'œuvre d'Enguerrand Charonton*, in *Gazette des Beaux-Arts*, 1939.

MASTER OF THE VILLENEUVE PIETÀ

C. de Mandach, *Un atelier provençal du XVe siècle*, in *Monuments et mémoires de la Fondation Piot*, XVI, 1909. — Pinder, *Die dichterische Wurzel der Pietà*, in *Repertorium für Kunstwissenschaft*, 1920. — James B. Ford & G. S. Vickers, in *Art Bulletin*, March 1939. — G. Bazin, *La Pietà d'Avignon*, Geneva 1941.

NICOLAS FROMENT

Trabaud, *La résurrection de Lazare, triptyque de Nicolas Froment*, in *Gazette des Beaux-Arts*, February 1895. — G. Lafenestre, *Nicolas Froment d'Avignon*, in *Revue de l'Art ancien et moderne*, November 1897. — L. Chamson, *Nicolas Froment et l'école avignonnaise du XVe*, Paris 1931. — L. H. Labande, *Notes sur quelques primitifs de Provence, Nicolas Froment*, in *Gazette des Beaux-Arts*, February 1933. — M. Marignane, *Nicolas Froment*, Paris 1936.

PAINTING IN ITALY

GENERAL

G. Vasari, *Le Vite de' più eccellenti pittori, scultori e architetti*, edited by G. Milanesi, Florence 1878. — L. Lanzi, *Storia pittorica dell' Italia*, 1795. — G. B. Cavalcaselle & J. A. Crowe, *History of Painting in Italy*, 2nd edition, London 1902 etc. — A. Venturi, *Storia dell' Arte Italiana*, Milan 1901 etc. — R. van Marle, *The Development of the Italian Schools of Painting*, The Hague 1922 etc. — Thieme-Becker, *Allgemeines Lexikon der Bildenden Künstler*, Leipzig 1907-47 (with an exhaustive bibliography). — B. Berenson, *Italian Pictures of the Renaissance*, Oxford 1932.

FLORENTINE PAINTERS

B. Berenson, *The Florentine Painters of the Renaissance*, London 1896. — G. Fiocco, *Pittura toscana del '400*, Novara 1941. — A. Schmarsow, *Masolino-Masaccio*, Leipzig 1928. — M. Salmi, *Masaccio*, Rome 1932. — M. Pittaluga, *Masaccio*, Florence 1935. — R. Longhi, *Fatti di Masolino e di Masaccio*, in *Critica d'Arte*, XXV-XXVI, 1940. — U. Procacci, *Masaccio*, 1952; id., *Sulla cronologia di alcune opere di Masolino e Masaccio*, in *Rivista d'Arte*, 1953. — R. Langton Douglas, *Fra Angelico*, London 1901. — G. Bazin, *Fra Angelico*, Paris 1949. — J. Pope-Hennessy, *Fra Angelico*, London 1952. — G. C. Argan, *Fra Angelico*, Geneva 1955. — B. Berenson, *Fra Angelico, Fra Filippo e la cronologia*, in *Bollettino d'Arte*, July-August 1932. — M. Salmi, *La giovinezza di Fra Filippo Lippi*, in *Rivista d'Arte*, 1936. — R. Oertel, *Fra Filippo Lippi*, Vienna 1942. — A. Chastel, *Filippo Lippi*, Geneva & Paris 1948. — M. Pittaluga, *Filippo Lippi*, Florence 1949. — M. Salmi, *Paolo Uccello, Andrea del Castagno, Domenico Veneziano*, Rome 1938. — L. Venturi, *Paolo Uccello*, in *L'Arte*, I, 1930. — W. Boeck, *Paolo Uccello*, Berlin 1939. — M. Pittaluga, *Paolo Uccello*, Rome 1946. — M. Salmi, *Riflessioni su Paolo Uccello*, in *Commentari*, I, 1950. — J. Pope-Hennessy, *Paolo Uccello*, London 1950. — E. Carli, *Paolo Uccello*, Milan 1954. — G. Sinibaldi, *Andrea del Castagno*, in *L'Arte*, IV, 1933. — G. M. Richter, *Andrea del Castagno*, Chicago 1943. — R. Longhi, *Un frammento della pala di Domenico Veneziano*, in *L'Arte*, XXVIII, 1925. — R. Longhi, *Il Maestro di Pratevecchio*, in *Paragone*, 1952. — A. Venturi, *Piero della Francesca*, Florence 1922. — R. Longhi, *Piero della Francesca*, Rome 1927. — B. Berenson, *Piero della Francesca*, London 1951. — K. Clark, *Piero della Francesca*, London 1951. — H. Focillon, *Piero della Francesca*, Paris 1952. — L. Venturi, *Piero della Francesca*, Geneva 1954. — M. Cruttwell, *Pollaiolo*, London 1907. — C. Colacicchi, *Antonio del Pollaiolo*, Florence 1943. — A. Sabatini, *Antonio e Piero del Pollaiolo*, Florence 1944. — S. Ortolani, *Il Pollaiolo*, Milan 1948. — M. Cruttwell, *Verrocchio*, London 1904. — B. Berenson, *Verrocchio e Leonardo*, in *Bollettino d'Arte*, 1933. — C. L. Ragghianti, *Inizi di Leonardo*, in *Critica d'Arte*, 1954. — R. Wedgwood Kennedy, *Alessio Baldovinetti*, New Haven 1938. — G. Pacchioni, *Gli inizi artistici di Benozzo Gozzoli*, in *L'Arte*, 1910. — Y. Yashiro, *Botticelli*, 3 vols., Boston 1925. — C. Gamba, *Botticelli*, Milan 1935. — L. Venturi, *Botticelli*, Oxford 1937. — J. Mesnil, *Botticelli*, Paris 1938. — S. Bettini, *Botticelli*, Bergamo 1942. — A. Bertini, *Botticelli*, Milan 1952. — L. Biagi, *Domenico Ghirlandaio*, Florence 1928. — E. Steinmann, *Il Ghirlandaio*, Leghorn 1929. — C. L. Ragghianti, *La giovinezza e lo svolgimento artistico di Domenico Ghirlandaio*, in *L'Arte*, 1935. — J. Lauts, *Domenico Ghirlandaio*, Vienna 1943. — R. Langton Douglas, *Piero di Cosimo*, Chicago 1946. — A. Lorenzoni, *Cosimo Rosselli*, Florence 1921. — L. Dussler, *Luca Signorelli*, Stuttgart 1927. — M. Salmi, *Luca Signorelli*, Novara 1953. — K. B. Neilson, *Filippino Lippi*, Cambridge, Mass., 1938. — A. Scharf, *Filippino Lippi*, Vienna 1935.

SIENESE PAINTERS

R. Langton Douglas, *A History of Siena*, London 1902; id., *A Forgotten Painter (Sassetta)*, in *Burlington Magazine* 1903, p. 306. — B. Berenson, *Essays in the Study of Sienese Painting*, New York 1918. — G. H. Edgell, *A History of Sienese Painting*, New York 1932. — C. Brandi, *Quattrocentisti senesi*, Milan 1949. — J. Pope-Hennessy, *Sassetta*, London 1939. — E. Carli, *Sassetta's Borgo S. Sepolcro Altarpiece*, in *The Burlington Magazine*, May 1952. — C. Brandi, *Giovanni di Paolo*, Florence 1947.

UMBRIAN PAINTERS

C. Gamba, *Pittura umbra del Rinascimento*, Novara 1949. — U. Gnoli, *Pietro Perugino*, Spoleto 1923. — F. Canuti, *Il Perugino*, 2 vols., Siena 1931. — C. Ricci, *Pinturicchio*, Perugia 1912.

VENETIAN PAINTERS

B. Berenson, *The Venetian Painters of the Renaissance*, London 1894. — R. Longhi, *Viatico per cinque secoli di pittura veneziana*, Florence 1946. — V. Moschini, *I Vivarini*, Milan 1946. — F. Drey, *Carlo Crivelli und seine Schule*, Munich 1927. — V. Moschini, *Disegni di Iacopo Bellini*, Bergamo 1943. — G. Fiocco, *L'Arte di Andrea Mantegna*, Bologna 1927; id., *Mantegna*, Milan 1937. — Tietze-Conrat, *Andrea Mantegna*, London 1955. — R. Fry, *Giovanni Bellini*, London 1901. — C. Gamba, *Giovanni Bellini*, Milan 1937. — V. Moschini, *Giambellino*, Bergamo 1943. — T. Borenius, *I pittori di Vicenza*, Vicenza 1912. — G. Fiocco, *Carpaccio*, Rome n. d.

FERRARESE PAINTERS

R. Longhi, *Officina ferrarese*, Rome 1934; id., *Ampliamenti nell' officina ferrarese*, in *Critica d'Arte*, IV, Florence 1940. — S. Ortolani, *Cosme Tura, Francesco del Cossa, Ercole de' Roberti*, Milan 1941. — A. Neppi, *Cosme Tura*, Milan 1953.

PAINTERS OF THE ROMAGNA

R. Buscaroli, *La pittura romagnola del Quattrocento*, Faenza 1936. — C. Ricci, *Melozzo da Forlì*, Rome 1911. — R. Buscaroli, *Melozzo da Forlì*, Rome 1938.

LOMBARD PAINTERS

C. Baroni & S. Samek Ludovici, *La pittura lombarda del Quattrocento*, Messina & Florence 1952. — V. Costantini, *La pittura lombarda dal XIV al XVI secolo*, Milan 1922. — F. Wittgens, *Vincenzo Foppa*, Milan 1949.

PIEDMONTESE PAINTERS

A. M. Brizio, *La pittura in Piemonte dall' età romanica al 500*, Turin 1942. — V. Viale, *Gotico e Rinascimento in Piemonte*, Turin.

SICILIAN PAINTERS

J. Lauts, in the Vienna *Jahrbuch*, 1933, pp. 15 ff; id., *Antonello da Messina*, Vienna 1940. — S. Bottari, *La Pittura del 400 in Sicilia*, Florence 1953; id., *Antonello da Messina*, Milan & Messina 1953. — G. Vigni, *Antonello da Messina*, Milan 1954.

INDEX OF NAMES

THE COLORPLATES

CONTENTS

THIS VOLUME OF THE COLLECTION

THE GREAT CENTURIES OF PAINTING

WAS PRINTED

BOTH TEXT AND COLORPLATES

BY THE

SKIRA

COLOR STUDIO

AT IMPRIMERIES RÉUNIES S. A., LAUSANNE

FINISHED THE FIFTEENTH DAY OF AUGUST

NINETEEN HUNDRED AND FIFTY-FIVE

THE COLORPLATES WERE ENGRAVED BY GUEZELLE ET RENOUARD, PARIS, EXCEPT FOR THOSE ON PAGES 89, 91, 134 AND 177, ENGRAVED BY ALTIMANI, MILAN, AND THAT ON PAGE 17, ENGRAVED BY MALVAUX, BRUSSELS.

The works reproduced in this volume were photographed by Louis Laniepce, Paris (pages 11, 18, 21, 23, 25, 26, 33, 34, 36, 39, 40, 45, 51, 68, 77, 78, 79, 108, 110, 111, 113, 131, 133, 136, 137, 181, 182, 187, 191, 193, 205, 208, 209), by Claudio Emmer, Milan (pages 92, 95, 96, 99, 100, 103, 114, 117, 120, 123, 124, 125, 139, 153, 154, 157, 196, 197, 200, 201, 203, 211, 212, 213, 215), by Hans Hinz, Basel (pages 3, 37, 38, 41, 42, 52, 57, 58, 61, 62, 85, 115, 127, 128, 169, 171, 176, 195), by M. Loose, Brussels (pages 17, 24, 28, 29, 74, 145, 147, 148, 151, 159, 160, 161, 162, 165), by Ruth Berghaus, Munich (pages 166, 168, 172), by Altimani, Milan (pages 89, 91, 134), by Henry B. Beville, Washington (pages 30, 46, 47, 49, 105, 106, 140, 143, 175, 188), and by the photographic service of the Bibliothèque Nationale, Paris (pages 64, 65, 80).

Photographs were obligingly lent us by Editions Plon, Paris (page 177) and by the magazine Du, *Zurich (pages 71, 72, 73, 184).*

PRINTED IN SWITZERLAND